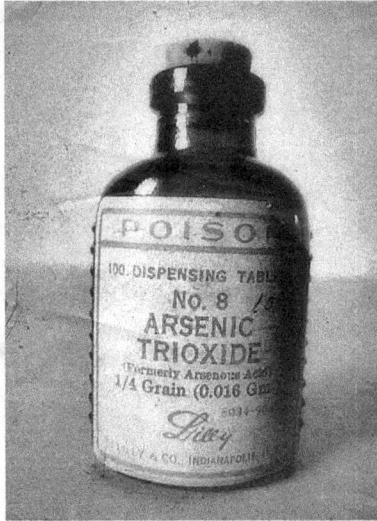

I know little of women.
But I've heard dread tales.
Harold Pinter

13 Spirits of the Wicked and the Wronged

HELL HATH NO FURY

TROY TAYLOR

An American Hauntings Ink Book

This Book is Published By:
American Hauntings Ink
Jacksonville, Illinois | 217.791.7859
Visit us on the Internet at http://www.americanhauntingsink.com

978-1-7352706-7-8
First Edition - July 2021

Printed in the United States of America

TABLE OF CONTENTS

INTRODUCTION

But the woman that God gave him, every fibre of her frame proves her launched for one sole issue, armed and engine for the same; And to serve that single issue, lest the generations fail, the female of the species must be deadlier than the male.
Rudyard Kipling

Rudyard Kipling made a simple statement in one of his poems, "The Female of the Species," that is always worth remembering - that the female is "much deadlier than the male." Kipling wasn't what most would consider enlightened, considering that he was a British imperialist during an era when misogyny was a word that didn't begin to describe how most men treated the women in their lives - but he was right about this.

We tend to forget that when we delve into the world of serial killers, murderers, mayhem, and the supernatural, but we shouldn't. Women are just as deadly - and perhaps, as Kipling said, even deadlier - as men. And often, that's because some man has driven her to it.

From "angels of mercy" to women who kill for money, love, and revenge, the so-called "fairer sex" has claimed more than its share of victims throughout American history. Female killers don't receive near the notoriety afforded to men, but they should because their crimes are often even more terrifying than those of the opposite sex. There have been many women who have caused troubled ghosts to remain behind. They are serial murderers, madwomen, vengeful lovers, and roadside ghosts who still demand attention long after their bodies have been consigned to the grave.

Women have also contributed much to the lore of the supernatural as lingering spirits. They stay with us as reminders of victims of murder and depravity who have refused to leave this world after their lives were snuffed out. They are often tragic figures whose stories need to be shared.

When I began writing of women who prey on others - and who have also been preyed upon - I realized there were far too many stories for a single book. I didn't want to cut things out - these are stories that deserve to be told. Some of the bloodcurdling tales within these pages may not be of a supernatural kind but were so strange and mysterious that they had to be included anyway. They are all tales of terror, bloodshed, suffering, death, and murder - and are not tales for the faint of heart.

Women are dangerous creatures - as you'll soon see. They should be approached with caution and should never be crossed. There is a reason that Shakespeare told us that "Hell hath no fury like a woman scorned..."

That's a warning always worth listening to.

Troy Taylor
Summer 2021

POLICE DEPARTMENT								
No. 22 (8) 9,000	No. 22069							
	CITY OF NEW YORK							
	Detective Bureau							

Bertillon Measurements						
	Head Length	Head Width	R. Ear	L. Foot	Mid. F.	Lit. F.	Fore A.
Height	1.55.3	18.1+			23.5+	10.7+	8.1+	41.9
Outer Arms.	1.56.0	14.5+					
Trunk.	32.0		Len. 5.7				

Name: Lillie Bates
Alias:
Crime: Badger
Age: 23   Height: 5 Ft 1-1/2
Weight: 142   Build: Medium
Hair: Brown   Eyes: Brown
Comp.: D.Med   Moustache:
Born: Mass.
Occupation: Housework
Date of Arrest: June 17th 1909
Officer: Burke, McCarthy &
Remarks: Cohen,   D. B.
Tat:- Wreath and 'FRED'
on left forearm

PART ONE:
THE WICKED

LEGACY OF EVIL
DELPHINE LALAURIE

During the late nineteenth century in New Orleans, if someone mentioned *the woman* or *the haunted house*, everyone knew who and what house they were talking about. It was the best-known haunted house in the French Quarter, and she was one of the most infamous characters in the history of the city - and yet her name was rarely spoken, and neither was the name of the house. There was no need.

She had done terrible things in that house - horrible enough to earn them both a reputation that still lingers more than two centuries later.

Marie Delphine Macarty was born into a wealthy New Orleans family in 1775. Her family boasted a mayor, a governor, three chevaliers of the French crown, Irish nobility, several slave traders, and some of the most prominent members of the city's wealthy Creole society. Her family was among the city's elite. She had two brothers and was regarded as an exceptionally beautiful child. There is nothing written about her childhood that would lead anyone to believe that she would become a monster -- but somehow, she did.

Delphine grew up in a typical Creole home. The Creole were essentially the ruling class and the upper crust of New Orleans society during the years Louisiana was run by the French, the Spanish, the French again, and finally, the United States. Her family owned a plantation north of the city and a house in the French Quarter. The Macarty plantation was a popular spot for parties and for visiting dignitaries, which would have given Delphine plenty of practice when refining her manners and charm. As the daughter of a well-bred family, she would have been taught to read and write, but the bulk of her education was likely in music, art, and etiquette. She would have learned what she needed to know about running a household from her mother.

In that era, Creole girls were introduced into society at the age of 15 and usually married by the time they were 16 or 17. For some unknown reason, Delphine was not married until she was about 24. It may be that her marriage was not late at all and that records were poorly kept, and her birthdate is wrong - or it could be a sign of a greater problem. Perhaps, despite her beauty, Delphine was seen as a "difficult" young woman and one for which a suitable husband was hard to find. No one knows for sure, but her first husband turned out to be a prominent figure in the Spanish government that ruled Louisiana at that time named Don Ramon Lopez y Angulo,

Little is known about their marriage, or even about Don Ramon himself, other than that he died in Havana, Cuba, as the couple returned from a trip to France. The pregnant Delphine became a widow, and she gave birth to a daughter named Marie, who was nicknamed "Borquita" because of her beauty.

In 1808, Delphine - now probably 32-years-old with an eight-year-old daughter -- married Jean Pierre Paulin Blanque, who had come to New Orleans in 1803. He was reputed to be an important man in

New Orleans business and politics. Stories say he was a handsome man with dark hair and eyes. After marrying Delphine, the family moved into a new home at 409 Royal Street.

Over the next eight years, the couple had four children: Marie Louise Jeanne (born 1810); Louise Marie Laure (born 1811); Jean Pierre Paulin (born 1815); and Marie Louise Pauline (born 1816). Borquita, Delphine's daughter from her previous marriage, also lived in the household until she herself was married. On the surface, Delphine and her family appeared to be living the respectable, comfortable life of a wealthy Creole family - but where Jean Blanque got his money was a bit of a mystery.

According to history -- mixed wildly with rumor, as a lot of history in New Orleans is -- Blanque was engaged in a slave smuggling business in New Orleans. Slavery importation had been outlawed in the United States in 1808, but New Orleans was exempted from this law until 1812. After that, smugglers still imported them illegally. Blanque's name appeared more than 350 times in the slave schedules, buying and selling slaves. It was also widely known that he owned boats that were used for smuggling and privateering.

He was on the New Orleans City Council, but his main claim to fame seems to have been his friendship with pirate and fellow slave smuggler Jean Lafitte.

In his book *The Pirates Lafitte*, author William C. Davis wrote of Jean Blanque as one of the "few less scrupulous New Orleans merchants... ffiwhoffl engaged sailors who plied both sides of the laws." In 1806, he had been taken to federal court for purchasing 27,000 pounds of illegally obtained coffee. Many merchants took advantage of the low prices and variety of goods offered by the pirates, but Blanque attracted so much attention with his purchases that he wound up in court.

He remained a man of influence in the city until 1818 when he either died or disappeared. No one seems to know which occurred, but he was gone, leaving Delphine with four children to raise on her own.

Delphine became a widow once more - officially or unofficially - but was in a much better place than she had been in the first time. She now lived in a grand home and had more money than she could possibly spend. Another decade passed before she seriously considered another husband.

On January 12, 1828, she married Dr. Leonard Louis Nicolas LaLaurie, who had arrived in New Orleans from France three years earlier.

Although not much is known about Dr. LaLaurie's personality, there are dozens of letters between him and his father, which are still housed with the Missouri Historical Society. His father, Francois Jean LaLaurie, wrote to his son about every two weeks. There are also many letters between him and his sisters, Victoire, Rosalie, and Helene, and he seems to have had a warm and loving relationship with them. There is no indication that he was anything other than a kind, personable man, although a rather poor medical student.

He arrived in New Orleans in February 1825, and about a month later, he sought to establish a surgical practice in the city, which was a little odd since he had only fully completed his studies at dental school. In a newspaper advertisement, he stated that he had graduated from an accredited French medical school, and while not entirely a lie, it certainly shaded the extent of his degree. The practice of medicine was almost unregulated in those days, so it wasn't unusual for doctors who studied in one field of medicine to randomly switch to another, as Dr. LaLaurie did. Even so, a switch from dentistry to surgery seems to be quite a leap.

There is no record to say that Dr. LaLaurie ever actually established a medical practice in New Orleans. However, there are several receipts and written requests for LaLaurie's services kept in historical archives. One acquaintance wrote to LaLaurie for assistance with a slave who was sick, and LaLaurie billed him for a potion. It should be noted that slaves were often the test subjects for a variety of untried medical potions and remedies. This was not illegal and not even considered unethical. Another client asked for a tooth to be removed, and LaLaurie later billed him for treatment. He was apparently working from home, which was not uncommon at the time.

Curiously, Dr. LaLaurie is mostly left out of the accounts of the atrocities that occurred in his home in the 1830s. He is occasionally mentioned as one of the perpetrators but is mainly seen as a background figure, hidden in the shadow of his wife's overpowering evil. This is strange, considering that in some erroneous accounts of the horror, medical experiments are mentioned. Since he was a doctor, who would have been more likely to conduct such experiments? He should have been the likely suspect as a doctor, but he never was. Perhaps this is because - in all the true, historical accounts of the terrible events - no medical experiments were ever mentioned. It is my personal belief that Dr. LaLaurie was truly an unwilling conspirator in the events that occurred both before and after April 1834.

Dr. LaLaurie and Delphine became acquainted at some point in 1827 and were married early the following year. Their son, Jean Louis, was born later in 1828.

The LaLauries moved into the mansion at 1140 Royal Street in 1832, four years into their marriage. The house, a beautiful two-story Creole-style building, had several balconies that allowed air to circulate through the house and a beautiful, shaded courtyard paved with bricks. The house had been built in 1831 and was one of the finest in the French Quarter. The LaLauries lavishly decorated the home, filling it with rich furniture and fine art. The couple threw lavish parties, which often saw them featured in the society pages of the day.

Delphine was a queen of Creole society, a woman to be admired, loved, and envied. For years, she handled her own business affairs and was respected for her intelligence and style. Her daughters were among the finest dressed girls in New Orleans. Those who received her attentions at her wonderful gatherings could not stop talking about her. Guests in her home were pampered as their hostess bustled about the house, seeing to their every need. They dined on European china and danced and rested on Oriental fabrics that had been imported at great expense. One of the things that nearly all her guests recalled about her was her extraordinary kindness.

But this was the side of Delphine that her friends and admirers were merely allowed to see. There was another side. Beneath her beautiful and refined exterior was a cruel, cold-blooded, and possibly insane woman that some only suspected. Still, others - namely the slaves who attended to her house -- knew as fact.

The LaLauries continued their privileged life during 1832, but then a strange incident took place later that year, on October 26. According to records, the LaLauries petitioned the courts to free a slave they owned named Devince, who was "about 40 or 45 years of age." The petition would be granted in August 1833.

Eight months later, Delphine and her husband would be revealed as the torturers, and possibly murderers, of slaves. So, why would they have freed one of their slaves just a short time before they were exposed? While the record remains unclear, I have an idea, primarily based on what happened soon after.

On November 16, 1832 - less than one month after the court petition - a summons was issued to Dr. LaLaurie, who was residing in Plaquemines Parish at the time. In the summons, Delphine petitioned for separation from her husband. She cited that "through a series of ill treatment from the said Louis LaLaurie that indeed the said LaLaurie acted toward her a long time since in such a manner as to render their living together insupportable." Delphine swore that LaLaurie beat and mistreated her on October 26, 1832. She asked to be allowed to separate from him and for the court to let her remain at the house on Royal Street. Judge Joshua Lawn signed an order that allowed her to sue her husband for legal separation.

It remains a mystery as to what happened that day, but it was serious enough to convince Delphine to separate from her husband, which was an uncommon occurrence at that time.

Note the date of the alleged beating - October 26 - this is the same day that the LaLauries were recorded as petitioning the court for the freedom of the slave Devince. What happened? Anyone who can say for sure is long dead, but based on what happened later, I have a theory. I believe that Dr. LaLaurie did, in fact, beat his wife that day - as a response to her brutal treatment of the slave, Devince. I think that he put a stop to her attack on the man and went as far as to strike her to prevent her from doing serious damage to him. LaLaurie was so shocked by her actions - and perhaps by his own - that he abandoned his wife and moved out of the house. At some point, however, he had a change of heart. It may have been his wife's legal summons, or perhaps something else, but he soon returned. Delphine never went forward with the case against her husband. I believe that the freeing of Devince was likely the price that Delphine had to pay to ensure her husband's silence about her cruelty, or perhaps Dr. LaLaurie freed the man out of guilt for allowing the cruelty to occur in the first place. Once again, we will never know for sure, but there is no question that the mistreatment of slaves was a serious offense in New Orleans in those days.

As early as 1727, New Orleans had set itself apart from other southern cities by adopting the "Code Noir" - a set of rules for the proper treatment of slaves. The so-called Black Codes were created to ensure the proper behavior of slaves, but they also offered the first protections for a slave from the tyranny, neglect, oppression, or cruelty of his master. The codes and laws were taken seriously because, in addition to thousands of slaves, New Orleans was also home to scores of free blacks, or "free persons of color," as they were referred to at the time. Free blacks in New Orleans could own property and seek justice in the courts, rights which were not given to them in any other American city. The mistreatment of slaves was a heavy offense in New Orleans, as the LaLauries would soon discover.

Those who attended the grand parties at the LaLaurie house often spoke of the quiet gracefulness of the house slaves. Nearly as elegant as the guests, these slaves went about their work with silent skill. They moved about the house like shadows, rarely speaking and never raising their eyes. Some wondered about them, and perhaps this is how the rumors began to circulate. However, it is more likely that no one spoke of Delphine's cruelty until after the incident in 1833. Years later, people whispered about the brutality that they never suspected and the terrible treatment they had somehow missed. She kept her cook chained to the fireplace in the kitchen, the stories said, forced to prepare the sumptuous dinners that they had enjoyed. There were also tales that were much worse - stories that went far beyond mere cruelty.

It was a neighbor on Royal Street, a man named Montreuil, who first began to suspect something was not quite right in the LaLaurie house. There were whispered conversations about how the LaLaurie slaves seemed to come and go quite often. Parlor maids would be replaced with no explanation, or the stable boy would suddenly just disappear, never to be seen again. He made a report to the authorities but, even though he was friends with several prominent people, nothing was done about it.

Then, in late 1833, another neighbor was climbing her own stairs when she heard a scream and witnessed Delphine chasing a young girl across her courtyard with a whip. The neighbor watched the girl being pursued from floor to floor until they, at last, appeared on the rooftop. The child ran down the steeply pitched roof and then vanished. Moments later, the neighbor heard a horrible thud as the small body struck the flagstones below. Late that night, the woman claimed that she saw one of Delphine's slaves carry a bundle into the courtyard and bury it. She believed that it was the body of the young girl, but it was never proven. She told her story to the police, and this time action was taken.

The LaLaurie slaves were impounded and sold at auction. Unfortunately for them, Delphine coaxed some relatives into buying them and then selling them back to her in secret. She explained to her friends that the entire incident had been a horrible accident. Some believed her, but many others did not, and the LaLaurie's social standing began to slowly decline.

The stories spread about the mistreatment of the LaLaurie slaves, and uneasy whispering spread among her former friends. A few party invitations were declined, dinner invitations were ignored, and the family was soon politely avoided by other members of the Creole society. Finally, in April of 1834, all the doubts about Delphine LaLaurie were realized at last.

On April 10, a fire broke out in the LaLaurie house. It started in the kitchen, accounts state, and then spread to the upper floors. As smoke billowed out the windows overlooking the street, it got the attention of passersby and neighbors who hurried to the house to lend assistance. Legend says that the fire was purposely started by the cook who was kept chained in the kitchen. She allegedly stated that she would rather burn to death than endure any more of the abuse she had suffered at the hands of Madame LaLaurie.

An alarm was sounded to the volunteer fire department, members of which were soon on the scene with water and to help evacuate the occupants and remove household items from the mansion. Locals crowded into the house, some to help, others perhaps out of sheer curiosity. Many rushed about the scene, shouting and adding to the growing chaos. Delphine remained calm in the midst of it all, directing volunteers and steering firefighters toward the worst of the flames. She was intent on saving the house, and everyone who recalled that day stated that she never panicked or raised her voice.

Montreuil, the neighbor who had first aroused suspicion about Delphine and her treatment of her servants, assisted during the fire. He demanded to know if any household slaves were in danger from the blaze and was allegedly told not to interfere in family business. Montreuil then appealed to his friend, Judge Canonge, and they began searching the house. They were accompanied by a man named Fernandez and many of the firefighters. Several of the servants were found as they climbed the stairs to the upper floors and sent out of the house.

According to a statement that Judge Canonge later gave, a man named Felix Lefebvre approached him in the house and told him that he had looked through a broken pane of glass and saw several slaves in a locked room. A man named Deponent, along with several others, went with Lefebvre and broke into the room. They found two slaves inside, both women. One of them had a heavy metal collar around her neck and chains attached to her feet. She directed the men to another nearby room where they found a third female slave stretched out on a bed. She was an older woman with a deep wound on her head. She was too weak to get out of bed on her own, and when the men helped her up, she was unable to walk. Deponent had several of the men hoist the mattress with her lying on it to carry her out of the house.

Meanwhile, Montreuil and Judge Canonge had finally reached the upper floor through the smoke to discover a wooden door that led to the attic. It was locked. According to the New Orleans Courier of April 11, 1834, Judge Canonge sought out Dr. LaLaurie, who was also present in the house. He is said to have asked him politely to open the attic door so that they could check for the presence of slaves, but the judge received a rude reply: "There are those who would be better employed if they would attend to their own affairs instead of officiously intermeddling with the concerns of others."

It's hard to know what to make of this statement by Dr. LaLaurie and his refusal to open the attic door. It is possible that he felt the attic was in no danger from the fire and didn't want the men poking around up there -- since he undoubtedly knew what they would find. It's also likely that he was referring to the presence of Montreuil, the neighbor who had already caused problems for the family over the treatment of their slaves.

Dr. LaLaurie had already tried to protect his wife -- or more likely, the family's reputation -- during the incident with the slave Devince by freeing the man so that the story would not become public. The couple had recently suffered embarrassment at having their slaves impounded, and a discovery of what was hidden in the attic would leave the family in ruin.

Perhaps Dr. LaLaurie felt his refusal to open the door would be enough to turn the men away, but he had not counted on the persistence of Montreuil and Judge Canonge. The judge ordered the firefighters to break open the door, and they forced themselves into the attic.

What greeted them behind the door shocked and dismayed the men. According to the *New Orleans Bee* for April 11, 1834:

> *Seven slaves, more or less horribly mutilated, were seen suspended by the neck, with their limbs apparently stretched and torn from one extremity to the other. These slaves had been confined by the woman LaLaurie for several months in the situation from which they had thus providentially been rescued and had been merely kept in existence to prolong their suffering and to make them taste all that the most refined cruelty could inflict.*

The *New Orleans Courier* added:

> *A most appalling sight was presented in the shape of several wretched negroes emerging from the fire, their bodies covered with scars and loaded with chains. Amongst them was a female slave, upwards of 60 years of age who could not move... We saw one of the miserable beings. The sight was so horrible that we could scarce not look at it. The most savage heart could not have witnessed the spectacle unmoved. He had a large hole in his head. His body was covered from head to foot with scars and filled with worms. The sight inspired us with such horror that even in the moment of writing this article we shudder from its effects.*

Those who have seen the others represent them to be
in similar condition.

In some accounts of the discovery -- modern, not contemporary -- behind the locked attic door, detailed descriptions of all sorts of perverse tortures and experiments have appeared. Tales have been told of makeshift operating tables, slaves locked in cages, bodies cut open, and holes that had been cut into human skulls so the victim's brains could be stirred.

In most cases, the *New Orleans Bee* is cited as the source for this horror, but a check of the actual newspaper accounts proves this to be untrue. All the stories and eyewitness accounts of the time confirm the discovery of the poorly treated slaves in the house and the horrific condition of the slaves kept in the attic. The story of the hole cut in the man's head "so that his brains could be stirred" undoubtedly came from the *Courier's* mention of the man with the hole in his head, wounds, and worms. This was actually referring to a deep wound, not an actual hole. Even so, he had been left in the attic with his wounds untreated for so long that maggots had been found in his cuts.

Later sources from the late nineteenth and early twentieth centuries, including some written by New Orleans natives who knew the case, also failed to mention anything other than the emaciated slaves who had wounds consistent with a long period of captivity and abuse. This doesn't make things any better. The slaves suffered horribly at the hands of a cruel and malicious master. Lurid tales of medical experiments take away from the fact that this was a horrible, vile situation.

The first mention that I located of the terrible experiments, which have since become a staple in the re-telling of the LaLaurie story, is in 1946. In the book *Ghost Stories of Old New Orleans*, author Jeanne deLavigne claims that the first men who entered the attic found:

> *...powerful male slaves, stark naked, chained to the wall, their eyes gouged out, their fingernails pulled out by the roots; others had their joints skinned and festering, great holes in their buttocks where their flesh had been sliced away, their ears hanging by shreds, their lips sewed together, their tongues drawn*

out and sewed to their chins, severed hands stitched to their bellies, legs pulled joint to joint. Female slaves there were, their mouths and ears crammed with ashes and chicken offal and bound tightly; others had been smeared with honey and were a mass of black ants. Intestines were pulled out and knotted around naked waists. There were holes in skulls, where a rough stick had been inserted to stir the brains. Some of the creatures were dead; some were unconscious; and a few were still breathing, suffering agonies beyond power to describe.

It's undoubtedly a terrifying scene - but there's not a shred of truth to it. The story created for the book was picked up, told, and re-told by various authors over the years. It's been repeated time and time again --and still is on the lesser ghost tours in New Orleans today -- often by people who should have known better. What Delphine LaLaurie did to her slaves was horrific but apparently, by the 1940s, just mistreating and abusing your slaves was not bad enough. To make the story even more frightening, it had to be taken one step further. Looking back on this story today, we can see what Delphine did in the house on Royal Street was the work of a sadist and a sociopath - and more than ample reason for the house to gain a reputation for being haunted.

As the mutilated slaves were carried and led out of the house, the crowd outside gathered. Only one of two friends remained beside Madame LaLaurie. By this time, Dr. LaLaurie was gone. There is no further mention of him in accounts of what happened next at the house, but we do know that he and his wife were separated after the fire. This time, it was for good.

Delphine managed to get someone to lock the house's doors and seal the wooden gates that led from the street into the courtyard. This effectively sealed the LaLaurie household off from the crowd outside, which was still milling about, waiting to see if any arrests were going to be made over the cruel treatment of the slaves. Several hours passed, and nothing happened. The fire was out by this time, and little damage had been done to the house.

But word spread of the atrocities discovered in the LaLaurie home, and people recalled the little girl that had allegedly been killed, the slaves that had been taken away from the LaLaurie family, and the rumors of the slaves that went missing and were never seen again. According to reports in the *New Orleans Gazette*, "at least 2,000 people" came to the courthouse to see the slaves that had been taken from the mansion. The slaves received food and medical care and were prodded with questions about their captivity and abuse. A long wooden table was filled with instruments of torture that had been brought from the attic. They included whips, shackles, and knives - some of which were said to be crusted with the red stain of dried blood.

One of the statements given came from a female slave who testified that Madame LaLaurie would sometimes beat and torture her captives while music and parties were going on below. She would enter the room, still clad in her ball gown, and whip the slaves as they cowered on the floor. After a few lashes, she would appear to be satisfied and would leave. One of the women also testified that Delphine once beat her own daughter for bringing food to the starving slaves.

Anger swept through New Orleans as curious crowds came to gape at the starving and brutalized slaves. As the wounded creatures gulped down the food given to them, Judge Canonge, Montreuil, Fernandez, and Felix Lefebvre all made formal statements about their discovery of the locked chamber.

Meanwhile, the mob was still waiting outside the gates to the house on Royal Street. They expected to see arrests made and for the authorities to demand entry to the house. Hours passed, and the police did not arrive. The mob continued to grow. More and more people came, and as each hour passed, they grew more restless and belligerent. Soon, threats were being shouted at the shuttered windows, and calls for vengeance were heard from the street.

Suddenly, late in the afternoon, the entry to the high-walled courtyard burst open, and a carriage roared out of the gates. The coach pushed through the crowd and disappeared, racing down Hospital Street toward the Bayou Road. It all happened so quickly that everyone was taken by surprise. Someone cried out that the carriage had only been a decoy -- that Madame LaLaurie was actually escaping through a rear door. While some went to look, others swore that she had been in the carriage alone. Dr. LaLaurie was nowhere to be found. Delphine's children -- it was rumored afterward -- had been forced to escape the house by climbing over a balcony and into a house next door.

But it was Delphine the angry mob was looking for, and she had easily escaped their clutches. The carriage drove furiously along the Bayou Road, and it is said that a sailing vessel waited for her there, which left at once for Mandeville. Another story claimed that she remained in hiding in New Orleans for several days and only left the city when she realized that public opinion was hopelessly against her. No one knows which of these stories is true, but we do know that she was in Mandeville nearly ten days later because she signed a power of attorney there that would allow an agent in New Orleans to handle her business affairs on her behalf.

Delphine LaLaurie had vanished - for a little while, at least.

The seething mob that remained behind on Royal Street continued to grow. Delphine's flight had enraged the crowd, and they decided to take their anger out on the mansion she had left behind. The *New Orleans Courier* reported that "doors and windows were broken open, the crowd rushed in, and the work of destruction began."

Featherbeds were ripped open and thrown out into the street while curtains were pulled down from the windows and pictures torn from the walls. Men carried furniture, pianos, tables, sofas, and chairs and hurled them out the windows to see them splinter on the streets below. After destroying nearly every belonging left in the house, the mob, still unsatisfied, began to tear apart the house itself. The mahogany railings were ripped away from the staircase; glass was broken, doors were torn from their hinges, and worse.

The *New Orleans Bee* for April 12, 1834, stated:

> *It was found necessary for the purpose of restoring order, for the sheriff and his officers to repair to the place of the riot and to interpose the authority of the state, which we are pleased to notice proved effectual, with the occurrence of any of those acts of violence, which are common on similar occasions... Nearly the whole of the edifice is demolished and scarcely anything remains but the walls, which the popular vengeance*

*have ornamented with various writings expressive of
their indignation and the justness of their punishment.*

It was later suggested that the house itself be completely torn
down, but cooler heads prevailed, and instead, the house was closed and
sealed. It remained that way for several years, silent, uninhabited, and
abandoned.

Or was it?

After her flight from New Orleans, Delphine set up residence
in Paris. The ghastly discovery in the attic had been enough to drive
the family, despite their wealth and social standing, out of the country.
Her husband, Dr. LaLaurie, did not flee to Paris with her. His
reputation had been destroyed, and as far as is known, Dr. LaLaurie
never saw his wife again. He eventually died in Cuba, although no
record of his death has ever been found. He remained exiled on the
island for the remainder of his life, his professional reputation in tatters
and his name all but destroyed. While never tortured, beaten, or killed
by her hand, Dr. Leonard Louis Nicolas LaLaurie was nevertheless a
victim of the sadistic cruelty of Delphine LaLaurie.

As for Delphine, she settled comfortably into her Paris life.
When she arrived, she was accompanied by her six-year-old son, Jean
Louis, and three of her adult children by Jean Blanque: daughters
Pauline and Laure and son, Paulin.

Despite some stories, she was never in hiding while living in
Paris. She could not be prosecuted for any of the crimes she had
committed in New Orleans, so her whereabouts were no secret. She
thrived in Paris, conducting her business in Louisiana from France. She
paid her taxes and financed the repair of a New Orleans' Marigny
District residence that was rented out. She would later return to New
Orleans and live in this house until her death.

By the early 1840s, she began to worry about money. Her son,
Paulin, would later write that he feared his mother was using her
concerns about her finances as a reason to return to New Orleans. Her
children were appalled that she would even consider such an action, but
they could not talk her out of it.

Unsuccessful in convincing her to stay in France, most of the
children returned with her to New Orleans. Only her son, Jean Louis,

maintained residences in Paris and New Orleans, traveling back and forth as he endeavored to handle his mother's business affairs. He took care of family business until his death in 1883 at the age of only 55.

Delphine's oldest daughter, Borquita, lived in New Orleans her entire life. There is no evidence that she ever visited her mother in Paris or record that she had any contact with her at all. What type of relationship they may have maintained, and whether or not the atrocities at the house on Royal Street had any effect on her life, is unknown.

Just as many erroneous stories about what happened to Delphine after she left New Orleans made the rounds, there were just as many rumors spread about her death. When she fled the city, some claimed that she spent the rest of her life in the forest along the north shore of Lake Pontchartrain. According to the author George W. Cable, Madame LaLaurie made her way to Mobile and then went on to Paris. He went on to say that her reputation preceded her to France and when she was confronted and recognized in Paris, she spent her days "skulking about in the provinces under assumed names."

Several different accounts of the death of Delphine LaLaurie have also been recorded. One claimed that she was killed by a wild boar while hunting in France. Another story, which appeared in the *Daily Picayune* in March 1892, insisted that she died among family and friends in Paris. Others claimed that she secretly returned to New Orleans and died there.

In the early 1900s, Eugene Backes, who served as sexton to St. Louis Cemetery #1 until 1924, was said to have discovered an old, cracked copper plate in Alley 4 of the cemetery. The inscription on the plate read: "Madame LaLaurie, née Marie Delphine Macarty, décédée à Paris, le 7 Décembre, 1842, à l'âge de 68 ans." No record of any burial has ever been found, however, further adding to the mystery.

More recently, other information has revealed that Delphine was alive for several years after 1842 - the year that she had returned to New Orleans from Paris. According to court papers, Delphine was apparently still alive in 1850, the year that her brother L.B. Macarty's estate was settled. Delphine was only supposed to receive a share of the estate, but somehow, she cleverly managed to not only seize control of all his money but she was also able to cheat the executors of the will out of their commission. She was not only alive in 1850, but she was still in control of her business, too.

Her name would only appear in records one more time - when she died. A newspaper advertisement appeared in the *New Orleans Times* in 1858 about the sale of "parcels" to settle her estate. However, no burial notice ever appeared in the newspapers. Based on how long it usually took to settle an estate in those days, Delphine probably died between 1855 and 1858, but no one knows for sure.

There is also a question about where she was interred. She could have been buried in any of the Macarty family crypts, those of the Forstall family, or some anonymous tomb. Nothing exists to say either way. The copper plaque -- with a mysterious death date -- offers only a tenuous connection to St. Louis Cemetery #1, but even that has been disputed.

What became of one of New Orleans' most infamous women? No one will ever know for sure. Those who can answer that question are now long dead.

Or are they? Many believe they know where Delphine lingers today - in her very haunted house on Royal Street.

Stories of a haunting at 1140 Royal Street began almost as soon as the LaLaurie carriage fled the house. According to legend, firefighters, police officers, and scavengers heard scratching and moaning sounds coming from the house for several days after the fire. Still, they were unable to find anyone - living or dead.

Ghastly tales circulated about the house as it remained vacant for a few years after its sacking by the mob, falling into a state of ruin and decay. Many people claimed to hear screams of agony coming from the empty house at night and saw the apparitions of slaves walking about on the balconies and in the yards. Some stories even claimed that vagrants who had gone into the house seeking shelter were never heard from again.

The LaLaurie family still owned the house until 1837, when it was finally sold. It was then rebuilt in its current, three-story configuration. When the LaLauries lived in the house, it was a typical two-story Creole home. While it is the same house that occupies the lot today, it was extensively renovated.

The man who purchased and remodeled the mansion only kept it for three months. He told his family and friends that he was plagued by strange noises, cries, and groans in the night, and he soon abandoned the place. He tried leasing the house to a barbershop and a store that rented the basement for a short time, but none of the occupants stayed for long. He tried to rent rooms out, but the tenants only remained for a few days at most. Finally, he gave up, and the house was abandoned.

Following the Civil War, Reconstruction turned the empty LaLaurie mansion into an integrated high school for "girls of the Lower District," but in 1874, the White League forced the black children to leave the school. Racist League members lined up the girls and questioned them about their family backgrounds, trying to determine which ones were colored and which were not. In a city as racially diverse as New Orleans, many had both white and black ancestors. To racists, even having a black ancestor several generations removed was enough to brand someone as "colored." Those girls were forcibly removed from the school.

Soon after the school was closed, the house was listed as a leaf tobacco business owned by Joseph Barnes. In addition, the 1938 New Orleans City Guide stated that the building was used as a gambling house in the 1870s. According to the guide, "Stories were told and retold of the strange lights and shadow objects that were seen flitting about in different apartments, their forms draped with sheets, skeleton heads protruding. Hoarse voices like unto those supposed to come only from the charnel house floated out on the fog-laden air on dismal and rainy nights, with the ominous sound of clanking chains coming from the servant's quarters, where foul crimes are said to have been committed." Needless to say, it's rather hard to take this entry in the guide too seriously. However, it does lend credence to the fact that stories were still circulating about Delphine and her victims many years after the events occurred.

In 1876, the *Daily Picayune* published an article about the house being up for auction. After that, it was used as the site of two different schools, a home for wayward boys, and as the headquarters for a fraternal organization. It changed owners five times over two decades.

At one point, in 1893, an article in the *Times Democrat* stated:

> *"F. Greco purchased the haunted house at Hospital and Royal ... yesterday he posted large flowing placards upon the walls of the building announcing in both Italian and English, 'The Haunted House.' There is an end to everything, so there is with ghosts. Come and be convinced. Admission ten cents."*

This was apparently New Orleans' very first ghost tour. How long this "attraction" ran is unknown, but by late in the decade, the house was empty once more.

By the end of the century, New Orleans had seen a considerable influx of Italian immigrants with few places for them to live. Landlords quickly bought up old and abandoned buildings to convert into cheap housing for this new wave of renters. The LaLaurie mansion, with its more than 40 rooms, became just such a house. For many of the tenants, though, even cheap rent was not enough to keep them there.

It was during this time that more accounts surfaced about strange, inexplicable events in the house. Among them was an encounter between an occupant and a naked black man in chains who attacked him. The man abruptly vanished. Others claimed that a phantom attacked children with a whip, that eerie figures appeared in shrouds, and, of course, the continuing sounds of screams, groans, and cries that echoed through the building at night. The sounds, they said, often came from the locked and abandoned attic, where the slaves had been discovered during the fire.

One young mother claimed to be terrified one night when she looked over to where her baby was sleeping and saw a dark-haired woman in elegant evening clothes bending over her sleeping infant. The ghostly woman was said to have been Delphine LaLaurie herself. When the mother let out a bloodcurdling cry, the apparition vanished.

It was never easy to keep tenants in the house, and finally, after word spread of the strange goings-on there, the mansion was deserted. By 1922, it was vacant once again.

Two decades later, in the middle of World War II, the mansion gained a new group of tenants. According to an *Associated Press* story from June 1943:

> *The sheet waving, bone rattling crew that has occupied New Orleans' most widely known haunted house for the last 111 years has been dispossessed to make way for war workers. Despite the kindness which this city - and the entire South - has always shown to its ghosts and 'ha'nts,' no investigation by the rental division of the OPA is anticipated. With the city's normal half-million population augmented by 50,000 war workers and an additional 12,000 workers anticipated to man now-building aircraft plants, the ghosts will have to shift for themselves.*

During the great immigration wave of the 1890s, New Orleans was flooded with new and temporary arrivals during the war years, and all of them were looking for places to live. With so many homes and empty buildings in the French Quarter, government services took over the old LaLaurie mansion and converted it into apartments for the workers. Their tenancy lasted until the end of the war when the house was put back on the market.

There is no record of any supernatural activity occurring in the house at this time, but the story stayed fresh in the minds of locals, which leads many to believe that tales were still being told. In 1945, the house's first floor was turned into a tavern, which the proprietor called the "Haunted Saloon." Taking advantage of the house's eerie history, he kept a record of the strange things experienced there by the staff and patrons.

After the bar closed, space was opened again as a furniture store. It did not fare well in the former LaLaurie house. The owner first suspected vandals when all his merchandise was found ruined on several occasions, covered in some sort of dark, stinking liquid. He finally waited one night with a shotgun, hoping the vandals would return. When dawn came, the furniture was all ruined again even though he knew that no one had entered the building. Exasperated and frightened, he closed the store and moved out.

The house was apparently empty for most of the early 1960s. An article that appeared in the *Times-Picayune* in 1964 reported that a preservation group, the Vieux Carre Commission, was trying to stop the deterioration and partial demolition of the former LaLaurie house. Evidently, people had been looting the abandoned house and stealing anything out of it that could be taken. The preservation group noted that "the building has been stripped of the floorboards in the upper balcony," among other things.

As it turned out, the house was saved, although, in 1969, it became an apartment building again. It had been divided into about 20 apartments for war workers in 1943, and they were now being rented out again - with ghostly results. Zella Funck, an artist who lived in one of the apartments, stated that the poltergeists in her place were "...playful. They're not around every day, but they do surprise visitors." She said that one of the ghosts she had seen was that of a handsome man in old-fashioned clothing, which may have been Dr. LaLaurie.

Another tenant, Mrs. Richards, reported numerous incidents in her apartment, such as opened water faucets, locked doors becoming unlocked, and showers that turned on by themselves.

In 2000, the mansion was purchased by a New Orleans doctor, who decided to restore the house. He renovated it with a living area in the front portion and five luxury apartments to the rear. He never spoke of any paranormal experiences while living in the house.

In 2007, actor Nicolas Cage bought the LaLaurie mansion through his Hancock Park Real Estate Company. Rumor had it that Cage lived in the front section of the house and rented out the back gallery, where the slave quarters were once located. Cage spent a lot of time in New Orleans in those days and even had a tomb built for himself at St. Louis Cemetery #1. If he was living in the mansion, however, his tenancy was short-lived. In 2008, the house was back on the market, listed at $3.5 million. A year later, the bank foreclosed on the home -- along with two other haunted homes in New Orleans that Cage had acquired -- and it was purchased by the Regions Financial Corporation in November 2009.

Today, the house is again privately owned and whether it is still haunted is unknown. Despite its appearance in television shows like *American Horror Story,* it seems to have been pretty quiet since the late 1970s. It certainly earned its place in supernatural history with the accounts of all the ghostly events that have taken place there, but today, it seems like a battery that has lost most of its charge.

I had the chance to go inside the mansion once several years ago, and I would be lying if I said that I hadn't hoped to see or feel something in the place. I went away with no supernatural encounter, but I did not go away disappointed.

It was a house alive with horrific history. I heard no phantom whispers or spectral wails, but I did leave with a sense of the evil legacy that Delphine LaLaurie left behind in that house. Her twisted heart and horrific actions created a legend that has lived on for nearly two centuries. Can a spirit like her, so infused with anger and evil, ever really find peace? Can her victims?

Those ghosts may no longer walk in the house on Royal Street, but history has left a dark and indelible impression there. The ghosts may be gone, but how much more "haunted" can one house be?

THE "MURDEROUS MATRON"
BERTHA GIFFORD

In 1928, a Missouri woman named Bertha Gifford was arrested on two charges of first-degree murder. The story might have been shocking to people who lived in nearby St. Louis, but those from Franklin County, where Bertha lived, were not surprised.

Some even wondered what had taken so long. Everyone seemed to know that this "angel of mercy" had a history of caring for people who suddenly became sick and died.

The story of how Bertha Gifford was able to carry out her crimes and get away with them for so long is bizarre, to say the least. What's equally as curious is that she is one of the most infamous criminals in the history of the area, but so few people living there today have heard anything about the case - although many know of a place where she allegedly once lived and worked - a hotel with a reputation for being haunted.

Bertha Alice Williams was born in 1876, just outside the small, unincorporated community of Morse Mill. The village, located about 40 miles south of St. Louis, had grown up around a house and grain mill owned by John H. Morse. The house, built in 1816, would later be turned into a hotel where Bertha worked for a time.

The Williams family were some of the first settlers in the area. W.P. and Matilda Williams had ten children, although two died in infancy. Bertha was the ninth child to be born.

The family was well-respected and belonged to a fundamentalist Christian sect known as the Church of God, Faith of Abraham. They were a reserved and studious sect that believed the Bible was meant to be taken literally - the world was 6,000 years old; it had been washed clean by a flood, that sort of thing. Those who criticized the church called them "soul sleepers" because they believed the dead weren't actually dead and were only sleeping in their graves, waiting for the return of Jesus. They didn't believe that human souls went to heaven. Instead, the righteous would be literally resurrected to enjoy immortality on earth. They also believed in peace and that no Christian "ought ever take up arms and kill their enemies."

Bertha didn't learn much from her church's message of peace and redemption, but she did learn to imitate the calm façade of the most solemn members of the faith. She also learned that ministering to the sick was good for the soul - or at least it was a good way to get attention.

Bertha grew up to be an exceptionally beautiful young woman and was believed to be the prettiest girl in Jefferson County. She had long, black hair, flashing eyes, and a bright smile. She loved music, loved to dance, and was very social, which helped attract young men from all over the area. She loved the attention they gave her.

On December 20, 1894, at the age of 22, Bertha married a man named Henry Graham. He had been born in Morse Mill in 1872, and his family had been in the region for generations. Henry had three sisters and four brothers, one of which, Peter, had committed suicide by swallowing carbolic acid.

They were an attractive and happy couple. They ran a boardinghouse together - which became the Morse Mill Hotel - and in July 1896, had a daughter, Lila. They had the appearance of an ideal family, even though by 1900, they were living with Bertha's brother, Albert. Henry helped out as a farmhand, and Bertha kept house for the family.

Something happened to shatter their marital bliss, but what it might have been remains a mystery. What we do know is that Henry started carrying on with another woman, but Bertha, still a beautiful woman, wasted little time worrying about her husband's infidelity. Instead, she started spending time with Eugene Gifford, a young man seven years her junior. He fell in love with her and broke off his engagement to another young woman.

Eugene was a strapping farmer and carpenter with thick brown hair and blue eyes. At nearly six feet tall, he was almost a foot taller than Bertha and was clearly enamored with her. Their relationship - as well as Henry's affair - became a badly-kept secret in the community.

But the Graham marital drama came to an abrupt halt when Henry became gravely ill. He was initially diagnosed with pneumonia. Bertha refused to leave his side, nursing him around the clock as Henry's condition became worse.

He died in agony on November 30, 1906, suffering from terrible stomach pain - which was not a symptom of pneumonia. Doctors shrugged it off, and no one questioned their findings. He was buried in the cemetery in Morse Mill, near the graves of his parents.

In 1907, after a respectable mourning period, Bertha married Eugene Gifford, and the couple moved to neighboring Franklin County, just far enough away to escape the gossip of Morse Mill. Lila moved there with her mother, but in 1914, she married Ernest West and moved to Detroit. She lived until 1978 - probably only because she was far away from her mother.

In Franklin County, the Giffords moved into a small house in the tiny rural community of Catawissa. The town had sprung up along the Union Pacific Railroad tracks and the Meramec River, and only about 150 people lived there when the Gifford arrived. When residents bought groceries or wanted to catch up on news, they went to the slightly larger town of Pacific.

The first home where Bertha and Eugene lived in Catawissa was next to the railroad tracks and had a dark history attached to it - the previous owners had both been hit and killed by a train.

Eugene took up farming again, and after making some money, they moved to a white farmhouse on Old Bend Road, overlooking the Meramec River.

It was in this house where Bertha would poison nine of her victims.

But before people started dying, the Giffords had a fine reputation. The neighbors, other families who lived on "The Bend" were tightly knit and welcoming. Everybody liked Eugene. He was a hard worker and had a great sense of humor. He ran the farm, and Bertha, who fed the hired hands, became a figure beloved for her incredible cooking. Her biscuits were things of beauty, and her potato soup was the best in the county. She was happy to have neighbors over for supper, and she often brought food to families when someone was sick. This is likely how she gained a reputation for caring for the ill and as a respected country nurse.

At first, her bedside care was little more than a comforting presence and a cold cloth on a fevered brow. Soon, though, she was treating people with "potions." What was in them was unknown, but she had a different one for headaches, insomnia, and fevers. She carried them with her in a black medical bag whenever she visited a sick neighbor.

Bertha had no medical training or skills with herbs. She was making things up as she went along. However, in a small rural community with the closest doctor being many miles away, she was a kindhearted "angel of mercy." She was known to walk or ride for miles to help a sick or injured person. She always remained calm and collected during an emergency and never flinched when stitching or bandaging even the most gruesome farm injury.

At some point, something changed. We'll never know what happened with Bertha - the inner workings of her mind remain a secret - but whether evil or insane, she eventually became an "angel of death." From 1912 through the early 1920s, many of her patients, including several children, died from unknown causes. They were neighbors, friends, even relatives.

But few people, if any, thought the deaths suspicious. That would, of course, eventually change.

In 1911, Eugene moved his widowed mother, Emilie, and his little brother, James, into the farmhouse on Old Bend Road. Bertha was, of course, warm and welcoming. The new arrivals loved Bertha and enjoyed her fabulous cooking.

Apparently, though, the unsuspecting Emilie wore out her welcome quickly. She soon became violently ill, suffering from vomiting and intense stomach cramps. Her health declined, and she died on January 24, 1912. With her husband wracked by grief, Bertha kindly took care of the funeral arrangements. It would be the first of many funerals that Bertha would attend. She dressed in her finest mourning dress and always spoke at the funerals of the "poor souls" who died under her care.

Eugene's brother, James, continued to live with Bertha and his brother for another year, but on May 12, 1913, the 12-year-old boy began suffering from the same ailment his mother had died from. His death certificate would read that he had died of "strangulation due to accumulation of mucus with inability to expectorate" - he choked to death on his own mucus. The secondary cause of death was whooping cough.

It is possible that James did not die by Bertha's hand. The symptoms listed on his death certificate don't match those of any kind of poisoning, but it's hard to ignore the fact that he was weakened initially by stomach cramps and vomiting. He also might have already been sick when he was poisoned. If he already had whooping cough, it wouldn't have taken much to push him into the grave.

In 1915, Bernard Stuhlfelder, the 15-month-old son of the Giffords' closest neighbors, George and Martha Stuhlfelder, became ill with pneumonia. Bertha immediately came to the young family's aid. She tended to Bernard for a few days before "complications" occurred. The little boy began screaming and writhing in his crib as he suffered from stomach cramps. After three days of this, Bernard mercifully died. His parents were grateful to Bertha for trying to help him and sang her praises to other neighbors.

One night in 1917, the Giffords had an unwelcome visitor - a relative of Eugene's named Sherman Pounds. He showed up that night on their doorstep so drunk that he could barely stand. Sherman was a decent fellow. He was well-liked, funny, and at 53, was a widower who cared for five young children. He provided well for his family, but on weekends he liked to drink - a lot. Bertha was not happy to see him. She helped Eugene get him into bed, and she mixed a tonic for him to help with the terrible hangover that he was bound to wake up with. But Sherman never woke up. In the middle of the night, he began screaming in pain, plagued with merciless stomach cramps. He was dead by the time the sun rose. Dr. W.H. Hemker, the only physician in the large rural area, declared that Sherman had died from alcohol poisoning.

Neighbors sadly shook their heads at Sherman's funeral. It was only a matter of time before something like this happened. His heavy drinking just couldn't continue. He'd never been the same since the death of his wife.

About eight months later, Jim Ogle, a farmhand who worked for the Giffords, began squabbling with Eugene over unpaid wages. He became sick a short time later. Dr. Hemker diagnosed his illness as malaria. Of course, Bertha offered to nurse Jim back to health.

On November 17, 1917, Bertha traveled to Pacific to do her monthly shopping. She stopped in at the drug store and told the pharmacist that rats were biting her chickenS and stealing eggs. He sold her a package of common arsenic-based rat poison to deal with the problem. To purchase it, though, Bertha had to sign a poison registry. She must have believed that she was above suspicion because she signed it with her own name and left the store with some very dangerous poison.

The next day, Jim Ogle suddenly got much worse. He began complaining of sharp stomach pains. Dr. Hemker was called once again and explained that the stomach pains were another symptom of malaria. And he was right, stomach pains, nausea, and diarrhea can all be symptoms of malaria, but a high fever always accompanies them. Jim didn't have one. He suffered for two more days before he died on November 20. Dr. Hemker's cause of death? Acute gastritis.

In 1918, a nine-year-old girl named Beulah Pounds also died from acute gastritis. Her parents, Jesse and Margarite Pounds had taken her to Bertha for help. It didn't help. Another area doctor named Parker signed the death certificate this time.

That same year, Margaret, the two-year-old daughter of George and Frances Stuhlfelder, whose son, Bernard, had died under Bertha's care in 1915, came down with pneumonia. They summoned Dr. Hemker to treat her, and he prescribed a medication for her that had little effect. When Margaret's condition got worse, they turned to Bertha, who immediately came to the house with her bag of tonics. She gravely explained that Margaret was desperately ill and unlikely to recover but would do her best to care for the toddler anyway. She remained next to the little girl's bed for the next two days, and then Margaret suddenly began crying in pain and vomiting uncontrollably. She died the next day, on February 28, 1921. Dr. Hemker listed the cause of death as acute gastritis.

On December 26, 1922, Bertha was caring for a little girl while her mother was away on a shopping trip in Pacific. Ironically, her name was Beulah Pounds. She was a relative of the girl who had died under Bertha's care in 1918. She was also the granddaughter of Sherman Pounds, who had died at the Giffords' home in 1917. By the time that Beulah's mother, Essie, returned from her trip, the little girl was crying from a bad stomachache. Bertha offered to care for the girl overnight, and Essie agreed. She stayed up with the girl all night, and by morning Beulah was much worse. Her panicked mother sent for Dr. Hemker, but the child was dead by the time he arrived. Bertha described Beulah's symptoms to the physician, and he once again listed "gastritis" as the cause of death.

Beulah wasn't buried until January 5, 1923. Her aunt had insisted on a postmortem for the child. She seemed to be the only person that thought it was suspicious that another child from the same family had died from the same thing under Bertha's care. However, Dr. Hemker dismissed the idea of anything resembling foul play. Bertha was furious that anyone would suspect that she caused the little girl's death when she had only been trying to help.

Essie Pounds would later tell a local newspaper, "My sister thought things looked pretty funny because my father also died in Mrs. Gifford's house after he was taken with acute stomach pains there. Mrs. Gifford was usually a quiet woman, but she sure got mad. She said terrible things."

The death caused a rift between Bertha and the Pounds family, causing them to exclude her from the funeral. Beulah's funeral was the only one that she missed during her years in Catawissa.

A third child from the Stuhlfelder family, seven-year-old Irene, became sick shortly after Beulah's death. Frances, Irene's mother, later told a grand jury, "Irene had always been troubled with worms and when she got sick in 1923, we called Dr. Hemker. He prescribed some stomach powder and she seemed to be getting along very well when Mrs. Gifford came by. Mrs. Gifford nursed her, and she started to vomit. She was sick nine days when she died."

This was the third child within the Stuhlfelder family that had died under Bertha's care. When the grand jury later asked her if she was troubled by this, Mrs. Stuhlfelder said, "We did not think anything strange about the death of our children. Everyone in this part of the country knows that Mrs. Gifford has a wide reputation as a nurse."

Two years passed quietly, and then in June 1925, Ethel Schamel, a Gifford neighbor, became sick. Ethel and her husband, George, were, by all appearances, close friends of Eugene and Bertha. They were even related to them, cousins somewhere down the line. George often helped Eugene around the farm, and the couples often had suppers together. When Ethel became ill, Bertha, of course, offered to nurse her back to health. A few days later, Ethel died. She was only 33 years old.

About two months later, Ethel and George's son, Lloyd, died very suddenly. He was nine years old and in fine health - until he spent the night at the Gifford house. Two months after that, his seven-year-old brother, Elmer, also died while under Bertha's care.

And then, a month after that, Leona Schamel, George's sister, became sick. She was confined to her bed with stomach pains and vomiting, and Bertha quickly stepped in to care for her. Leona died two days later. She was 37. Dr. Hemker signed all four of the Schamel death certificates - but he did so reluctantly. Up until this point, he seemed to be completely clueless, inexperienced, or both. But now, he was starting to wonder about what was going on. He had recommended an autopsy after Elmer Schamel had died, but George wouldn't agree to it. Deciding not to press the issue, he cited the cause of death on Elmer's death certificate as "acute unknown disease" and "acute gastritis." This was wording similar to what he had written on the death certificates of several of Bertha's previous patients, but not quite the same.

Too many people had died, and Bertha Gifford had been around all of them. Even a simple country doctor began to think that something wasn't right.

And he wasn't the only one. After the Schamel deaths, Bertha's neighbors started whispering about possible foul play. Mortality rates were high in rural Missouri in the 1920s but not that high. Almost all the people who had died had been healthy and strong one day and mortally ill the next. And they had all died at Eugene and Bertha Giffords' house. Rumors spread, and a few people even wrote anonymous letters to Franklin County prosecuting attorney Frank Jenny urging an investigation, but no action was taken.

Bertha was safe - for now, anyway.

During Prohibition, Eugene - much like so many others in the rural county - kept a still in his barn to make homemade liquor. It was good quality, and he sold off the excess to neighbors and townsfolk, which earned the Giffords some extra money.

Eugene had a friend named Gus Unnerstall who helped him with distribution. At some point, Gus and Eugene got into an argument over money. It became so heated that Bertha ended up running Gus off the property with a butcher's knife. Gus came back a few days later, feeling shamed, but Bertha wasn't having it. Before he could get out of his truck, she was on the porch with the knife in her hand. She told him that if he set foot on her property, she'd cut him up into pieces. Gus called the sheriff, and Bertha was arrested, but no charges were filed against her.

Then, in 1926, Gus's mother, Clementine, became sick, and Bertha offered to care for her. One might think that Gus would be leery of letting a woman who had threatened to kill him with a knife take care of his mother, especially one about whom rumors were spreading about suspicious deaths, but he wasn't. He just assumed that Bertha had forgiven him for the recent dispute.

She hadn't.

Clementine died on February 9, just days after Bertha started nursing her. Her death certificate stated the cause of death as chronic myocarditis, or heart failure.

Things were quiet until early 1927 when Prohibition agents dropped in at the farm and destroyed Eugene's still. He was arrested and fined for the illegal operation but didn't spend any time in jail. Bertha was outraged. When the agents had first shown up, she tried to chase them off the farm with a shotgun, but this wasn't like scaring away a local farm boy. Federal agents took their job seriously. Even so, Bertha insisted that Eugene had done nothing wrong. Times were tough, and he was only trying to make ends meet. Everyone on The Bend - most of whom made their own liquor - felt the same way. The fine was a financial blow for the couple, and Bertha was angry.

Bertha's next victim landed - literally–on her doorstep on May 15, 1927. One of Eugene's farmhands, 49-year-old Ed Brinley, collapsed drunk that evening on the Giffords' porch. Eugene and Bertha managed to get him into the house and put him into the spare room bed to sleep it off. When Brinley woke the following day, Bertha gave him some homemade lemonade to help with his hangover. But his headache was quickly forgotten when he began experiencing stabbing stomach pains. A few hours later, he died in agony.

Dr. Hemker was called but was nervous about recording another death as "acute gastritis," so he summoned a second doctor from Pacific for his opinion. They could not agree on a cause of death, so Hemker again wrote "acute unknown disease" and "acute gastritis" on the death certificate.

Bertha took charge of Brinley's funeral arrangements and had his body picked up by the local undertaker. Brinley's estranged wife was unhappy about this and arranged to have the man's body taken to Pacific instead. The undertaker there, John Theibes, Jr., did excellent work. The high quality of that work would later come back to haunt Bertha Gifford.

After Ed Brinley's death, tongues started wagging again, and more anonymous letters were sent to the prosecutor, urging an investigation into Bertha's actions - and maybe those of Dr. Hemker, too.

In hindsight, it almost looks as if Dr. Hemker was Bertha's accomplice, covering up for her murders. But this wasn't the case. Hemker did suspect her of poisoning people but was unable to prove it. He was a simple country doctor with little formal training. He had never seen anyone poisoned before. After Bertha was eventually arrested, he stated that he had not spoken up because he feared Gifford would sue him for libel. He wasn't the only one who felt that way. Others were also suspicious, but no one wanted to be the first to speak up.

Even so, this seemed to be one too many strange deaths for the tiny town of Catawissa. Neighbors looked at everything Bertha did with suspicion. Bertha ignored the gossip. She came to Ed Brinley's funeral wearing her best black mourning dress and quietly took charge of the proceedings, greeting the mourners as if Ed had been her husband and not merely one of the Giffords' farmhands.

As news of this latest death continued to spread, the prosecutor continued to ignore the situation. It finally took a newspaper reporter from St. Louis to get the authorities to take action. After receiving an anonymous letter, he came to the county to look into the story. After nosing around town, he wrote a story naming at least five people who had died mysteriously while under Bertha Gifford's care. There were more, but that was a start - the suspicions about Bertha were finally a matter of public record.

In November of 1927, Frank Jenny finally empaneled a grand jury to investigate Ed Brinley's death. Bertha was enraged. She told anyone who would listen that all she had ever done was to try and help people. She began threatening libel suits against anyone who spoke against her. Eugene remained loyal to her and assisted in the harassment, even swearing at old friends in the middle of the street if they dared speak out against his wife. The Giffords managed to intimidate their neighbors to such an extent that no one was willing to testify against Bertha. As a result, the grand jury failed to indict her.

Finally, Bertha and Eugene moved to Eureka, Missouri, hoping to make a fresh start. However, her former neighbors - anonymously, of course -- kept up the pressure on Prosecutor Jenny, who summoned another grand jury in August of 1928. It remained an uphill battle, though. No one wanted to testify against Bertha. Things changed after Jenny managed to get the poison books from the two pharmacies in Pacific. He had now had details of the large amounts of arsenic that Bertha had been buying since 1911. Each time she had signed for it, she had written: "for rats." Once Jenny had hard evidence in hand, witnesses were finally willing to talk.

While the grand jury was hearing evidence about Bertha's poison purchases and listening to Frank Jenny's suspicions that she had killed at least nine people, other witnesses were finally gathering their courage. They contacted the prosecutor with their own stories of suspicious deaths, which Jenny then cross-referenced with Bertha's poison purchases.

She had killed, he believed, 17 people, making her one of the most prolific female killers in American history.

A grand jury indictment was returned against Bertha Gifford on August 23, 1928. Although Frank Jenny was able to show the jury at least four instances when patients in her care died within four days of her purchasing poison, she was only formally charged with two counts of first-degree murder. For the deaths of Ed Brinley and seven-year-old Elmer Schamel.

Bertha was arrested on the morning of August 25 by police detective Andrew McDonnell. He allowed her to powder her face before he placed her in the car. The woman he arrested that morning no longer resembled the dark-haired beauty that had once been known as "the prettiest girl in Jefferson County." Newspapers would later describe the gray-haired, heavy-set matron as having a deeply lined face and a grim expression. Her eyes, one reporter wrote, looked "dead." She was arrested in Eureka, which is in St. Louis County, but officers seemed to have no intention of transferring her to Franklin County, where her crimes had taken place.

Bertha was taken to the police station in Union, Missouri, where she was given a cup of tea and sat down to chat with Detective McDonnell. And that's when she started talking.

Curiously, she started complaining about the rumors going around claiming she had killed Sherman Pounds and little Beulah Pounds with poison. She denied giving arsenic to Beulah but did admit that she had given poison to Ed Brinley and Elmer and Lloyd Schamel to try and alleviate their pain. She had not done it to kill them. And strange as it sounds, that could have been the truth. Arsenic was often used throughout history as a medical treatment - although not in the size of dose Bertha used.

But she got into trouble when she mentioned offhandedly that she might have given "medicinal" arsenic to a few other people, too.

Detective McDonnell wrote down everything she said, and her statement was printed in newspapers the following day:

> *I, Bertha Gifford, hereby state of my own free will, without threat or promise of immunity, that my husband and I lived near Catawissa about August 8, 1925, when George Schamel brought his son, Lloyd, nine, and his son, Elmer John, about seven, to our house where he and they made their home with us.*
>
> *Lloyd was sick at the time. Doctor Hemker waited on him. I put some arsenic in his medicine before I gave it to him, and Lloyd died on August 31.*
>
> *About September 8, 1925, Elmer John took sick. Dr. Hemker was called and left some medicine for him and I put some arsenic in it, and Elmer John died about September 22.*
>
> *About May 15, 1927, Edward Brinley, forty-eight, drove up to our house in an old Ford. He was drunk. He came in, sat down for a little while, then got up and went out and fell down on the concrete walk.*
>
> *My husband went out and brought him in and fixed the bed for him in the front room and laid him on the bed. His mother came over and insisted we call a doctor. So I called Dr. Hemker.*
>
> *He left some medicine for him and I put some arsenic in the medicine. He died on May 16.*
>
> *In all three cases, the patients were suffering from severe pains in the stomach, and I put arsenic in the medicine to quiet their pains.*

When Bertha learned that her "confession" was in the newspaper, she was horrified. She frantically denied everything she'd said, claiming that McDonnell had made up the whole story. Eugene, still convinced of his wife's innocence, loudly told everyone that she had been bullied into a false confession. He then quickly hired a prominent lawyer named James Booth to defend Bertha. Booth promptly began trying to makeover his client's image, paying for her hair to be colored and cut into a stylish bob. The last thing that he wanted was for her to look like the murderous, middle-aged matron that she was.

In September, the court ordered the bodies of Ed Brinley and Lloyd Schamel to be exhumed. No autopsies had ever been conducted on the bodies, and Frank Jenny was confident in what a post-mortem would reveal. The exams were conducted by Dr. Ralph Thompson, a nationally recognized pathologist from St. Louis. He removed the stomachs and livers for testing and found the stomachs showed signs of distress with ulcers and signs of an angry, red rash. Considerable amounts of arsenic - much more than merely a "medicinal" amount - were found in the livers of both bodies.

While Bertha waited in jail for her trial, her legend grew. Stories spread about her behavior behind bars. There were stories that she was sleeping all day and performing strange rituals at night. One claimed that she paced her cell all night and, remarkably, howled like a wolf and put curses on anyone who walked past her iron-barred cell window. After refusing to eat for three days, it was said that Bertha requested ice cream and wanted to wear a nurse's uniform while she ate it. The rumor went on to say that she would only speak to Eugene and only while wearing that same nurse's uniform. The last story was actually true. The others were doubtful but proved entertaining in 1928.

Reporters began to refer to the Giffords' home on The Bend as the "House of Mystery." The neighbors never called it that - the newspapers made it up - but it managed to stick. People all over the area were finally talking. With Bertha behind bars, she couldn't sue anyone or chase them with a knife or a shotgun, so everyone wanted to tell their stories. They all had one, and each usually ended with a neighbor who had "suspected her all along."

But if that was true, then Bertha must have been a terrifying character to man, woman, and child alike. It seems hard to believe they could accept all that death and simply look the other way.

Bertha's trial began on November 19, 1928. Crowds of reporters and curiosity-seekers packed into the courthouse in Union, all eager to get a look at the defendant. A murder trial, especially involving women, was a rare thing in rural Missouri and everyone wanted to be part of it.

In the three months leading up to the trial, Bertha had lost a great deal of weight. Her black hair was still fashionably bobbed and waved, but her "dead" eyes stared out from hollow sockets. Her jailhouse pallor was not improved by the thick layer of powder on her face and the circle of rouge on each cheek.

Defense attorney James Booth entered a plea of not guilty for his client, which Judge R.A. Bruener accepted. The jury was composed of 12 men - eight farmers, a mail carrier, a shoe worker, a fruit dealer, and a restaurant owner.

Even though Bertha had been indicted on three counts of murder - Elmer Schamel's death was later added after Bertha's statement - the prosecution decided only to try her for Ed Brinley's murder. It's possible that Frank Jenny was holding the other two charges in reserve in case something went wrong with the first trial, but most likely, he just felt the Brinley case was the strongest.

Prosecutor Jenny began the proceedings by announcing in his opening statement that he planned to seek the death penalty in the case. The first witness called was a longtime neighbor, Mary Grodie. She testified that Bertha had said to her about Ed Brinley, "I hope he don't die in my house." It was an understandable statement and not really incriminating. She also added that Brinley's mother, not Bertha, had given him the lemonade that made him so sick.

Next on the stand was Ludelphia Brinley, the dead man's wife. She testified that on the day he died, Bertha told her that Ed's mother "would be a heap better off" with her troublemaking, drunken son dead and buried. Few who knew Ed would deny that was true, but it probably wasn't the best thing to say. Even so, Ludelphia didn't seem all that upset about her estranged husband's demise. When cross-examined, she explained that they had been separated for two years, largely due to his drinking. They were so out of touch that Ludelphia, who lived in the town of Kirkwood, did not even know that Ed was dead until his mother, Mary, told her. She didn't say much about her relationship with Ed, other than to admit that she was still upset that they had lost the butcher's shop they had owned together because Ed had drunk away all the profits. However, she was also instrumental in getting his murder investigated. She still loved him, in spite of everything.

The day ended in Bertha's favor. Two of the state's witnesses had done nothing to damage Bertha's defense.

On the second day of the trial, Ed's mother, Mary, took the stand. She revealed that she had a conversation with Bertha a short time after the funeral about the rumors suggesting Ed's death was suspicious. She told Bertha that the police might exhume her son's body. Bertha had said to Mary, "Don't you let them dig up Ed's body."

Mary described seeing Ed at the Giffords' house on the day he died, and she denied giving him the lemonade, contradicting the testimony of Mary Grodie. When asked if her son grew sicker after drinking the lemonade, Mary said, "He was sick all that day. He was sick before he took the lemonade and after it."

Frank Jenny then called William Powers to the stand. He was the druggist from Pacific, and Bertha had bought an ounce of arsenic from him on the day that Ed died. He had the poison log to back it up. Bertha's signature, along with her terse comment of "For Rats," was on the paper for everyone in the courtroom to see.

Bertha appeared to be unfazed by the damning testimony of the second day. She was cool, calm, and seemingly disinterested in what was going on.

Dr. Hemker testified next. He refused to look at Bertha during his testimony, still intimidated by her. He stated that he had found Ed Brinley in "acute distress" with stomach pains when he arrived at the Giffords' house. When asked by James Booth whether Ed potentially sneaking alcohol after his "medicinal" lemonade could have made his stomach pain worse, Hemker agreed it was possible. However, he added, the mix was probably "not toxic."

Dr. Hemker - useless to the end.

The doctors who performed Ed Brinley's autopsy -- Dr. Ralph Thompson and Dr. Harry Bristow -- took the stand next. They stated that Ed's organs showed no sign of organic disease or infection that would have caused death. They noted that arsenic was found in both the liver and the stomach - enough poison to cause the man's death.

Although he knew the testimony was coming, James Booth was not pleased with this reveal. That afternoon, he had engaged in a very loud argument with Frank Jenny in front of the judge about whether Bertha's "confession" should be allowed into evidence. Booth insisted that it was never intended to be a confession or an admission to murder

- Bertha had just been trying to answer Detective McDonnell's questions honestly. The debate became so heated that the judge dismissed the jury for the day and called McDonnell to the stand. Evidently, Bertha and the detective's conversation continued after she finished her official statement when she admitted that she sometimes took arsenic herself to look younger because it was said to reduce puffiness under her eyes.

No one knows if this was true or not. It might seem strange, but it was not outrageous at the time. Arsenic had been used for a lot of things, including for cosmetic enhancement. In fact, in 1855, Kate Bennett, the wife of a wealthy St. Louis businessman, had died after ingesting arsenic for years. She had used it as a beauty treatment, never realizing that it was slowly killing her.

McDonnell's boss, County Sheriff Gorg, had also been present at the time of Bertha's questioning, and he believed her statements were true. He felt that she "attributed some mystical healing power to arsenic and gave it to patients without sinister motive." That point of view was not shared by Detective McConnell, Prosecutor Jenny, or this author.

Once again, the sheriff may not have been as misguided as he appeared. Doctors did, on occasion, give arsenic and strychnine - two deadly poisons - to patients as a heart stimulant. In fact, Dr. Hemker had done the same thing himself in the past. He even admitted to a reporter that because he felt the deaths of Ed Brinley and the two Schamel children were suspicious, he refrained from giving them arsenic or strychnine so that he "didn't complicate the postmortem inquiry." In this statement, Hemker admitted that he believed Bertha had poisoned her "patients" and didn't want to confuse the autopsy by adding his dose of poison to hers. Amazingly, Dr. Hemker was never charged with negligence and was allowed to continue to practice in the wake of Bertha's trial.

I'm just glad that I was never his patient.

Judge Bruener ultimately ruled that Bertha's confession could be admitted as evidence - a devastating blow to the defense. The jury returned to the courtroom, and the statement was read aloud to them. After a witness swore that he saw Bertha sign the confession, the prosecution rested its case.

The first thing James Booth did when the defense arguments began was to ask the judge to dismiss the case, claiming that the prosecution had failed to prove Bertha's guilt. He was overruled.

Eugene was the first to testify for the defense. Nervous and morose, he claimed that Bertha had suffered from emotional trauma her entire life. She had been suffering from terrible bouts of melancholy for at least ten years. He said that his wife sometimes went days without sleeping, paced around the house, and refused to speak. At times, she simply sat in a chair and stared silently at the wall for hours at a time.

There was no question that Eugene's testimony had been coached by Bertha's attorney. He wanted the jury to sympathize with Bertha, seeing her as a lost and harmless woman. It's doubtful that Eugene had any idea that Booth was building a case for an insanity defense. Booth knew that when Bertha's confession was allowed into evidence, there was no chance of proving her innocent. His strategy had now shifted.

Booth knew that Eugene's testimony was crucial to his case - and so did Bertha. As she watched her husband on the stand, she listened intently for the first time since the trial had started. Her knuckles were white as she pressed a clenched fist to her mouth.

But she didn't need to worry about Eugene. He'd do anything to protect her. He went on to describe the day that Ed Brinley showed up at their house. He insisted that he, Eugene, had made a ham sandwich for the other man. His testimony rambled, which made him even more sympathetic to everyone in the courtroom.

Booth called four more witnesses, each of them praising Bertha as a "kind" woman but adding that she was also nervous, excitable, and prone to depression. They had also been coached to make Bertha sound as unstable as possible.

After their testimony had concluded, Booth requested a recess to confer with the group of doctors that he had arranged to testify about Bertha's state of mind. When court resumed, Booth changed Bertha's plea from not guilty to not guilty by reason of insanity. The judge agreed to the change, and Booth's doctors took the stand.

Oddly, none of Booth's "experts" were psychiatrists. They were all local doctors, and it's assumed that Booth thought this would make them more credible to the jury. It was their conclusion that Bertha was suffering from "dementia praecox," which was something of a catch-all term for insanity caused by old age. The doctors used Bertha's morbid behavior - her obsession with deaths, funerals, and illness - as proof of her condition.

In hindsight, this seems ridiculous. Not only were none of Booth's doctors' experts on mental illness, but they failed to explain why - if Bertha was suffering from dementia caused by her advanced age - she had started poisoning her victims many years earlier.

Frank Jenny brought his own doctors to the stand. They were actually psychiatrists and rightfully considered experts. They had only met Bertha one time, when they had been called to consult on the case, and Jenny had obviously hoped they found her sane and guilty of her crimes. But calling the two psychiatrists to the stand turned out to be a misstep. They examined Bertha, and both declared, "She is unquestionably of unsound mind, suffering from chronic paranoia, incurable."

After that, the jury was sent out to decide Bertha's fate. She never took the stand in her own defense.

The jury returned to the courtroom after three hours of deliberation. It seemed that 11 of them had voted not guilty, but one hard-bitten old farmer wanted to see her punished. The judge sent them out again. They returned a little after 10:00 p.m., this time with a verdict.

Bertha was found "guilty on the sole ground that she was insane at the time of the commission of the offense and has not recovered from such insanity."

Bertha had no visible reaction to the verdict, even after the judge ordered that she be remanded to a hospital for the criminally insane for the rest of her life. Eugene whispered something in her ear when she was led away but what it was remains a mystery.

Even with Bertha behind the walls of an asylum for the rest of her life, it might be said that she paid for taking one life but got away with all the other murders that she also committed. No motive was ever discovered for the killings. There had been rumors that the Giffords had profited from some of the deaths, but this wasn't true. Bertha didn't even charge the sick people that she cared for who became well. One of the doctors who found her insane stated that she might have believed she was doing good by ending the suffering of the sick and sending them on to heaven.

It was never suggested during her trial that Bertha might simply be evil - a sadistic killer who relished taking the lives of those under her control. In 1928, it was unthinkable that a woman might be capable of such cruelty and depravity.

Today, though, we know better.

After the trial, Bertha was sent to State Hospital No. 4, located in Farmington, Missouri. Eugene visited regularly, and a few years later, he hired an attorney who petitioned the court for a three-day furlough so that Bertha could be taken to St. Louis to be examined by doctors. He believed she was no longer insane.

Franklin County prosecutor Anson Tibbe was strongly opposed to the furlough. In reply to the petition, he noted the many other murders that Bertha was suspected of committing and noted that the jury that had convicted her ordered that she be sent to an asylum because she was hopelessly insane. He added, "In my opinion, it would be better for the community at large if Mrs. Gifford continues to be confined."

Bertha Gifford was in the asylum to stay.

On August 20, 1951, Bertha Gifford died of a stroke. She had spent the last 23 years of her life in the state mental hospital. She had been a model prisoner, first working in the hospital beauty shop and then as a cook.

I assume any rat poison was kept out of her reach.

Eugene, who had long since found another woman to keep him company, shipped Bertha's body to Pacific and paid for a private funeral for her at Morse Mill. She was buried in an unmarked grave in the local cemetery. A few years later, he was buried a few feet away.

Bertha - if she rests in peace - lies in between the graves of her two husbands and just a short distance away from at least eight of her victims.

The cemetery is practically in the shadow of the old Morse Mill Hotel, the same building that had been run as a boardinghouse by Bertha and her first husband, Henry. The old hotel does have a reputation for being haunted, but if Bertha still walks here - as so many claim - she may not do so alone. The structure dates back to the start of the tiny village, survived the Civil War, and was used by bootleggers during Prohibition.

There is a long list of paranormal happenings connected to the place - from phantom footsteps to full-blown apparitions - and plenty of people believe that Bertha Gifford is one of the many spirits that linger here. Others have also noted the possible presence of Bertha's first husband, Henry, with whom she operated the place during the early years of their marriage. When things turned sour, Henry conveniently became sick and died. Has his spirit returned to the old hotel?

Contractor Patrick Sheehan bought the building in 2007 with plans to re-open it as a small hotel again. Soon after, workers began to notice strange happenings like tools mysteriously going missing, footsteps and voices on the upper floors, and the men being touched on the arm or the shoulder when working alone. Each time they turned to see who was with them, they found they were alone.

As work has slowly continued on the building, it has become a heavily visited location for those seeking spirits and ghostly activity. As mentioned, the laundry list of haunted happenings is long. It has included the same things the contractors heard, as well as people having their hair pulled, their clothing tugged on, and in a few rare cases, have had inexplicable marks and scratches appear on their body.

Visitors and staff members believe that, in addition to Bertha and Henry, as many as nine other entities haunted the old hotel. Various ghostly men, women, and children have engaged workers and visitors over the years. Some have been given nicknames and even backstories, although records or newspapers have verified a few resident spirits.

But if even half of the numerous stories from all the people who have tromped through the place over the years are true, then the Morse Mill Hotel is definitely a haunted place.

And maybe, just maybe, Bertha Gifford is among those who don't rest here in peace.

THE "HOUSE OF WEIRD DEATH"
DR. ALICE WYNEKOOP

The street where the Wynekoop Mansion was once located is a rather forlorn area near Garfield Park on Chicago's West Side. It was once an opulent neighborhood where prestigious brick homes lined the streets, but it's a far different place today. The fading, weather-beaten old homes that still stand next to the empty lots and decaying structures are ghost-like now, recalling days of past elegance.

The Wynekoop Mansion was torn down many years ago, but its stories linger today. The house still casts an odd shadow over the city of Chicago as a place best-known for its notorious nickname - "The House of Weird Death."

Doctors Frank and Alice Wynekoop built the mansion at 3406 West Monroe Street in 1901. They closely supervised the construction, planning to turn the red brick home into a safe and loving environment for their family. The house seemed to be a warm and welcoming place, but then events conspired to make words like "haunted" and "cursed" better adjectives to describe it. The house became marked by death, illness, and scandal, but no single occurrence affected the house like the death of Rheta Wynekoop in 1933.

In the years before that horrific event, it seemed to be a wonderful place for the family. The Wynekoops had three children - Walker, Earle, and Catherine - and later adopted a second daughter, Marie, who died at an early age. All the children, who brought Alice many years of happiness, thrived in the environment of learning and respect that was fostered in the family home. Their only sadness came with the death of Dr. Frank Wynekoop, who died while several of the children were still young. He left them in the care of their more than capable mother.

Dr. Alice Lindsay Wynekoop was an early advocate of women's rights and promoter of the suffrage movement. In addition to being a graduate of the Women's Medical School at Northwestern University, she was a pillar of the community and was much loved and admired for her charitable deeds and work on behalf of those in need. She was also a civic leader and a pioneer in the movement for children's health. Dr. Alice maintained her office in her home, in a basement suite built for that purpose, accessible from West Monroe Street.

Her children continued to bring her joy as adults. Her oldest son, Walker, became a respected businessperson in Wilmette. He was married and had two children of his own. Catherine, the youngest of the family, also studied medicine and became a surgeon and highly respected member of the staff of the Cook County Hospital.

The pride of Dr. Wynekoop's life, though, was her son, Earle. What she saw in him remains a mystery, even today. Earle never had a job, was lazy, and almost constantly in trouble of some sort. He was a continual embarrassment to the rest of the family - except for Alice, of course. She never saw him as bad since he was quite charming despite his many faults and was very attentive to his mother.

At the age of 27, Earle was still being supported by his mother and still residing in her fashionable brownstone. By this time, his younger sister was finishing her medical training, and his brother had married and moved to Wilmette. Earle was living a carefree life of travel and, while visiting Indianapolis, met an attractive, well-to-do redheaded heiress named Rheta Gardner. She was an entertainer at a concert he attended, and when he returned to Chicago, he began corresponding with her. Less than a year later, he had coaxed her into coming to the city and convinced her that they should be married. Since Rheta was only 18, Alice insisted that Earle obtain consent for the marriage from the girl's father, an Indianapolis flour and salt merchant named Burdine H. Gardner. It was given -- somewhat grudgingly -- and Gardner did not attend the wedding.

A celebration was held on the wedding day, but Rheta refused to spend her wedding night in the Wynekoop mansion. After a night in a hotel, they left on their honeymoon. While they were away on their trip, Alice redecorated and refinished a suite of rooms on the second floor so that it would be ready for the newlyweds when they returned.

When Rheta returned from the honeymoon, she likely wondered what she had gotten herself involved in as she tried to fit in with the unusual group of people who lived in the looming three-story townhouse.

Earle was not what she expected when she got to know him better. He still had no plans to look for employment, although he was now married. His mother, Alice, was a brilliant doctor but privately an eccentric and odd woman. Marie, Earle's adopted sister, lurked about the house, staying mostly out of sight and always recovering from some sort of illness. Catherine seemed to be the only normal family member, but she was rarely there since her medical practice kept her so busy.

And then there was the household invalid, a middle-aged woman named Catherine Porter. She was rooming in the house and being treated by Dr. Alice for cancer and heart disease. The patient and the doctor were devoted friends and shared a $2,000 bank account.

Finally, there were two other tenants, a schoolteacher named Enid Hennessey and her father. They shared rooms on the second floor.

Rheta did her best to try and immerse herself in the household routines, but this was difficult because she had to do it alone. Earle largely abandoned her after the honeymoon, also regretting their hasty marriage. He was rarely home, so Rheta had to try and make the best of the situation. She became stranded in Dr. Alice's gloomy mansion, playing her violin, and wishing for her old life back. She had been an accomplished musician on her way to a distinguished career, and now everything had been derailed.

Meanwhile, Earle was keeping busy in his pursuit of other young women. His address book contained the names of more than 50 women he had slept with during the 1933 World's Fair. He had even proposed marriage to several of these poor, and lovesick girls, most of whom worked at concession stands on the fairgrounds. He escorted them about the fair, bought them food and small trinkets, and whispered about the future they would have together. He took particular care to avoid areas of the fair where his other "sweethearts" might be working. According to reports, when the details of Earle's many affairs were later revealed, his numerous "fiancées" accused him of making love to them in strange ways that were "shocking and repulsive."

I have no idea what that means, but that's probably best.

Earle's behavior made things worse for Rheta. She had become increasingly less happy the longer she was in Chicago. She had been all but forgotten by her handsome husband and had been left with only the companionship of her aging mother-in-law and a middle-aged schoolteacher. The only bright spots in her life were her music and the friendship of Marie and Catherine. Tragically, though, Marie died. Then Alice's friend, Catherine Porter, and Miss Hennessy's father died a short time later. Not long after that, Catherine left and moved to be closer to the hospital where she worked.

Rheta plunged into a dark depression. She was terrified of becoming mentally ill. When she had been only seven years old, her mother had been confined to an insane asylum and had died there, from tuberculosis, about a decade later. Now, Rheta had a great fear of any kind of illness and an even greater fear of insanity.

She roamed about the house doing mundane chores, playing her violin, and treating herself to an occasional purchase of sheet music. That seemed to be her only joy. She felt like she had become another tenant of Dr. Alice's, who appeared to resent Rheta increasingly each day, believing that her precious Earle had chosen poorly when he picked Rheta as his wife.

As for Rheta, we can't possibly know what went through her mind as she was trapped in the house day after day, but it couldn't have been good. She had no idea where her husband was, where he spent his nights, or what would happen to her in the future. Her life seemed very uncertain, adding to her anxiety.

Sadly, though, there would be no need to ponder her future for much longer.

On November 21, 1933, around 10:00 p.m., Catherine Wynekoop was called away from her duties in the children's department at Cook County Hospital for an urgent telephone call. When she picked up the receiver, she heard her mother's voice on the other end of the line. She sounded shaky and unsure as she told Catherine, "something terrible has happened here... It's Rheta. She's dead. She's been shot."

Catherine called the police. The call sent police officers from the Fillmore Street Station to the mansion on West Monroe Street. The officer in charge of Squad Car 15 later reported: "We went directly there and were met at the front door by a lady who told us to come inside. The lady we met first we later found to be Miss Enid Hennessey, a schoolteacher, and roomer there. When we got inside, we met the defendant, Dr. Wynekoop. She was seated in a chair in the library. Mr. Ahearn, an undertaker, was there. We asked the defendant what happened. She said, 'something terrible has happened; come on downstairs, and I will show you.' We went downstairs."

The police officers followed Dr. Alice downstairs and found Rheta lying on the operating table in the basement. She was nude, partially covered by a thick blanket, and her clothing was in a pile on the floor next to the table. She had a bullet wound in her breast, just under her left shoulder. Next to the body, they found a chloroform mask and the murder weapon. Three shots had been fired from it, and it had been left just over the girl's head. She had some burns on her face, later said to be a reaction to chloroform.

The crowd of police attracted onlookers outside, but it made things very tense inside of the house. Detectives, who soon arrived on the scene, began questioning everyone, including Alice. At one point, she muttered, "It must have been a burglar... We've had robberies here before when burglars took some money and some drugs, I keep in the glass case over there in the corner. It must have been a burglar..."

While the police were there, Dr. Alice kept speaking. She continually changed her story, confusing the police, the coroner, and even members of the household. Many wondered if the beloved doctor might be incoherent over the girl's death. She advanced the theory that Rheta may have killed herself in a fit of depression and then again suggested that a burglar was responsible for the crime, declaring that both money and drugs were missing from the house.

The police didn't arrest anyone on the night of the murder. They took Rheta's body to the coroner's office and allowed Captain John Stege - one of Chicago's finest and a rarity in the Windy City in that he was an honest cop - to take over the case. To Captain Stege, the manner of Rheta's murder didn't suggest that she had surprised a burglar. He also ruled out suicide because of the angle of the shot and because of chloroform burns that were present on the girl's face.

There was a lot that Stege needed to know about the murder, and once word of the sensational incident leaked to the press, there was a lot the public needed to know, too.

For instance, where was Earle Wynekoop on the night of the murder?

According to Earle, he traveled west to photograph the Grand Canyon for the Santa Fe Railroad, accompanied by a friend named Stanley, at the time of his wife's death. He claimed that he had started west for Arizona several days before the murder, but rumor had it that he had been seen in Chicago less than 24 hours before the crime. He was taken into custody when he arrived from Kansas City by train, and his friend "Stanley" turned out to be an attractive brunette that he had met at the fair. She thought his name was "Michael" and he had told her that he wasn't married.

When Earle stepped off the train, he was met by detectives and by a group of reporters who badgered him with questions. Earle, naturally, enjoyed the limelight and told reporters that Rheta "was sickly, had tuberculosis, and was also mentally deranged. You know she once tried to poison my entire family by putting drugs and iron filings in our food? The marriage, gentlemen, was an utter failure."

When one of the reporters quizzed him about his attractive companion, the young woman slipped away in the crowd.

Earle laughed as she ran off and waved his address book. "I've got 50 more just like her listed here!" This probably wasn't the best thing to brag about just after his wife was murdered, but no one claimed Earle was smart. He did agree with his mother, though, and dismissed Rheta's murder as the work of a "burglar" or, less helpfully, "a moron."

While Earle was making wild statements to the press, Rheta's father, Burdine H. Gardner, was rushing to Chicago. He met with Dr. Alice and then dramatically took his daughter's body home for burial. Alice had advised him to tell others that complications from tuberculosis had caused Rheta's death. He would later state that he found the living arrangements at the Wynekoop house to be rather odd, and Dr. Alice even more so. "She struck me as a most peculiar person," he told a newspaper reporter.

The police continued the investigation, grilling Alice and the other members of the household. Confused by the large and eccentric collection of characters who lived in the house, they questioned them and found the bizarre group fiercely loyal to Dr. Alice. When detectives hinted to Miss Hennessey that Alice might have been responsible for Rheta's death, she became hysterical and began screaming, "It's a lie! It's a lie!" She stood faithfully by the doctor until the trial when she finally realized her friend was a murderer.

During her interrogations, Dr. Alice continued to explain Rheta's death as being caused by "burglars" and "drug fiends." In recent months, she claimed, her basement office had been broken into, and drugs had been stolen. She suggested that Rheta might have caught them in the act. But when detectives searched for any reports of a burglary, they found nothing. They continued to grill Dr. Alice, but she refused to say anything that would incriminate herself or Earle.

On the morning of November 24, 1933, Captain Stege entered the office where Dr. Alice was being held. She was lying on a couch with an overcoat covering her. She sat up when Stege entered the room.

"Good morning, doctor," Stege greeted her.

"Good morning, captain."

"Did you have any breakfast?"

"No, I didn't want any, but I would like some coffee."

Captain Stege turned to an officer in the room and sent him to get some coffee for Dr. Alice. He returned a few moments later, and she took a sip from the cup. She turned to Stege, "Captain, what would happen if I told the story about killing Rheta?"

Stege shook his head. "Doctor, I don't want any story from you. All I want is the truth."

Captain Stege then told her that he had recently learned that Earle had taken out a $5,000 insurance policy on Rheta. This convinced him that Earle was the killer.

And that did the trick - Dr. Alice confessed.

She confessed that it had been she, not Earle, who had pulled the trigger, but only after Rheta had already expired from the deadly anesthetic. It had all been an accident, she said. Dr. Alice explained that she had been about to perform a painful surgical procedure on the young woman for a pain in her side that was troubling her. The mysterious "pain" was never explained. Alice said that she had asked Rheta herself to pour some chloroform into the mask to ease the pain of the surgery, but the dosage had proven to be too much. Minutes later, the girl had lapsed into a coma. Fearing public humiliation and a ruined reputation, she panicked and fired the fatal shot into the girl so that she could claim the crime had been committed by imaginary "drug fiends." The burns on Rheta's face, thought to be from chloroform, were actually powder burns from the pistol.

The sensational confession raised doubts among the detectives. They still believed that "charming" Earle had masterminded the crime, and his mother had taken the blame for it to save her "little boy."

Earle visited his mother in jail before her confession. He was in custody at the time, but he was allowed to speak with her. Officers overheard part of their conversation.

"For God's sake, mother," Earle whispered, "if you did this on account of the bond of love between us, go ahead and confess."

"But Earle - I did not kill Rheta."

"Mother - mother..."

The investigation found love letters that had been written between mother and son, suggesting a relationship that was anything but normal. One such letter became public, and it had been written after a secret meeting that had taken place between Alice and Earle on the Sunday evening before the murder. Assistant State's Attorney Charles S. Doughtery believed Alice had made up her mind to murder Rheta after this meeting. No one knows what was said at that meeting --- and never will --- but after her return home, Alice wrote Earle a frantic note that read:

Sunday night ---

Precious ----

I'm choked --- you are gone --- you have called me up ---- and after 10 minutes or so, I called and called ---- no answer ---- maybe you are sleeping ---- you need to be ---- but I want to hear your voice again tonight ---- I would give anything I had --- to spend an hour ---- in real talk with you ---- tonight --- and I cannot ---- Good night.

Dr. Alice apparently believed that the sickly, moody Rheta had caused Earle to feel hemmed in and made him miserable. After talking with her son at great length about his unhappy marriage, Dr. Alice became determined to kill Rheta so that he could find happiness elsewhere. She simply wanted to ensure her son's love for her by getting rid of his unwanted wife.

And there might have been another, less complicated motive, as well. Dr. Alice was deeply in debt. If Rheta was dead, the family could collect on her life insurance policy.

Earle refused to believe his mother's confession, branding it false. He later made five obviously false confessions of his own, culminating in a wild story about how he had slipped into the Wynekoop home on Tuesday afternoon, hid in the basement for his wife, seized her, threw her onto the operating table, killed her, and then fled by airplane to Kansas City. He tried to re-enact how he had done all of this but so badly bungled the "crime" that detectives laughed at him.

His entire story was dismissed, and his confession debunked when it was proven that his alibi was solid. He really was out of state at the time of the murder.

Prosecutors were convinced that Dr. Alice was responsible for the murder, killing Rheta because she needed money and hated her daughter-in-law for making her son so miserable.

The Wynekoop case stayed in the newspaper headlines. On November 28, Alice became seriously ill with a bronchial cough and high blood pressure. From her sickbed in the prison hospital, she reversed her confession and claimed that the police had coerced her into making it after 60 hours (about two and a half days) of questioning.

She said she had been given no food or drink during that time, save for a single cup of coffee. Two days later, she changed her story again and, this time, stated that she had only made the confession because she did not think she would live to stand trial.

The trial was scheduled for January, but the Wynekoops stayed in the public eye in the meantime. On December 2, Earle announced that the family had hired a private detective to solve the mystery and prove his mother's innocence. Apparently, though, nothing ever came of that investigation, for it was never spoken of again.

A few days later, newspapers carried reports that Rheta's body had been exhumed in Indianapolis. The coroner announced that there was no trace of chloroform in her body, thus repudiating one portion of Alice's story.

In the middle of December, two events occurred that, while having nothing to do with Rheta's murder, managed to keep the Wynekoops in the headlines. On December 14, Earle ran over a nine-year-old boy with his automobile. His sister, Dr. Catherine Wynekoop, was in the car with him at the time. Shortly after, Alice's brother-in-law, Dr. Gilbert Wynekoop, was found to be insane by a jury that was trying him for attacking a nurse. He was sent to St. Luke's Hospital for an indefinite stay.

These happenings helped put Chicago into a state of great excitement by the time the trial opened in January. While on the stand, Enid Hennessey finally became convinced of Dr. Alice's guilt - and actually shuddered on the stand when she pondered the events that occurred on the day of the murder. The murder had occurred in the afternoon, but soon after, when Miss Hennessey arrived home for the day, she met Dr. Alice, who acted as though nothing was amiss. The doctor prepared a supper of pork chops and mashed potatoes for the two of them, and after eating, they sat in the study and quietly discussed some of the recent books they had read.

All the while, Rheta had been lying dead in the downstairs surgery.

The case dragged on for days, but it must have been Enid Hennessey's testimony of the cool, callous killer that convinced the jury of Alice Wynekoop's guilt in just 14 hours. On March 6, 1934, they returned the verdict, and while the public and the press were divided about whether justice had been served, Alice was sentenced to 25 years in prison.

She was sent to the Women's Reformatory in Dwight, Illinois, and was paroled in 1949. She was 79 years old when she got out, and she died two years later, her life and reputation destroyed.

Somehow, the rest of the family managed not to be destroyed along with her. Walter Wynekoop continued his successful business career, and Catherine became an esteemed physician, long associated with the Children's Clinic of the Cook County Hospital.

Only Earle vanished completely from the public eye. In 1945, he was working as an auto mechanic, but that was the last time that anyone heard from him. He undoubtedly died many years ago, but no trace of him has been found.

Dr. Alice's grim mansion - which the newspapers called "The House of Weird Death" - was torn down many decades ago. For years, rumors about the house circulated. It was considered by many to be haunted, and stories claimed that the ghostly strains of Rheta's violin could sometimes be heard coming from the ruins of the building. She seemed to be trapped in the house, with Dr. Alice herself, who was sometimes reported peering out the broken windows of the mansion.

True or fiction? No one knows. This baffling case extends from the crime to the ghost stories that surround it. Was Dr. Alice insane, or was she a devious killer who murdered her daughter-in-law without regret - just so that her beloved son would be happy? If I had to bet, I would say it was the latter, but we'll never know for sure.

The neighborhood around Garfield Park is now a crime-ridden area and where the mansions once stood, mostly just empty garbage-strewn lots remain. Rheta, Dr. Alice, and the rest of the oddballs who once lived in the house are now long forgotten.

And if their ghosts still walk here, they walk alone.

THE "TIGER WOMAN" CLARA PHILLIPS

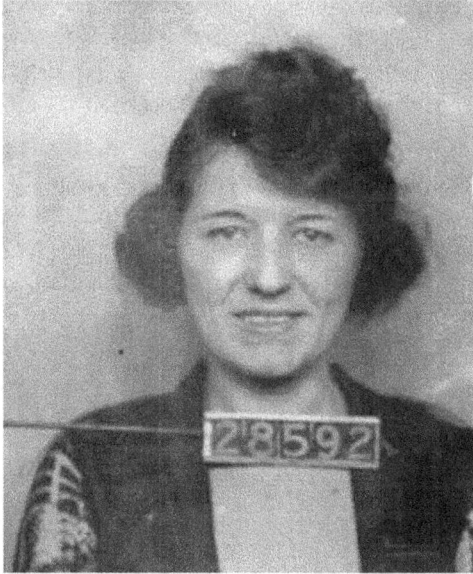

On July 10, 1922, a young woman named Clara Phillips walked into the hardware department of a local five-and-dime store. She picked up a 15-cent hammer, hefted it in her hand, and then turned to the clerk and asked him if he thought it was heavy enough to kill a woman with.

The clerk, thinking she was joking, replied, "Yes, it is, if you hit her hard enough with it."

Clara bought the hammer from him.

The following day, she used the hammer - just for the purpose she'd asked the clerk about. The murder she committed came to be regarded as one of the most vicious to ever occur in Southern California history.

But Clara didn't start off as a killer. Some might even say that her husband drove her to it.

Armour L. Phillips was part of the oil boom of 1922 in Los Angeles. Wildcatters were drilling everywhere back then. Oil derricks sprang up like dandelions after a spring rain. Oil magnates - would-be, has-been, and a few of the real thing - started companies in what is now Long Beach, Venice, Culver City, and a dozen other locales around L.A. Oil fever spread like an epidemic across the city. Anyone, it seemed, could get rich. If you couldn't drill for oil, you could buy land. Gasoline was produced from oil, and gasoline was needed to fuel the thousands of automobiles already starting to clog the city streets.

Big, charming, handsome, and young, Armour Phillips started calling himself an oil stock salesman. He bought himself fine suits, a flashy automobile, and a big house for his wife, Clara, a former vaudeville dancer that was just 23 years old. She was dark-haired, dimpled, and cute with a bright, captivating smile.

Armour furnished their home with imported rugs, expensive furniture, a built-in bar, and three sets of silver. And he did it all with the expectation that there was a lot of oil still left to be discovered. He believed that more new companies would float more new stock issues, that more and more people would buy these oil stocks, and that he would soon be rolling in dough. So, he bought everything on credit - easy credit that the banks were more than willing to offer.

But not everything went according to plan. Armour had stocks to sell but too few prospects who wanted to buy them. As his credit dwindled, he asked for more, making excuses about his payments while trying to keep up appearances and watching his dreams unravel.

Perhaps seeking distraction - or possibly her late husband's money - Armour turned his attentions to a tall, stylish, and beautiful young widow named Alberta Meadows. In the spring of 1922, he was spending most evenings and weekends with her, using the excuse with Clara that oil stock salesman kept strange hours. They were always running around town, going to prospect's homes, or taking investors out to the oil fields so they could see what their money was paying for. Clara might not enjoy his absences, he said but hoped she knew they were necessary.

But Clara wasn't as dumb as Armour thought she was. She was suspicious, and she wasn't shy about protecting what was hers. Back in her showbiz days, she was known for fighting any woman - and some men - who took what didn't belong to them. Clara spent most of June eavesdropping on Armour's late-night telephone calls from the extension upstairs. She followed him in taxicabs, snuck into restaurants, and soon discovered that he was having an affair. She quickly developed a hatred of Alberta Meadows.

By the first week of July, Clara had decided how she wanted to handle the matter and dropped in a local five and dime to buy a claw hammer.

Clara spent the next day in a speakeasy in Long Beach with her best friend, chorus girl Peggy Caffee. She spilled the whole story of Armour's affair over their drinks, telling Peggy that she had listened in on one call and heard Armour say that he was in love with Alberta and wanted to run away with her.

That was just too much for Clara to take. Several hours - and a lot of cocktails later - she'd decided to get rid of the rival for her husband's affections once and for all.

Clara and Peggy - a bit unsteady and more than a little tipsy but otherwise presentable - went to the bank where Alberta worked and waited in the parking lot for her to leave for the day. When Alberta came out to her car, they asked her for a lift to Peggy's sister's house in Montecito Heights. Alberta, who didn't know who Clara was, agreed to take them.

Clara was chatty on the way. She complimented Alberta on her fine car, commented on her dress, commiserated with her on the loss of her husband, and talked about how nice the weather had been lately.

Montecito was a new subdivision with a few grand homes near the top of a winding road that passed through an arroyo, winding its way toward the green and largely vacant hilltop. As they reached a secluded bend in the road, Clara asked Alberta to pull over for a private conversation. Alberta stopped and turned off the engine.

Clara didn't seem so chatty now. In a quiet voice, she confessed that she was bothered by what appeared to be new tires on Alberta's car and by her lovely gold wristwatch. Wasn't it true that Armour Phillips had bought those things for her? The same Armour Phillips that was Clara's husband?

Alberta denied it, but Clara insisted it was true. She was now visibly angry. She punched Alberta in the face, and the other woman tumbled out of the open car onto the road. Alberta stumbled to her feet and began to run down the hill with Clara in pursuit. When a heel broke on Alberta's shoe, the chase ended.

Clara had already pulled the 15-cent hammer from her purse, and she swung it squarely into Alberta's face. And then she swung it again, cracking her skull. Clara began to rain hammer blows down on Alberta's head and body. She beat her face to a bloody pulp and then used the hammer's claw to disembowel the young women. Finally, the wooden handle broke, leaving the head of the hammer embedded in Alberta's skull. Even then, Clara choked her and rolled a 50-pound boulder onto her chest.

Peggy Caffee witnessed the whole thing from the car but, not wanting to end up like Alberta, she tried to keep silent, even as she vomited all over the back seat of the vehicle.

Clara had broken a finger on the hand she'd used to swing the hammer but was unaware of it as she removed her bloody wedding rings and dropped them into Alberta's purse. She got into Alberta's car, leaving bloodstains all over the seats. She smiled strangely at Peggy, "It's all right now, dear, time to go home."

Clara dropped Peggy off at her house in Long Beach and then drove home. Her waiting husband was shaken when she arrived in Alberta's car - especially when he saw all the blood inside of it and all over Clara's hands and clothing.

"I guess it's murder," she said. "I killed your lover, Alberta." She poured herself a drink and then smiled at him and told him she was going to cook him the best dinner he'd ever had because she was so happy. Clara had decided to turn herself over to the police the next day.

In the morning - after having presumably the "best dinner he'd ever had" and tossing and turning all night - Armour decided that he didn't want Clara to turn herself in. "You've got to escape and get out," he told her, and soon he was in his own car, following Clara in Alberta's, on his way to Pomona, about 30 miles away. There, they abandoned Alberta's Ford. It might be months, if ever, before anyone reported it or linked it to the murder. People frequently abandoned cars when they couldn't keep up with the payments or couldn't afford to fix them. It would be just another stranded automobile that the state government couldn't keep track of.

Returning to Los Angeles, Armour scraped up all the money he could to put Clara on the next train to El Paso. There, she would cross the border. Mexico, troubled by bandits and insurrections, was still angry about the U.S. Army invasion of 1917 under General John "Black Jack" Pershing and had no extradition treaty with the United States.

Clara could vanish over the border and stay gone for good. She'd be free, and Armour would be free of his troublesome wife.

Meanwhile, the police were in the process of making a gruesome discovery on Montecito Heights. One of the cops who took a look at Alberta's disemboweled corpse said loud enough for a reporter to hear him, "It looks like she's been attacked by a tiger." Even veteran newsmen who rushed to the scene were sick to their stomachs. But they recovered quickly - it was the slow summer season, and pages needed to be filled. This grisly murder promised to grab big headlines.

What sort of monster was loose in L.A.?

Was he attacking beautiful women?

And whose corpse was this, wearing silk underwear, with no identification and no face to photograph?

They had their headlines, and the people of the city shivered with delicious fear.

Back at home, Armour Philips was having second thoughts about helping Clara escape. His lover was gone, and his killer wife had vanished. He didn't want to be charged as an accessory, so he called his lawyer and spilled his guts. His attorney, John Haas, was unsympathetic, and he called Undersheriff Gene Biscailuz, a legendary figure in Los Angeles law enforcement and an old friend of Haas. The attorney had arranged a meeting between the lawman and his client, and Armour wept as he told his story again.

Biscailuz made some calls, and Clara was pulled off the train in Tucson. She spent two nights in a filthy, airless cell, sleeping without a blanket and a mattress on a rusty iron cot, and was barely fed.

But back in Los Angeles, the newspapers were creating her legend. Who was the monster who had mauled Alberta Meadows, crushed her skull, and ripped out her guts? It was Clara Phillips, the "Tiger Woman!"

Clara rode back to L.A. in style, accompanied by County Sheriff Bill Traeger himself. The sheriff's wife shared a Pullman car with the prisoner. En route, Clara was confronted by a distraught Peggy Caffee, held in protective custody by a detective. Peggy identified Clara as Alberta's killer. Clara coolly ignored her.

When she stepped off the train, she was greeted by throngs of reporters, photographers, and bizarrely, admirers. The "Tiger Woman" had consented to be interviewed on the way back to Los Angeles. She told reporters that she enjoyed driving cars, riding bicycles, horses, and motorcycles, but she knew nothing about murder. She was wearing a smartly tailored suit when she arrived at the station, and she posed for pictures, showing off her broad smile and dimples.

Clara's admirers - men and women alike - sent letters, boxes of candy, and bouquets of flowers to her cell. They scorned her lousy husband, who had cheated on her, and then ratted her out. Even so, Armour borrowed more money to pay for her lawyers.

The trial was a sensation. Peggy Caffee arrived to give testimony in a very lowcut green blouse and a short skirt. She stuttered and stammered her way through it and eventually mumbled that Clara was Alberta's killer.

Clara denied it all. She'd had words with Alberta and called her a few names on the side Montecito Drive, but that was all. "Alberta, you're just as dirty as a dog!" she claimed to have yelled. Alberta, who was taller and heavier, then slapped Clara across the face. They had struggled, which had caused Clara's broken finger. And then it was Peggy who lost her head and started hitting Alberta with the hammer. Peggy Caffee had been the killer, not Clara.

It was an inventive story, but it didn't work. Clara's attorney shifted gears. Clara must be insane, he said. The mutilation of Alberta's body could have only been done by someone who was insane. Both sides called psychiatrists to make their cases. The doctors who testified for the prosecution fared far better with the jury. Clara was convicted on charges of second-degree murder, with a sentence of 10 years to life in prison.

But that was far from the end of Clara's story.

During the trial, Clara had made the very slight and public acquaintance of a spectator whose name was Jesse Carson. Unable to get a seat in the crowded courtroom, he'd stood outside and watched her arrive each day as she was taken from her cell at the county jail to the courtroom. One day, he announced to her, very quietly, that if things went badly and she was convicted, he'd break her out. Clara's attorney heard the exchange. He knew a crackpot when he saw one, and he laughed the whole thing off.

But Jesse wasn't laughing, and neither was her attorney when, on the morning of December 5, a jail matron came to Clara's cell to bring her breakfast and discovered that the cell was empty. Clara was gone!

It turned out that Jesse Carson wasn't some "crackpot." He was a soldier of fortune, gun runner, and smuggler who had become enamored with the "Tiger Woman." He had slipped a hacksaw blade into Clara's cell, and she spent three nights cutting the iron bars on the window, using chewing gum to hold them in place. On the night of December 4, Clara slipped her slender shoulders and hips through the narrow window opening. Perched on a ledge, she reached up and grabbed the cornice of the roof. Hand over hand, she inched along the building to the drainpipe in the corner and then shimmied down it to a roof above. Jesse had left a rope hanging there, and she used it to lower herself five stories to the alley below. After jumping a steel fence at the end of the alley and into Jesse's waiting car, she was free.

They hid out in Pomona - not far from where Clara had abandoned Alberta's car - in a cold, damp house while the manhunt for the "Tiger Woman" unfolded. The weather wasn't kind to Clara, and she came down with tonsilitis. So, Jesse moved them east to Redlands and into a duplex that they shared with an older woman who could neither read nor write, so she hadn't seen the papers. By January 4, Clara was well enough to move again.

She bleached her hair blond, put on a pair of dark glasses and a hat, and they took off. They traveled east, and in St. Louis, they had their only brush with the law. Their taxi skidded into another car on a rain-slicked street, and the police took witnesses' names and addresses. But Clara was inventive, and even though her face had been on the front pages of St. Louis newspapers, too, no one had any idea that the "Tiger Woman" had passed through town.

In New Orleans, they rented a room for a while, and then Clara sailed alone to Vera Cruz. It was the first time she had been able to relax in months.

Clara Phillips was free - for now.

Back in Los Angeles it wasn't the police who managed to pick up Clara's trail; it was Morris Lavine, a reporter for the *Los Angeles Examiner.* Morris visited the rooftop from which Clara escaped and found two sets of footprints - his and hers. He knew that Clara would need money when she got out of jail. If she went to friends or relatives in L.A., the police would be all over her. But if she left the area, someone could send her money - and money always leaves a trail.

He remembered that Alberta Meadows had worked at a bank, and he found a friendly teller there who was willing to share some of the secrets of the Armour Phillips' accounts. He discovered that Armour had been borrowing heavily and making withdrawals. But there were no checks or money orders drawn on the account, so where was the money going? Morris knew that most of the financial transactions between U.S. and Mexican firms were done by the Bank of Montreal's Mexican branch or the Mexico City Banking Corporation during this time of mutual antagonism. So, he got in touch with his newspaper's correspondent in Mexico City, Julio Trens, who started poking around south of the border. He soon learned that money from Los Angeles was going to Galveston, Texas, and from Galveston, it went to Jesse Carson in Mexico. He received cash in an envelope with the return address of a local church on it - a church where Amour Phillips' sister taught Sunday School.

Morris shared the information he'd dug up with the authorities, and they sent a telegram to Mexico, asking for cooperation and an arrest of the "Tiger Woman." But it was too late. She'd gone to Guatemala. They wired Guatemala City but were too late again. She was now in Honduras, a country with an extradition treaty with the United States and a consulate in Los Angeles. Clara was soon taken into custody, and with her, Etta May Jackson, her younger sister. Undersheriff Biscailuz, his wife, and a deputy set sail for San Salvador, the closest port to where Clara was being held in Tegucigalpa.

The situation in Honduras was complicated and unstable. The country was on the brink of revolution, and Jesse Carson, who had run guns to Honduras for the rebels, was behind bars. Since it was customary during revolutions in the so-called "Banana Republics" for the jails to be emptied, he wouldn't be locked up much longer - and neither would Clara.

She continued to be her charming self, winning over the chief of police and many of the local officials. They were smitten with her, as was the public. The prevailing sentiment seemed to be that what Clara had done to Alberta with that hammer was no more than the woman deserved and no more than what many of them would have done in the same situation.

With both an election and a revolution brewing, Clara's extradition became a political lightning rod of controversy. Should Honduras just turn over Clara just because the Yankee government demanded it? Wasn't Honduras an independent nation with its own sense of pride? Clara was being held at the jail in spacious second-floor rooms without bars on the windows. Sympathetic locals knew how easy it would be to break her out.

Into this odd situation arrived Morris Lavine. He paid a call on Franklin Morales, the American ambassador. There was going to be a special session of the Chamber of Deputies, and it was likely that they would refuse to turn Clara over to the U.S. authorities. It had become a matter of pride to them. But Franklin Morales managed to get the ear of the Honduran president. He told him that a certain large American firm might pay a substantial advance on their Honduran taxes - but only if the extradition was not discussed in the meeting. This had a certain, under-the-table appeal to the president.

While all this was brewing, Eugene Biscailuz and company arrived. He conducted negotiations in Spanish, and all parties - except for the revolutionaries - were included. After a few days, it was agreed to remove Clara from the jail and take her overland to Puerto Cortez on the north coast. From there, they would take a ship to New Orleans. The party would leave Tegucigalpa as soon as the formal extradition request papers arrived from Washington.

A mounted messenger was dispatched 100 miles to pick up the diplomatic pouch. When he returned, it was opened, but there were no extradition papers inside - and it would be at least another week before the next pouch arrived. One of the officials who had become friendly with Clara pointed out that Honduras had already held Clara longer than the treaty required. There were no papers, he said, so she needed to be let go.

With her release looming, Biscailuz and Ambassador Morales hurried to see the president. An unscheduled cabinet meeting was held, and a decision was made - undoubtedly greased by American dollars - to move Clara to Puerto Cortez and to keep an eye on her until the extradition papers arrived. After the papers arrived, the Chamber of Deputies would formally consider the request, but the president would make sure they were honored.

Clara was taken from Tegucigalpa in the middle of the night, without a chance to use a telephone to reach Jesse Carson. Biscailuz and his party drove out of town, crossed a large lake in dugout canoes, and then stopped to make camp in the tiny jungle village of Jaral.

Morris Lavine had his first chance to sit down and interview the "Tiger Woman." She insisted that she was innocent and that she had been convicted because of the newspaper headlines. She had never, she claimed, had the chance to tell her side of the story.

The next morning the party arrived in San Pedro by narrow gauge railway. They were met by the local military commander, who demanded that Clara be released by the authority of orders from Tegucigalpa. More negotiations took place, and more money exchanged hands. The party was soon on its way again toward Puerto Cortez, this time by tramp steamer. They were wedged onboard between bundles of bananas.

When they arrived in Puerto Cortez, they were greeted by a wire from the capital stating that the extradition papers had finally arrived - and they were worthless. Apparently, the language was incorrect, and the following day the Honduran Supreme Court planned to order Clara's freedom.

Biscailuz called a meeting. He only had $40 left. Morris Lavine had only a little more. He was considering loading Clara onto a boat and getting her out of the country. The governments could decide this between themselves later on. The drawback to that plan was the three Honduran gunboats in the harbor and the chance of starting an international incident that could lead to war between Honduras and the United States.

Morris had a better idea. He would talk to Clara and try and convince her to waive her extradition rights and come back voluntarily. It was a long shot but worth a try.

When he sat down with Clara, he asked her why she had been convicted if she was innocent. According to Clara, the detectives had never bothered to find out who bought the murder weapon, the hammer that killed Alberta. If they had, they would have found out that Peggy had bought it. Clara had been convicted in court, but it was all a mistake.

Morris nodded and seemed to contemplate what she'd told him. Then why, he suggested, didn't she just come back and clear her name. "Set the record straight," he told her. New evidence was a basis for a new trial, and her attorney should be able to find the sales clerk who sold the hammer. Her attorney, he reminded her, had already filed an appeal in her case, so the ball was already rolling. Morris didn't mention that her attorney had died on the day she escaped from jail - another reason he wasn't laughing at Jesse Carson, I guess.

Clara hesitated. Morris had appealed to her vanity. If she was truly innocent, she should come back. But if she really was the "Tiger Woman," she had better stay in Honduras, where she was soon to be set free.

Finally, Clara voluntarily boarded the boat for New Orleans in the early morning hours. When they arrived, they caught a train bound for Los Angeles. At Colton, near San Bernardino, Los Angeles District Attorney Asa Keyes boarded the train. With him were Sheriff Traeger and John Richardson, Clara's new attorney.

They had bad news.

California law required that appeals be filed within five days of sentencing, but Clara's original attorney had inexplicably waited nine days. The law was clear - Clara had no way to appeal. She would be sent to prison without a second trial. The only good news was that she would be given a guaranteed parole date since she had chosen not to fight her extradition.

More than 2,000 Los Angeles residents met the train that brought her back to the city in June 1923. Standing on the observation platform of a railroad car, she and Armour Phillips kissed and embraced for the benefit of the crowds and the press. And then the train kept going - all the way to San Quentin and later, to the new women's prison at Tehachapi.

Behind prison bars, Clara learned the saxophone and organized and conducted a seven-piece orchestra made up of female inmates. She wrote and performed in a theatrical production and learned to be a dental assistant.

Clara came up for parole in the spring of 1935. She would have gotten out sooner, but she lost some good behavior time after getting caught writing dirty notes to Thomas Price, a young convict working as an electrician.

By the time she got out of prison, her strange celebrity was a thing of the past. She never returned to the front pages of the newspaper. She moved to La Mesa, near San Diego, and lived with her mother and three sisters.

In 1938, she divorced Armour Phillips, who had moved back to his native city of Galveston, Texas, several years before. He continued to work in the oil business until his death in 1972. She announced that she planned to marry again, but her husband was never publicly identified. Clara worked as a dental assistant until 1961 when she moved to Texas and disappeared completely from the pages of history.

"The Tiger Woman" only claimed one victim, but her case was such a sensation that she still hasn't been forgotten.

"HIGH PRIESTESS OF THE BLUEBEARD CLIQUE"
OTTILIE "TILLIE" KLIMEK

On November 20, 1936, a Chicago woman named Tillie Klimek died in prison. She had been convicted of only a single murder, but the authorities suspected that she had killed many more, including neighbors, relatives, and three of her husbands. However, Tillie wasn't just a murderer - she was also a self-proclaimed psychic who was able to determine a person's exact date of death.

It was a convenient ability to have for a woman who killed with poison.

She was born Ottilie Gburek in Poland in 1876. She came to America with her parents when she was an infant, and the family settled in Chicago. As a young girl, she began working in a northside sweatshop, a fate shared by many poor immigrants in the city in those days. By the age of 20, Tillie had given up on the idea of ever finding a husband. To be charitable, those who knew her said she was not exactly the sort of girl to attract a man. She was short, broad, muscular, and red-faced, plus she dressed poorly in mannish-looking clothes. However, she was said to be a superb cook, one of the best in the Little Poland neighborhood - a skill that would someday bring Tillie into the public eye.

Unlucky enough to find a husband on her own, Tillie took $50 that she had saved over a three-year period and invested the cash with a marriage broker. Her investment gained her a prospect - a dull young man named John Mitkiewitz, who promptly proposed to her. Mitkiewitz had also been lacking in marriage prospects but largely because he was a lazy, shiftless, would-be handyman and jack-of-all-trades who never had steady work. He knew his bride-to-be had a job and was the best cook in the community, and he planned to take advantage of that fact. So, Tillie settled for a man whose best efforts were directed toward starting, or recovering from, a serious hangover.

She put up with John for years, but by 1911, she decided that she'd had enough - she was tired of being berated by her supervisor in the sweatshop, neglected by her husband, and taken advantage of by her neighbors. She was renowned as a cook - her carefully guarded stew recipe was a favorite - but she wanted more.

Tillie decided that she would become a prophet.

One hot summer evening in 1911, Tillie was sitting on a fire escape with a neighbor woman, and she pointed to a yellow mongrel dog that was sniffing around for food in the alley below. She told the neighbor that the dog would be dead within a week. When asked how she knew this, Tillie replied, "My powers tell me so."

On the seventh day, the dog was found lying stiff and dead, and Tillie's fabulous career as a seer began.

Over the next three years, Tillie predicted the deaths of neighborhood cats and dogs with stunning accuracy, enhancing her claims of being able to foretell the future.

As a result, Little Poland learned to respect and fear her. She found the butcher would give her excellent prices on the meat that she bought for her stews when she hinted that evil might befall him if he overcharged her. The iceman made sure that his deliveries reached

Tillie's house first, especially after she mentioned to him that she disliked his product to be melted when it arrived.

Men, women, and children went out of their way to be nice to her. When they didn't, the results could be dire.

In 1912, Stanley Zakrzewski, a cousin of Tillie's died at the age of only 16. A feud had started between Tillie and the family, so she tried to patch things up with one of her "special" stews. Stanley's sisters, Helen and Stelle, also died after becoming "sick." Tillie personally nursed each of them before their deaths.

Another cousin with whom Tillie bickered, Nick Micko, became mysteriously sick one day after eating one of Tillie's stews, but he recovered.

Each time, Tillie predicted the death of those who became sick, just as she had predicted the deaths of neighborhood cats and dogs. The only one she got wrong was Nick, which was an impressive track record to friends and neighbors.

In fact, the only person not impressed by Tillie's claims of prophecy was her husband. That, as it turned out, was to John Mitkiewitz's misfortune.

One night in 1914, Tillie was sitting outside with a neighbor and made a strange and spooky comment to the other woman. She said, "I don't think John is long for this world. The powers tell me that I will be a widow within three weeks."

One morning, exactly three weeks later, Tillie went into the local butcher's shop to buy some meat for a stew and announced, rather indifferently, that her husband had died. The butcher inquired about the cause of death. "He just got numb all over, and then he stopped breathing," she replied. Tillie then purchased her stew meat and left the store without another word.

She didn't shed a single tear as her husband was lowered into the ground at All Saint's Cemetery. After the funeral, she invited friends to her home for dinner and an impromptu celebration. Toward the end of the party, she let it be known that, although her husband had been a miserable drunk, she considered marriage to be a fine institution and was contemplating finding another mate.

Even though John Mitkiewitz was "barely cold," as the saying goes, Tillie returned to the marriage broker a few weeks later. She had received, she admitted, $1,000 from an insurance company after her husband had died. Her money, along with her prowess as a cook, was enough, the broker believed, to counterbalance her lack of physical attraction when it came to arranging another match. Six weeks after the funeral of John Mitkiewitz, Tillie married again, this time to a man named John Ruskowski, who had recently taken a job as a section hand with the Pennsylvania Railroad and who, as luck would have it, carried a large insurance policy for $2,000.

Ruskowski, a man known for his enormous appetite, was pleased with his new bride. He often boasted to his friends and neighbors about how well Tillie kept him fed. He had no idea what she put in those stews of hers, he told everyone, but he had never tasted anything like them.

One night, after their first month of marriage, Ruskowski noticed that something seemed different about that evening's stew. He asked Tillie what she had added to it, and she simply told him that it was "a new spice."

The following afternoon, Tillie was gathered with some of her friends and told them that she was about to make another prophecy - her powers had previewed a new death in the neighborhood. Her friends asked her who was going to die. She replied, "Don't say anything about it to him because it would worry him - but it's my husband."

Two weeks later, Tillie was in the butcher shop buying meat for another stew, and just before she left, she informed the butcher that she had become a widow again during the night. She explained, "It was the same thing that happened to my first husband; he just got numb and died."

John Ruskowski was laid to rest in All Saint's Cemetery, just a short distance away from Tillie's first husband. Once again, she showed little emotion at the gravesite, and later, at another party in her home, she expressed to her friends that she had every intention of finding another husband.

A hulking, ugly man by the name of Joseph Grantkowski had put in a bid for a wife with the same marriage broker that Tillie consulted with about a third husband. Grantkowski, a railroad laborer, was known to his friends as "Blunt Joe" because he honestly spoke his mind about everything. If he didn't like the looks of someone, he told them, no matter what the consequences. When he met Tillie, he definitely did not like her looks. Despite his own, flat-faced countenance, he had hoped for a wife who was young and pretty and said so to the marriage broker while still in Tillie's presence. Tillie kept her feelings about the man's comments to herself and, in fact, acted so grateful to him that Grantkowski felt ashamed of himself and agreed to move into Tillie's home on a trial basis. His notions about what a bride should be were somewhat alleviated by the fact that Tillie was such an excellent cook and that she had a bank account, thanks to the insurance payments from her two dead husbands, that was quite substantial in those days.

Grantkowski became quite taken with Tillie's cooking, and eventually, he overlooked her plain appearance and asked her to marry him. Tillie delayed the marriage, though, shortly after finding out that "Blunt Joe" carried no life insurance policy. However, still remembering his stinging remarks about her looks, she continued to feed him her "special" stew. Within two months of her last husband's death, Grantkowski had taken to his bed. Tillie told an impressed neighbor, "He's numb all over, poor man. My powers tell me that he has less than two weeks of this life." He died a short time later and was laid to rest in All Saint's Cemetery.

In 1919, Tillie married for the third time. This unlucky soul was Frank Kupczyk, a friendly, easy-going man who worked at the same factory where Tillie had worked for so many years. For whatever reason, Frank believed that Tillie was the most attractive woman that he had ever met. This was a new experience for Tillie. It was the first time she was married to a man who liked her for herself and not only for her cooking. Many believe that Tillie, now in her 40's, was in love for the first time in her life.

On the day of the wedding, Tillie and Frank threw a wild party in their home, serving huge quantities of food and drink. The party went on for hours, but the only person who did not take part in the merrymaking was a young woman named Rose Chudzinski, a distant relative of the bride who lived in a nearby apartment. Many of the guests tried to get Rose to join in the party, but she refused. Finally, Tillie demanded to know what was wrong with her. Rose's reply had an ominous tone, "I have been wondering how long your new husband is going to live."

Tillie grew angry and demanded to know what she meant by the remark. Rose told her that she thought it was odd how soon after marrying her, her previous husbands had died. Tillie threw her out of the house, and Rose left without another word.

Several of Tillie's friends, who had been temporarily sobered by the incident, waited in embarrassed silence for some sort of explanation from the bride. Tillie had been unnerved, but she quickly recovered herself. She shook her head before she spoke, "Poor child. We must be sorry for her rather than angry because she's soon going to die."

Her friends expressed shock that a girl as young and vibrant might die, but Tillie told them there was nothing to be done. Her powers foretold Rose's death - and there was nothing Tillie could do to stop the future from coming to pass.

Tillie enjoyed such a status as a prophet in the neighborhood that no one who heard her wedding night pronouncement ever made any connection between the coming death of Rose Chudzinski and the fact that the girl had made some very pointed remarks to Tillie. These same witnesses were, in fact, greatly impressed when it became known that Tillie was making frequent visits to Rose's home in an effort to patch things up between the two of them. When Rose died within six weeks of Tillie's third wedding, Tillie, rather than drawing suspicion to herself, took on added stature as a prophet. She had foretold, ten days earlier, the exact day of Rose's death.

In retrospect, it seems incredible that Tillie could have been so closely associated with so many deaths within such a short space of time without drawing official suspicion to herself. The neighborhood where she lived, however, offers much in the way of explanation. To speak out against a seer in Little Poland in those days, let alone suspect one of ulterior motives, was considered the same as signing one's death warrant by way of courting a prophet's curse. Rose Chudzinski had cast aspersions on Tillie, and the young woman's fresh grave was a frightening reminder of the terrible things that could happen to anyone who entertained ideas similar to those expressed by Rose.

In addition, Tillie had also seen to it that different doctors and different undertakers had been summoned following the deaths of her husbands. Two different insurance companies had paid out on their policies, and therefore, no outsider in possession of sufficient facts upon which to draw a suspicious inference could be found. Since no one brought the deaths to the attention of the Chicago Police Department, there was no one to investigate her mysterious "special" stews.

Following the death of Rose Chudzinski, things were quiet in the neighborhood for a time. Tillie left the sweatshop where she had toiled for so many years and was content to stay home and cook for her adoring husband. Just to maintain her reputation, she continued to predict the deaths of neighborhood dogs and cats. Her predictions, of course, were never wrong.

In 1920, circumstances arose that caused Tillie to be glad that she had maintained her reputation as a seer. She had gotten into arguments with the parents of three small children, and the children died, one by one, just as Tillie had predicted they would.

Shortly after the third child's death, Tillie turned her attentions to Frank, whose affections had somewhat cooled toward her over the last few years. Moreover, during a fire escape chat with a neighbor lady, Tillie also learned that Frank had developed a roving eye. By strange coincidence, her "powers" revealed to Tillie that Frank was not long for this world at the same time she discovered that his romantic interests lay elsewhere.

Tillie went into a neighborhood store and bought some black cloth, which she announced was for her husband's funeral, who was going to die in 10 days. Tillie's next stop was at the undertaker's establishment, where she bought the cheapest casket available. While Frank was at work, she had it delivered to the basement of the tenement where she lived.

Frank, who was a great believer in his wife's supernatural powers, noticed that she was sewing a black hat one evening, and he asked her what it was for, commenting that it looked like a mourning hat. Tillie told him that it was and added that her powers told her that a death was coming in eight days and that she would have to attend a funeral.

Six days later, Frank was confined to his bed, unable to rise, suffering from severe pains in his legs and stomach. He was dead within two days, and Tillie had him laid out in his coffin for the wake. She threw another party on the night of Frank's funeral and, with a mug of beer in her hand, remarked to a neighbor woman that it was unfortunate that she had such bad luck with husbands. The neighbor was shocked when Tillie said, "I hope the next one lasts a little longer."

In 1921, Tillie married Joseph Anton Klimek, a short, mild-mannered man in his fifties. Tillie left the old apartment, where three husbands and a prospective groom had died, and moved to another street in Little Poland. It was a fresh start, and Tillie and Joe were quite happy during the first few months of their marriage - but it wouldn't last.

A rift formed over two large dogs, which Joe had owned for several years, and he insisted on keeping them in their apartment. Tillie complained to a friend one day that Joe spent more time with his dogs than he did with her. Her "powers," though, provided a solution to the problem. She predicted that the dogs were going to die within one hour of each other. Joe was not told about this prophecy, and the first that he heard about it was one night in October when, returning from the brewery, he stumbled over the bodies of both dogs as he let himself into the apartment.

Klimek went around to tell his brother, John, who ran a blacksmith shop, about his misfortune. John stared at his brother curiously as he told the story, and while he expressed condolences about Joe's beloved dogs, he stated that he was more worried about his brother's life. When asked why John told him that his face was puffed up and had a purple cast, he wondered if Joe might be coming down with something.

The following day, Joe called on his brother again and told him that he had pains in his legs and that something seemed to be wrong with his hearing. John began to question his brother about his wife's previous husbands, a subject that Anton knew very little about. When he arrived home, he asked Tillie about them, and she dismissed the subject chaulking up their deaths to bad luck. Joe's aches and pains were nothing that a hearty meal couldn't cure. Even though her stew tasted bitter, she coerced him into eating a bowl of it anyway.

John Klimek saved his brother's life; He rushed Joe to the hospital and notified the police. Joe's doctors suspected arsenic poisoning. Luckily for Joe, he survived, and Tillie was arrested after tests confirmed the doctor's suspicions.

When police officers arrived at Tillie's apartment on October 27, 1921, she was taken into custody after a struggle. Tillie fought them savagely and injured several officers before she could be tossed into a patrol car. It's reported that as she was driven away, she turned to one officer and said, "The next one I want to cook dinner for is you. You made all my trouble."

The body of Frank Kupczyk, her most recently deceased husband, was exhumed, and his corpse was found to contain lethal quantities of arsenic. The police also learned of other neighbors and relatives in the neighborhood who had died unexpectedly. After Tillie was arrested, her cousin, Nellie Koulik, was arrested, too. Tillie may have been the "high priestess of the Bluebeard clique" in Little Poland, but Nellie - and possibly others - were willing followers.

In 1918, Nellie had come to Tillie complaining about her husband, Wojek Strummer, saying that she wanted to divorce him. Tillie had a better idea and gave her a box of rat poison. Nellie claimed she never used it, but somehow, Wojek mysteriously died a short time later.

And he wasn't the only one.

Soon, Nellie's daughter, Sophie, also died, followed by her twin brother, Ben, a month later. The death of Nellie's granddaughter, Dorothy, age two, occurred soon after that, followed by the poisoning of Nellie's daughter, Lillian. She survived, as did her brother, John. They both believed that their mother had poisoned them. Why? Because Tillie told them that she had. But it wasn't true. Nellie was later acquitted after spending a year in prison during her drawn-out trial.

As for Tillie, her trial was a circus, and she was the star in the center ring. She strutted around, posed for the newspaper cameras, sneered at the prosecutor, and even made another prediction - that she would escape the gallows. And she did. She was found guilty of the murder of Frank Kupczyk in March 1923 and was sentenced to life in prison -- the harshest sentence ever given to a woman in Chicago.

Like all the other inmates, Tillie was put to work in prison, although officials expressly ordered that she never be allowed to cook for her fellow inmates.

She died behind bars on November 20, 1836, with her days as a psychic seer long behind her.

"ANGEL OF DEATH" JANE TOPPAN

The sprawling building has been standing since 1854, nearly five decades before its most notorious resident took up residence there. Built in the "bat-wing" design of all the old Kirkbride structures, it looms over the neglected lawn like some sort of menacing creature. It seems almost impossible to believe that this building had been designed to bring comfort to the mentally ill. There seems to be no comfort in its brick walls, dark windows, and crumbling walls today.

The Taunton State Hospital has seen more than its share of residents over the years. When it opened, it was called the "State Lunatic Hospital at Taunton," but improvements in mental health caused its title to be changed many times. Fires, accidents, and the passage of time doomed the old hospital, but all life is not yet gone from its hallways, staircases, and patient rooms. Its current - and probably final - incarnation is an addiction treatment center for women.

But legends say that these women are not the only occupants of the building. There are others - inmates from the past who are unable to find peace, even long after their deaths. Most of them are faceless, nameless spirits, souls who were lost long before they took their final breath.

But if they truly do walk here, they do not walk alone.

One spirit among them has earned a place of infamy in New England history - an "angel of death" who took the lives of at least 31 people that she treated as a nurse.

"My desire is to kill more people, more desperate people, from every man and every woman who has lived to this day," she once said.

Is it any wonder that her malevolent spirit still walks?

Jane Toppan was born Honora Kelley on March 31, 1854, in Boston, Massachusetts. She was the daughter of Irish immigrants and had three older sisters, Mary, Ellen, and Delia. Her mother, Bridget, and her father, Peter, lived in rather desperate conditions, taking in boarders to help pay the bills because Peter foolishly spent all the money he could get his hands on. He was well-known as an eccentric and an abusive alcoholic, nicknamed by those who knew him "Kelley the Crack" - as in "crackpot." In later years, Peter became the source of many local rumors about his alleged insanity, including that his madness drove him to sew his eyelids closed while working as a tailor.

In 1857, Bridget died from tuberculosis, and her death sent Peter completely over the edge. People who knew the family could easily believe that Honora -- or "Jane" as she would become - was insane. They believed that she inherited it from her father. Her sister, Ellen, became "violently insane" in her 20s and was committed to the Medfield Insane Asylum for life.

After his wife's death, Peter sent his oldest daughters, Mary and Ellen, to live with family friends. The two youngest girls, eight-year-old Delia and six-year-old Honora, were taken to the Boston Female Asylum, an orphanage for indigent girls. He abandoned them there and never saw them again. Documents from the asylum make note that they were "rescued from a very miserable home."

Two years later, Peter Kelley was dead. He drank himself to death.

No records exist of Delia and Honora's experiences during their time in the asylum, but they could not have been good. Honora went on to become one of the most prolific female serial killers in history, and Delia reportedly ended her life as a prostitute and alcoholic.

The Boston Female Asylum depended on donors to keep the doors open. The girls were served three meals each day, but the menu rarely changed. Week after week, they received boiled rice with molasses or milk porridge thickened with flour for breakfast, depending on the season. Dinner was soup on Monday and Wednesday, boiled meat on Tuesday, pork and beans on Thursday, lamb broth on Friday, fish on Saturday, and roasted meat and pudding on Sunday.

The asylum claimed to teach the young girls "useful things suitable to their age, sex, and station," which, in truth, meant very little. They were taught to read, spell, and work their sums, but only as "far as necessary." Their main objective was to teach them to be domestic servants, which was likely as far as they could ever hope to rise. They learned sewing, cooking, and housekeeping. Once a girl turned 11, she was "placed" with a family. A few girls were adopted, but most became servants.

That was precisely what happened to Honora. In November 1864, a widow named Ann Toppan from Lowell, Massachusetts appeared before the asylum board with the desire to adopt her. She was only seven, but the asylum made an exception, and Honora became an indentured servant.

Contrary to what she had told the board, Ann Toppan never formally adopted Honora. Rather, in an attempt to hide the little girl's Irish heritage, Ann changed her name to Jane after her favorite aunt. With Jane's dark hair and eyes and olive complexion, she easily passed for Italian, which was considered much better than Irish in those days. She even coached the girl on a new life story. If anyone asked, Jane was to say that her birth parents had died while coring the ocean to America from Italy. She later took on the surname of the family and became known as Toppan.

With her entire life story now a lie, Jane became known as a clever and engaging storyteller. She was "pretty, smart, and an exceedingly clever child," who was popular and active in the

Congregational church in Lowell and the Sunday School. She made many friends, but others would hold lifelong grudges against her. As a notorious gossip, Jane spread nasty rumors about classmates that she had a grudge against or was jealous of. By ingratiating herself with her teachers, she was able to pin her misdeeds on others and serve as the classroom snitch.

And yet, she won the heart of her first lover, a 16-year-old boy who showered her with flowers and even proposed marriage. When he broke things off with her, though, Jane was crushed. Privately, she had terrible issues with self-esteem, knowing that she was a servant at home, not a member of the family, no matter how Ann Toppan and her daughter, Elizabeth, acted when they were all out in public.

Jane remained with the Toppans during her teen years and into her 20s. She had settled into spinsterhood by then, neglecting herself and allowing her once trim figure to balloon in size.

Shortly after Ann Toppan died in 1874, Elizabeth married a local merchant named O.A. Brigham. The relations between the two foster sisters became strained, while the differences in their stations became more apparent. Jane lived in the Toppan house for another 11 years but was now nothing more than a servant - an arrangement that must have been a bitter one. Jane eventually left the family home at the age of 28 in 1885.

No accounts remain to say whether Elizabeth asked Jane to leave or whether she did so on her own. She was assured, though, that she could return whenever she wanted, and there would always be a room waiting for her.

And Jane did come back every year - even after she murdered Elizabeth.

Out in the world on her own, Jane found herself with no skills other than domestic duties, no money, and no husband. For a time, she stayed with friends and then, in 1887, decided to become a nurse.

For the next two years, she trained at the nursing school affiliated with Cambridge Hospital, working seven days a week, 50 weeks (about 11 and a half months) per year, with no time off for holidays. She slept in a cramped, dimly lit, and poorly heated room with three other students, rose each day at 5:30 a.m., had breakfast, and was at work on the ward by 7:00. Between shifts - which lasted 12-14 hours a day - she had roughly an hour for a break and to eat both lunch and supper.

For the first months of nursing school, she scrubbed floors, emptied chamber pots, and washed dirty sheets. Later, the school added patients that Jane bathed, treated wounds, administered enemas, and dispensed medications.

Everyone loved her. She was well-liked, bright, friendly, and even earned the nickname of "Jolly Jane." She became close with her patients - young and old - and picked her favorite ones.

She also began to experiment on her patients, giving them doses of morphine and atropine to witness the results. She would later confess that she derived "the most exquisite pleasure" from watching people die. She didn't realize it until she witnessed her first death and then, after that, did all she could to carefully kill others. She would stand by their bedside - and, in one case, crawl into bed with a victim - so that she would feel their breath grow fainter and see the light vanish from their eyes. Even better, after a large dose of morphine, they would suffer "violent convulsions." That way, Jane could hold them in her arms as they shivered, shook, and expired.

But, of course, she couldn't kill every patient. There were hundreds of them that she nursed back to health, including the survivors of a particularly nasty typhoid epidemic that hit the city.

Jane excelled in her studies and was recommended for the nursing program at the prestigious Massachusetts General Hospital in 1889. But the physicians on staff at the hospital were a little more suspicious than those at the nursing school. When an inordinate number of patients seemed to die under Jane's care, she was discharged. No wrongdoing against her could be proven, so she left the hospital with her nursing diploma and a new position as a private nurse.

That same summer, Jane claimed what may have been her most satisfying victim - her foster sister, Elizabeth Brigham. Elizabeth had come to Lowell to try and reconnect with her sister, but Jane had something else in mind.

Over the years, the two women had maintained a cordial relationship, although deep down, Jane always resented Elizabeth. Two decades older, Elizabeth had always been everything that Jane wasn't. Elizabeth had always been pampered by Ann Toppan, while Jane was little more than a servant. She was wealthy, attractive, and married to a respected deacon of his church and the Boston and Main Railroad depot manager. Jane, who never married or was even courted by a suitable man, wasn't even mentioned in her foster mother's will.

On August 26, the two of them were having a holiday on Cape Cod, and Jane suggested a picnic on the beach. They went down to Scotch House Cove and spent several hours chatting and munching on cold corned beef sandwiches and taffy. By the end of the day, Elizabeth was exhausted by the sun and surf and went to bed early. The next morning, Jane called her down for breakfast, but she didn't respond. Instead of checking on her, Jane rushed next door to the landlord's house and asked them to call a doctor because "her sister had taken sick." Jane then sent a telegram to Elizabeth's husband, telling him that his wife was in grave condition.

Alarmed, O.A. Brigham took the first train to Cape Cod. By the time he arrived, Elizabeth was in a coma. She died in the early morning hours of August 29. The doctor believed that she had died from a stroke.

But, of course, Jane knew it was strychnine.

Jane eventually began spending every summer in the peaceful Cape Cod community of Cataumet. She rented a cottage from Alden Davis, one of the town's most influential residents. He ran a successful marble business, owned a general store, and was the man responsible for bringing the railroad to Cape Cod.

Over the years, the folks of Cataumet got to know Jane quite well - or so they thought. She was often seen cavorting with the children in town, walking on the beach, and playing on the bluffs with them. She could always be counted on to take the children on picnics and made sure they had plenty to eat. Many wondered how she could afford all the frivolous spending, but they didn't wonder for long. Everyone adored "Jolly Jane," and her kindness and her bright smile touched the hearts of everyone she met.

But while living in Cataumet, Jane signed numerous notes for unpaid rents and personal loans totaling thousands of dollars. However, the Davis family was so fond of Jane that none of them pressured her for the money - until June 25, 1901, when Mattie Davis finally stopped being so generous.

On that morning, Mattie made plans to go to Cambridge to reluctantly confront Jane about the money. She was a good friend, but

Mattie and her husband, Alden, felt they had been patient long enough. Mattie planned to combine the trip with a visit to see her daughter, Genevieve Gordon, who lived in Chicago. She was in the area visiting her in-laws, who lived in Somerville, Massachusetts. She planned to visit Genevieve after seeing Jane about the money. Mattie expected no problems with Jane. In fact, she planned to ask Jane if she was going to summer with them again that season.

In poor health because of diabetes, Mattie was moving slowly that day, largely because of the hot and humid conditions of the past week. To help his wife, Alden offered to go to the station and hold the Boston train for a few minutes, so she makes it onboard. He made it just in time and chatted with the conductor while his wife hurried to the train. As she was coming down a short hill, she suddenly tripped and fell, landing hard in front of the passengers on the train.

Alden saw it happen through the window and rushed out to help her. But by the time he reached her, Mattie had gotten shakily to her feet and was limping toward the platform.

Disheveled and embarrassed, she clung to her husband's arm as he assisted her to a seat in the second car. Conductor Charles Hammond helped her to get settled before he started collecting tickets from other passengers.

By the time the train left the station, Mattie had settled her nerves. Another passenger, Willard Hill, who had witnessed her fall, took a seat across from Mattie and asked her if she was all right.

"Nothing hurt but my dignity," she replied.

They chatted during the remainder of the trip, and Mattie shared with Hill the reason for her trip to Cambridge. Hill was disappointed when he learned that Jane had been so careless about paying her bills. He and his wife knew Jane and always thought highly of her, but it was now clear that she had been taking advantage of the Davis family. He told Mattie that if he were in her position, he wouldn't leave Cambridge until Jane had paid her debts.

When she left the train in Cambridge, Mattie went to 31 Wendell Street, the home of a former city councilman named Melvin Beedle and his wife, Eliza. Jane was a boarder in their home, and Mattie hoped to work everything out with Jane without causing a scene.

And that makes it clear that Mattie Davis really didn't know Jane Toppan at all.

Before Jane had boarded with the Beedles, she had been living at 10 Wendell Street with Israel and Lovey Dunham. As part of her room and board, she offered nursing care to Israel Dunham, who was in his late 70s. With all his aches and pains, Jane believed that a little morphine could do him some good.

Israel Dunham died on May 26, 1895.

Jane continued rooming at the Dunham house, helping take care of Mrs. Dunham for the next two years. Often bothered by arthritis at her advanced age, Jane offered to ease her frequent pain - leading to her death on September 19, 1897.

After dispatching the Dunhams, Jane moved to the Beedle home. They, however, had a live-in housekeeper named Mary Sullivan. Jane felt that Mary's services were no longer needed, so Jane drugged her with morphine and then arranged for Mrs. Beedle to find the girl in a stupor on her bed. Jane insisted that Mary had a drinking problem - often consuming hard liquor while on the job - and Mrs. Beedle fired her on the spot.

Now in control of the household, Jane casually poisoned the Beedles to keep them in line. Occasionally, she would slip something into their food to cause stomach problems as a way of reminding them how lucky they were to have a nurse as a boarder. This ensured that she would always have a roof over her head and not have to worry about eviction.

When Mattie Davis arrived at the Beedle home that June afternoon, the family was just sitting down for the noontime meal. Jane went into the kitchen and returned to the dining room with a glass of mineral water for Mattie, insisting that she must be thirsty after her trip.

During the meal, Mattie told the embarrassing story of falling on her way to the train. She could laugh about it now, but it had been very embarrassing at the time. As she talked and ate, she finished off the glass of water that Jane had fetched for her.

As they were finishing, Jane suggested that they take a walk together to the bank so that she would withdraw the funds to pay Mattie what she owed her. Mattie agreed, but she became so dizzy when she stood up from the table that she collapsed back into her chair.

Jane appeared to be worried. Could it be from her fall? Had Mattie's injuries been worse than she thought? But Mattie insisted she was fine. She didn't say it aloud, but she was anxious to finally get the money her family was owed. She wasn't going to let a little dizziness keep her from achieving this goal.

But once Mattie stepped outside into the afternoon heat, she let out a loud groan and crumpled to the street. Jane pulled her up and half-carried her back toward the house. Melvin Beedle had seen Mattie fall, and he hurried out to help. The two of them managed to get the half-conscious woman into the guest room, and Melvin went to get a glass of water for her. He assumed that she had fainted from the heat.

With Melvin out of the way, Jane darted into her room and grabbed a glass syringe and a needle from her bag. Soon, Mattie was silent.

"I gave her another small dose of morphia," Jane later confessed. "And that quieted her."

Later that evening, Jane sent an urgent telegram to Alden Davis and explained that his wife had arrived at the Beedle house in a "dazed" state, and now she was quite ill. She also sent a telegram to Mattie's daughter, Genevieve, who was worried that her mother had never arrived to see her.

Genevieve arrived at the Beedles' home the following day to find her mother lying unconscious in a darkened room hung with ice sheets. Jane was stationed at her bedside. Even though Jane insisted that she could care for Mattie alone, Genevieve insisted on calling a doctor to examine her.

But that was easier said than done. The summer was off to a brutally warm start, and many had fled the cities. The Beedles called four different physicians before finding one who would see Mattie. Dr. John T.G. Nichols arrived at the house and was greeted by Jane, who informed him that Mattie had diabetes. She claimed that Mattie had ignored her warnings and treated herself to a large slice of cake at dinnertime. She collapsed soon after Jane said, and no, there was no need for the doctor to take more urine from the patient; Jane had collected a sample for him before he arrived.

Over the next several days, Jane secretly toyed with the amount of morphine that she gave to her victim, making it appear that she might recover.

She didn't. Mattie died on July 4, 1901.

No one in Cataumet was surprised to learn of Mattie's death. Her health was often described as delicate, and the early summer heatwave had already killed nearly 9,500 people. No one suspected that Jane had anything to do with her death. In fact, Genevieve begged Jane to come to Cape Cod with her because she couldn't bear to take her mother's body back alone.

Reluctantly, Jane agreed. By killing Mattie, she had postponed the repayment of the debt that she owed to the Davis family, but, of course, it had not gone away. The only thing that might see her debt disappear would be if something happened to the entire family.

Jane Toppan's mind began to turn.

The funeral took place on another brutally hot day, and then the mourners gathered at the Davis cottage, which was known as Jachin House.

Some of the guests noticed that Genevieve was not looking well. But how could she be? Her mother's death had been a great shock, and the heat was leaving her looking "pale and worn." Jane knew just what she needed - a cool glass of mineral water. Soon, Genevieve took a turn for the worse and was confined to bed. With his daughter's condition so grave, Alden Davis pleaded with Jane to stay in Cataumet. Once again, she agreed.

Late that same night, Minnie Gibbs, Genevieve's younger sister, hurried into Jane's room to rouse her from her sleep. Something was wrong with Genevieve.

Jane hurriedly got out of bed, seemingly in a panic. She confided in Minnie that she had overheard Genevieve threatening to commit suicide, and she prayed the young woman had not decided to poison herself. Unknown to everyone else, Jane had also sent a telegram to Genevieve's husband, Harry, and told him that his wife had threatened to kill herself.

Jane's "fears" had been confirmed - Genevieve was unconscious and in a terrible state. She must have taken some poison, Jane told the family. She promised to watch over and nurse her, just as she had done for Genevieve's mother. Over the next two weeks, Genevieve suffered. Sometimes it seemed as though she was improving, but then she always took a turn for the worse. She continued "sinking" until the evening of July 31.

On that night, Genevieve joined her mother in death.

But Jane was still worried. Afraid that Alden Davis might become suspicious about her proximity to both his wife and daughter just before their deaths, she now set her sights on him. At first, she hoped that Alden might consider marrying her, but when that wasn't to be, she decided that he would leave her something in his will.

But for that to happen, Alden Davis would have to die. And, conveniently, he did on August 5.

Jane reported the news to Captain Paul Gibbs, Minnie's father-in-law, who arrived that morning for a visit. According to Jane, Alden had died in his bedroom just before breakfast. The doctor, she said, told her the cause of death was from a cerebral hemorrhage.

No one in town was really surprised. The Davis family had recently seen more than their share of grief. Perhaps it had simply been more than Alden's heart could stand.

Even now, no one suspected Jane Toppan of her role in the family's deaths.

After another funeral, Captain Gibbs tried to convince Minnie to go back home to Pocasset with her two young sons and wait for her husband, Irving, to return from the sea. He was out on the schooner, *Golden Ball*, from which his father had retired two years earlier.

But Minnie was needed in Cataumet. With her father, mother, and sister all dying unexpectedly, there was much to do to settle the estate. She told her father-in-law she would be fine because Jane had agreed to stay and help her, and her cousin, Beulah Jacobs, was coming down from Cambridge to lend a hand. Genevieve's widowed husband, Harry, also offered to help. After receiving Jane's telegram, he hurried to Cape Cod and staying a little longer to help Minnie was not a problem.

There was nothing that Paul could say to change her mind, so he offered to care for his grandsons while she settled her family matters. He was worried, but Minnie seemed fine. She was sad but was in good health and was certainly not ill.

And that was why Paul was so alarmed when he received an urgent message to return to Cataumet less than two weeks later. When he arrived at Jachin House, he found Minnie tucked away in a darkened upstairs room, comatose and gasping for air. How could something like this happen?

As he was leaning over his beloved daughter-in-law, a figure appeared in the doorway. It was the nurse, Jane, and she had a needle and syringe in her hand. "The doctor had ordered Mrs. Gibbs to be kept absolutely quiet," she said firmly. "I must ask you to leave immediately."

Jane injected Minnie with the contents of the syringe and then followed Captain Gibbs into the hallway. She explained that Minnie had gone shopping in Falmouth for the day and had not been feeling well when she returned. Perhaps the heat and her emotional distress had just been too much for her, Jane said and promised to nurse her back to health.

Paul had no reason to doubt her or to doubt that Minnie was in capable hands. He left the house and returned the next morning to find that Minnie seemed even worse, though. He now insisted that a doctor see her.

Two different physicians - a doctor named Latter, and Dr. Frank P. Hudnut of Boston, who was vacationing on the Upper Cape - were summoned to the house by Paul and by Harry Gordon. Both men were concerned by Minnie's paleness and her dilated pupils, but neither could offer any answers for the family. They were both puzzled by Minnie's condition.

Then, around 4:00 p.m. on August 13, Minnie took her final breath and died.

Minnie's death was just too much for Captain Gibbs. When the undertaker arrived, he announced that he planned to ask for an autopsy. Jane scoffed at the idea, stating there had been no suspicious circumstances. If it were necessary, she added, one of the doctors would have requested one. But there was no changing Paul's mind. He insisted that four deaths in one family in such a short amount of time went beyond coincidence.

The doctors agreed with Jane. Diabetes and exhaustion had both been listed on Minnie's death certificate, but this didn't satisfy Paul. He knew something was wrong. He sent a telegram to his son, whose ship had just docked in Virginia, and told him the terrible news. He was soon on his way to Cataumet.

On Thursday, August 15, mourners gathered at the Methodist Church in town for Minnie's funeral. When it was over, she was buried in the nearby cemetery.

Captain Gibbs was both heartbroken and simmering with anger. When Irving arrived for his wife's burial, he told him that he had misgivings about Jane Toppan, the nurse who had cared for Minnie and the rest of the family before they died. He still wanted Minnie's body to be examined, even though she had already been buried.

Finally, he met with Dr. Latter and tried to explain his suspicions. The doctor agreed that the case was puzzling but dismissed Paul's fears about the nurse. "I have not a shred of evidence against Nurse Toppan," he said.

"Nor have I," Captain Gibbs replied, "but that last day I was at the house - when Minnie seemed unconscious - watching Nurse Toppan give her the injection gave me the shivers, I'm frank to say."

Dr. Latter stared at Paul in confusion, and the next words he uttered sealed the fate of Jane Toppan.

"I didn't order an injection," he said.

A strange twist of fate followed the realization that Jane Toppan might have murdered the Davis family - Dr. Latter died. There truly was nothing suspicious about his death. He died from natural causes, but now Captain Gibbs had no one to back up his claims against Jane Toppan.

Or so he thought. He actually did have an ally, but that man had not yet been revealed to him.

His name was Dr. Ira Cushing, and he had happened to travel by train with Alden Davis on August 7. He didn't think much of it at the time, but when he learned about Alden's death, he found the circumstances to be very strange. To his expert eye, Alden had seemed very healthy on the train, and now that his daughter Minnie had also died, Dr. Cushing hoped that Captain Gibbs would act on behalf of the Davis family.

Unfortunately, Dr. Cushing didn't know Paul Gibbs and didn't feel he should contact him directly. But they did share a mutual friend - Captain Ed Robinson - and he urged him to speak with Paul about the possibility that arsenic poisoning might be to blame in the Davis family deaths.

When Paul received the suggestion about poison, he knew that it had merit. There was a problem, though. Since Dr. Latter had recently died, he had no physician to corroborate his claims against Jane Toppan. But Paul Gibbs, a "bluff, honest sailor" with experience from all over the world, was not a man to accept defeat.

He reached out to two friends - Pocasset native Dr. Leonard Wood, the governor-general of the Philippines, who was vacationing on the Cape, and his brother, Dr. Edward S. Wood, professor of pathology at Harvard Medical. The two men agreed that the deaths of Alden and Mattie Davis were not that unusual since both of them were of advanced age and had other health problems, but they were concerned about two healthy women in the prime of their lives dying within days of each other. The deaths of Minnie and Genevieve simply made no sense. The situation needed to be investigated, and both men urged Captain Gibbs to make a plea to the authorities.

Paul told his story to State Police Captain Rufus Wade, who assigned the case to General Jophanus Whitney to investigate further. He could understand Paul's concerns, but the most pressing question he had was - what motive could Jane Toppan have to murder the Davis family?

After Alden's funeral, Minnie told Paul that Jane had tried to persuade her to sign a document forgiving her debt to the Davis estate. Minnie had refused.

There was also missing money. When Alden died, he had roughly $300 in his pocketbook, and it had vanished. As his nurse, Jane could easily have taken it. Mattie and Genevieve had also had considerable sums of money when they fell ill, and yet when the undertakers arrived to take them to prepare for viewing, neither had more than a dollar or two on them. Before dealing with her parents' estate, Minnie had stashed $150 in her home, not far from Jachin House. Since she hadn't any money on her at the time of her sudden illness, it was not taken. Captain Gibbs was unable to say with any certainty how much money each family member had when they died, but he estimated the total was upwards of several hundred dollars.

Jane had been with each member of the David family when they became ill and when they died. She washed and dressed the bodies, and there was not a section of the house to which she didn't have access. The motive and the opportunity were both presented to the police.

It was soon learned that Jane was in serious debt. She had briefly closed her private nursing business in 1900 but owed several hundred dollars from that. She was also under the threat of several civil suits, as well.

Jane had also taken a new job under suspicious circumstances. After Sarah Connors died while under Jane's care, Jane took over her lucrative job as the proprietress of the dining hall at Woods Holl Summer School on the Cape. This new job paid nearly $1,000 per year.

As it happened, Captain Gibbs' daughter worked alongside Jane as the bookkeeper at Woods Holl. One day, $100 that had been set aside for the cook's wages went missing. She thought perhaps the cook had received it, but the cook was able to prove that she hadn't. The funds were replaced, but Paul's daughter believed that Jane Toppan had taken the money.

Jane was greedy. That much was clear. And while money might have driven her to murder, there was still no evidence to prove that she had committed it.

Meanwhile, Jane had left Cataumet and stopped in Cambridge to visit Harry Gordon's father, Henry, Sr., to speak with him about the David murders. Jane was nervous and wanted to find out what was being said.

When she asked him, the old man shrugged his shoulders and expressed the clueless opinion that "the family was an old one, it was dying out." Murder hadn't crossed his mind. Somehow, he believed the deaths had all been from natural causes.

After her visit, Jane boarded a train for Lowell, satisfied that she was not a suspect. She was wrong but had no way of knowing that just yet. Or she just ignored the possibility because she had other plans in mind.

Ever since she had murdered her foster sister, Elizabeth, two years earlier, Jane secretly fantasized about marrying her widowed brother-in-law, O.A. Brigham. But her fantasy wasn't just about being a married woman - it was because marriage to Brigham was the only way to get her hands on the Toppan fortune.

When Ann Toppan died, her estate had been left to her biological daughter, Elizabeth, and she and her husband moved into the family home. Jane lived there for a while before finally moving out. When Elizabeth died, Jane believed that the estate should have gone to her. Instead, she received $200 and a gold watch. The fortune went to Elizbeth's closest relative - her husband.

According to Jane, Brigham had come to see her the previous summer at Cataumet. They went swimming on the beach and went sailing and, Jane claimed, he asked her to marry him. He begged her to come and see him in Lowell in the early Fall and make plans for their wedding. When Jane arrived in Lowell, she was surprised by the coolness that Brigham showed her. He no longer wanted to talk of marriage. When she pushed for a reason, he told her that he planned to marry someone else - a young woman named Florence Calkins.

Florence didn't live long enough to walk down the aisle with Brigham. She died from a "mysterious ailment" before the wedding could ever take place.

Eight months later, Jane was on her way back to Lowell to try again. Brigham remained unmarried, and Jane believed that she still had a chance to be his wife.

But fate had other ideas.

On August 26, 1901, one week after Jane returned to the Toppan house in Lowell - General Jophanus Whitney of the Massachusetts District Police came calling.

After presenting his credentials to Jane, he explained that he was investigating the deaths of the Davis family. Since Jane had been in attendance at the death beds of all of them, he wanted to hear a narrative of their decline and deaths directly from Jane. "I don't want to question you," he explained, "but you have to tell me the story as you know it."

Jane began the story, starting with how Mattie had taken ill at the Beedles' home in Cambridge and then died, either from the heat or from her fall outside the train station in Cataumet. Some of the details were not entirely clear - such as how two sisters in their 30s died within days of each other - but Whitney listened to the story. He was especially curious about Minnie's death since it had been the catalyst for a murder investigation into the entire Davis family.

Jane detailed the story for him, never hesitating or losing her calm, professional demeanor. She was simply an observer, trying to provide details of what she had seen as an attending nurse and nothing else. She didn't seem nervous or anxious, no matter what Whitney asked.

Whitney continued his questions even when O.A. Brigham came into the room. "Did you not think it would be a good thing to have an autopsy on the body?" he asked Jane. "If these people died from natural causes, it would be better for all parties concerned. Don't you think it would be better?"

Jane didn't answer. Instead, she turned to Brigham and asked his opinion. "I think it would be better to have an autopsy, and then it would settle the matter," he shrugged.

Jane didn't agree. "I don't know that it would."

The second to last thing she wanted was an autopsy - while the one thing she wanted most was for General Whitney to leave the house. Unknown to the policeman, another of Jane's "patients" was right then dying in the next room.

Soon after Jane arrived at Brigham's home, O.A.'s sister, Edna Bannister, stopped for a visit on her way to the Pan-American Exposition in Buffalo, New York. This World's Fair ran from May 1 to November 2, 1901, and drew visitors from across the country. It would be the location of the assassination of President William McKinley.

Brigham had covered his sister's traveling expenses to visit the fair and invited her to stay for a few days to break up the long trip. Edna was not a well woman. She suffered from heart disease and had been traveling in the terrible summer heat.

Jane was not happy about her arrival. The last thing she wanted was another woman in the house. She was bound to interfere in what Jane hoped would be a rekindling of their love affair. As usual, when Jane was unhappy, someone else was bound to be soon.

By August 27, Edna was dead.

Dr. William Lathrop, a general practitioner in town for almost 35 years, called at the Brigham house that same day, only to learn that Edna had passed. Rather than examine her body, he took her nurse's word for her condition.

"Edna died from a long-standing disease of the heart," Jane told him, "after a sudden and severe attack of characteristic breathing."

Dr. Lathrop had no reason to doubt her. He'd known Jane for almost a decade. Even though she had never worked for him, she had a fine reputation as a nurse.

She also had a few questions for the doctor. "If a body had been poisoned and died and then was embalmed, would those poisonous drugs be found if they exhumed the body, that is, had an autopsy?"

"If they were a mineral poison," Lathrop told her, unbelievably not wondering what she asked since they were literally standing over a body that was not even cold, "they would be in the body, but if they were a vegetable, they would be absorbed."

Jane listed several drugs, asking which was mineral and which was vegetable, and then thanked him for his time - bringing an end to a surreal and shockingly ridiculous conversation, which didn't seem to faze the doctor at all.

Jane now believed that she could relax. She was safe, she thought. Now all she had to do was convince O.A. Brigham - the man she had killed three women for - to marry her.

But Jane shouldn't have relaxed. The state police had already ordered exhumations of the Davis family.

The bodies were exhumed on an autumn night by Captain Paul Gibbs, his son, Irving, General Jophanus Whitney, Medical Examiner Dr. Robert H. Faunce, Professor Edward Wood from Harvard, State Police officer Simeon Lettney, and Reverend James Dicking of the Methodist Church in Cataumet. The corpses were taken to a nearby barn that belonged to Major Allen Swift.

One by one, Dr. Faunce opened the bodies of Alden and Mattie Davis, Genevieve Gordon, and Minnie Gibbs. He removed all the vital organs, including the stomachs, to test for poisons. Professor Wood took the samples back to his laboratory in Cambridge. He would alert the police if anything out of the ordinary were found. No arrest could be made until the toxicology reports had been created.

Jane had become General Whitney's main suspect, even if he couldn't prove she had done anything wrong. The list of her possible victims had grown, and he was worried about who she might poison next. In order to keep an eye on her, he assigned a detective named

John S. Patterson to keep track of her every move. Patterson followed her everywhere she went. He even rented a room under an assumed name that was near the Brigham house. For the next few weeks, wherever Jane went - post office, druggist, or even a morning stroll - Patterson was nearby.

To everyone else, Jane appeared to be a plump, mid-40s spinster with a pleasing face and dark hair that was lightly streaked with silver. Her brown eyes were kind, and she almost always wore a smile on her face.

But James Patterson was convinced she was a cold-blooded killer.

While Jane was being followed whenever she left the house, there was no one to keep an eye on her while she was inside. Her feelings of romance for O.A. Brigham - or for his money -- had become an obsession. She devised a plan to start adding a little bit of poison into Brigham's tea, then when he became sick, she would nurse him back to health and win him over.

Jane was sure that her plan was working - and then Detective Patterson called to speak with Brigham. "After he left," Jane later wrote, "a change came over Mr. Brigham."

Patterson's message to Brigham had been a simple one: "Be careful of that woman, or she will poison you." Patterson had noted Brigham's sudden change in health and knew he had to warn him.

The words sent a chill up Brigham's spine. As soon as the detective left the house, Brigham struggled out of bed, weak from the morphia Jane had been dosing him with and ordered her to leave the house.

Jane was now frantic. Everything had been lost - her "lover," the home she had counted on, and her fortune. Worst of all, she had been discovered!

Later that afternoon, Sunday, September 29, Jane took an overdose of the same poison she had been giving her patients for years. When Brigham looked into her bedroom to make sure she was packing her things, he found her unconscious. He called Dr. Lathrop to the house to help. When he arrived, he injected her with an emetic to induce vomiting.

"I want to die," Jane said when she awoke from her stupor.

Dr. Lathrop tried to get her to tell him what she had taken, but Jane refused to answer. She just continually repeated that she wanted to die. Rather than take the chance that she might succeed, Dr. Lathrop sent for a private nurse, Ann Tyler, to stay at Jane's bedside. Before he left the house, he told Brigham that Jane had evidently self-medicated by taking some sort of narcotic. He promised to return in the morning to check on her.

Jane was angry and bitter, blaming Brigham for the fact that she was still alive. "If you had left me alone, I would have been out of this world by now."

By morning, though, her spirits seemed improved, so Nurse Tayler had no reservations about leaving her alone so she could eat breakfast downstairs.

When she returned to Jane's room, she discovered that Jane had taken another massive dose of poison. She was so sick that she could no longer swallow, her lower jaw sagged open, and she was barely breathing. Her face had turned a ghastly shade of white. After two suicide attempts in as many days, Jane would have succeeded this time if Dr. Lathrop had not already arrived at the house.

Hearing Nurse Tyler's cry, he rushed up the stairs and injected both of Jane's arms with apomorphine, a morphine that mimics dopamine and, in high doses, is effective in causing vomiting. Within a few moments, Jane was vomiting into the chamber pot. She was alive.

When Dr. Lathrop asked her why she wanted to die so badly, Jane replied, "I'm tired of life. I know that people are talking about me. I just want to die."

If Jane was looking for sympathy, she didn't find it from O.A. Brigham. He ordered her away from the house, and with nowhere else to go, she admitted herself into Lowell General Hospital for "rest and treatment."

Detective Patterson also got himself admitted into the hospital and managed to get a bed in an adjoining ward.

When she was eventually discharged from the hospital, Jane took a train to Amherst, New Hampshire, to visit a long-time friend named George Nichols, who lived with his sister, Sarah.

Detective Patterson was on the same train.

On October 27, Professor Wood finally received the reports of the autopsies he had performed on the Davis family - Minnie's body contained traces of morphine, and all four bodies had high levels of arsenic in their intestines.

District Attorney LeBaron Holmes went straight to the Barnstable courthouse and obtained an arrest warrant for Jane Toppan. They decided to make Minnie's murder the primary case with which to charge Jane. She would also be charged for the deaths of Alden, Mattie, and Genevieve if enough evidence could be found.

Two days later, General Whitney arrived in Amherst with two Nashua police officers, Inspector Thomas Flood and Deputy Marshall Wheeler. After finding Detective Patterson at a nearby boarding house - from where he had continued watching Jane's movements - the four lawmen went to the bright yellow farmhouse that belonged to George and Sarah Nichols.

Warrant in hand, Whitney informed Jane that she was under arrest for the murder of Minnie Gibbs.

This was absurd, Jane said and scoffed at the warrant. "I wouldn't kill a chicken," she smirked. "If there is any justice in Massachusetts, they will let me go."

Whitney ordered her to pack her belongings, and Jane didn't protest. She was not surprised by the arrest, but George and Sarah certainly were. They had no idea how lucky they were.

Jane later wrote, "I might have killed George Nichols and his sister at Amherst, New Hampshire, where I was arrested, if I had stayed long enough. But Detective Whitney came to the house in the night and took me away."

Jane never explained what George and Sarah had done so that she would turn her murderous attentions toward them. Maybe she simply missed committing murder after a four-week dry spell, or perhaps she sensed that George was becoming concerned about her presence.

After Jane's arrest, he told a reporter from the *Boston Herald*:

We first formed the acquaintance of Miss Toppan in Cambridge, Massachusetts. She became acquainted with my sister, who lives with me. I knew Miss Toppan merely as a trained nurse of much ability. It was several years ago that she commenced to make visits to Amherst. She hardly ever stayed longer than a day or two.

I always entertained a high regard for her, and it is hard for me to suspect her of wrongdoing. She was always fond of talking about her business, and, according to her statements, enjoyed the work of nursing very much. She liked to be present when patients were operated upon, and I am informed she was considered a valuable assistant on those occasions. I recall one time when Dr. Marcy and another Cambridge physician sent for her when about to perform an operation.

Very many times during her stay at my house, Miss Toppan talked of surgical operations and autopsies. Her mind seemed to run entirely in that channel, but not for a moment did I suspect that something might be weighing on her mind. Whenever she talked of these subjects there was a distant look in her eyes. It was these actions that, toward the last of her stay, rather made me nervous. I was afraid her mind was unbalanced, and for that reason, kept a close watch over my sister, being fearful that something might happen.

The reporter asked George if there had been any sickness in the household while Jane was there.

"Well, no. Yes - there was a day or two when my sister was ill."

"Did Jane attend her?"

"I think she assisted her somewhat."

The reporter then asked if Jane had cared for anyone as a nurse during the time she was in Amherst. He was obviously fishing for more for his story.

George replied, "No, I think not. Whenever she was here, she stopped at my house. She occasionally visited with the people of this place for a few hours at a time."

"Did she go about much on her last visit to your house?"

"Not very much. The fact of the matter is, when Jane came to Amherst, she was what I would call an invalid. Why she came to my place I do not know, other than it was the only one she had to go to. I do not know how long she intended to remain. I had not thought of turning her out of doors as long as she behaved herself."

"What about Miss Toppan's finances?" the reporter asked.

"As far as I know, she was plentifully supplied with money. As a trained nurse, she commanded good wages, and not being of extravagant tastes, I think $3 a day ought to keep a woman like her in good shape. If Jane Toppan was responsible for the alleged poisoning cases in Massachusetts, I don't believe it was money she was after. In my belief, if she committed the deeds charged to her, she must have been laboring under a hallucination of some kind."

George Nichols shook his head. "While Miss Toppan was at my house, I read about the autopsies being held over the bodies in Massachusetts. I believed I remarked to my sister that Jane Toppan had nursed the families at that time. Notwithstanding this, we had no suspicion regarding Miss Toppan, and we were as much surprised as anyone else in this town when Detective Whitney and the Nashua officers made the arrest."

On the carriage ride from Amherst to Nashua, Jane asked Whitney if she would need an attorney, and he recommended it. "It is a very serious matter for you and the best lawyer you can get will be none too good for you," he replied.

Once they arrived at the Nashua jail, Whitney arranged for the matron of the station to stay with Jane all night in case she became suicidal again. In the morning, at the prisoner's request, he purchased "a veil for her and some other little things." Before they went into court, Jane agreed to return to Massachusetts without an extradition hearing, which made things easier for Whitney. The judge was informed, and they were soon on their way to Boston by train.

During the trip, Whitney got Jane to admit that she had purchased morphine tablets at various drug stores in Falmouth, Wareham, and Cataumet, but Jane told him this was normal for someone in her profession. She claimed to be innocent of Minnie's death.

The train stopped at the North Station in Boston, where Whitney turned Jane over to Detective Simeon Letteney, a state police officer based on Cape Cod. They switched trains and promptly left South Station for Bourne. Letteney was reading the afternoon newspaper and keeping an eye on Jane who he described as having "an ever-changing smile, her half-shut eyes twinkling with amusement."

When Letteney brought up the Davis family, Jane continued to insist that she had not killed them. "Those people all died of natural causes," she insisted. "Excepting old man Davis. He was crazy, and I think he poisoned himself."

Upbeat and relaxed, Letteney said that Jane "chatted pleasantly" and even "laughed and joked about the stories of her arrest and alleged crimes which she read in the newspapers on the train."

That afternoon, the train stopped at Bourne, and Jane was hustled through the depot, followed by a crowd of reporters. The people of Cataumet who knew her came out to gawk as she was taken to the brick jail in Barnstable. Jane smiled and waved at acquaintances as the carriage passed by them on the streets.

Though the Commonwealth had only charged Jane with the murder of Minnie Gibbs, she was the prime suspect in many other cases. Captain Paul Gibbs, and his son, Irving, were greatly affected by Jane's arrest. They were relieved that she couldn't hurt anyone else, but they now knew that Minnie had died at the hands of a monster that she had believed was her friend.

But the full horror of Jane Toppan was yet to be revealed.

Jane was locked up at the Barnstable Jail, where she was watched over by the jailer's wife, Mrs. Cash. Reporters loitered about outside, looking for any kind of scoop. Papers all over New England wrote in lavish detail about the "serial poisoner" who was locked away, awaiting trial.

She had been appointed an attorney, James Stuart Murphy of Lowell, who also happened to be a childhood friend. He insisted that Jane would be cleared of all charges. He believed that she should not have been arrested because the state could not prove its case against her. They had only arrested her, he claimed, because she had attempted suicide. The state was claiming this proved she was guilty, but he believed otherwise.

He told a reporter, "From the time Miss Toppan left Cataumet until she was put under arrest in Amherst, the government knew her whereabouts. She did not attempt to hide, but all the time she was in Amherst she corresponded with friends. She worried considerably over the suspicions she realized the government had of her, after Officer Whitney talked with her about the Davis deaths, and it does not seem strange to me that a woman whose friends had turned against her should seek to destroy herself. Jane verbalized what a terrible position these suspicions had placed her in, and she did not care to remain in the world with them hanging over her. You must consider, how a knowledge that she was suspected of murder would affect any woman, and does it not seem strange, does it, that she would want to die?"

O.A. Brigham, who first stated that he had been told not to talk about the case, changed his mind and told a reporter from the *Boston Herald* that he now suspected there was something suspicious about this wife's death. When she had gone to Cataumet to see Jane, she was in fine health, but within 48 hours, she was dead. The doctor had told him that she'd died from heart failure and a stroke, but he had come to believe that Jane had killed her in light of the other poisonings.

Dr. Lathrop was also interviewed by the same reporter, who said that he had no reason to believe - at the time - that Elizabeth had been poisoned."

Jane's attorney agreed with this and once more insisted that Jane would be cleared of all the charges against her. "She is an innocent woman," he said, "who would have absolutely no reason to kill people she considered her best friends. When her story has been heard, I am sure the tide of public opinion will turn in her favor. She has made no statement since her arrest, by my orders. She has told the state officers everything that happened in the Davis house and she has told them the truth, but she will say no more until the proper time comes."

Murphy was a passionate defender for Jane but, on the day of her arraignment, he missed the train to Barnstable and Jane had to appear in the courtroom alone. Led in by Detective Letteney, her face was pale and drawn as she was led into the courtroom in a black tailored dress. She had dark circles under her eyes, which led reporters to speculate that she had "suffered a restless sleep" during her first night in jail.

Jane was seated on a bench in the prisoner's dock, a four-foot-high wooden box used to confine the accused during trials at the Barnstable Courthouse. When the clerk called her name, she reached for the wood rail in front of her and unsteadily pulled herself to her feet.

The clerk recited a capital charge of murder against her and then asked how she replied to the complaint. "Not guilty," Jane said quietly.

The trial was scheduled to being on November 8, and she was remanded back to the jail. The entire thing took less than 10 minutes. As Letteney led her out of the courtroom, Jane ran her hand along the wall for support. They walked together down the courthouse steps, and Jane's gloves slipped from her shaking hands. Letteney bent to retrieve them as any gentleman would then guided her back to the second floor of the jail, where the women were kept. As the door clanged shut behind her, Jane stripped off her jacket and fell back on the cot.

Numerous messages had arrived for her at the jail, Letteney told her, adding that the newspapers would be glad to publish anything that Jane wanted to say in her defense.

"Thank them very much," she replied, "but I think I shall keep my own counsel until I have an opportunity to talk with my attorney." Jane swore to him that she knew nothing about the deaths of the Davis family, except to suppose "they all died of natural causes." She was angry that she was being taken to task for something she knew nothing about. "I am very sorry that I am obliged to endure this wide publicity, and the only wish I could offer would be that my name does not appear in the papers anymore."

While incarcerated, waiting for her trial to start, Jane developed an affection for Mrs. Cash, the jailer's wife, and her four-year-old granddaughter, Lucy. She became very attached to the little girl, and reporters called her visits "the brightest moments of Miss Toppan's prison life."

When not chatting with Lucy, she spent most of her time reading. Mrs. Cash loaned her various novels, and her favorites were the love stories, the more sentimental, the better.

A typical day in the Barnstable jail included rising early with the other female inmates. She read, did some sewing, and performed simple household tasks as needed. In the evenings, "less violent" inmates were allowed to attend "theatrical entertainments" and dances, but Jane remained locked in her cell. She usually spent those times talking with Mrs. Cash - who had no doubt about Jane's guilt.

"The moment I laid eyes on that woman, I thought she was guilty," she told a reporter, who was interviewing Jane at the same time. "The evening she arrived, I took her up to her room and locked her in. Before the next morning, I had made up my mind she was a murderess, even before she confessed."

"Why?" Jane interrupted.

Mrs. Cash said that it was simply intuition. She just knew it.

Jane laughed. "I never said I didn't do it, did I?"

Jane's first trial was postponed - there was more trouble coming. On December 6, 1901, a grand jury filed further indictments against her for the murders of Genevieve Gordon, Alden Davis, and Mattie Davis. Jane was again escorted to the courthouse.

The clerk addressed the court, "Each is in four counts and charges death was caused by 10 grains of morphine, by 10 grains of atropine, by 10 grains of morphine and atropine combined, and by poisons unknown to the jury."

When the clerk read enough of the first indictment to reveal the nature of the poisons, James S. Murphy waived further reading of the charges, and Jane entered a plea of "not guilty" to the additional three murders.

Because Jane had little or no money, Murphy asked if additional counsel could be assigned. He had taken on the case for free. The judge took it under advisement, adjourned the court, and sent Jane back to the jail.

District Attorney Holmes told the press that he didn't expect the trial to start until sometime in April, leaving reporters a long time to wait for the next part of the sensational story.

When reporters have to wait, they get bored and move on to the next story. By January, Jane's crimes had faded from the headlines, but then District Attorney Holmes announced that not only did he believe that Jane had killed the entire Davis family, but he also suspected her of seven other deaths, too.

And then the death toll rose to 11:

Elizabeth Brigham

Sarah Connors

Mary McNear - she ran a theological school, and Jane wanted her job

Israel and Lovey Dunham - Jane's former landlords

Edna Bannister - O.A.'s sister

Florence Calkins - O.A.'s housekeeper

And then, of course, Minnie Gibbs, Genevieve Gordon, and Alden and Mattie Davis.

James S. Murphy was freed from Jane's case, and Fred M. Bixby was assigned as his replacement. He was a justice of the Brockton police court and a summer resident of Hyannis on the Cape. He had a "good working knowledge of the law, good abilities as a public speaker, and a remarkable capacity for seeing a point quickly and turning it promptly to his own advantage."

He was undoubtedly a good lawyer, but he'd certainly never had a client quite like Jane Toppan.

Of course, Jane blamed all the deaths on the list - and there were undoubtedly more, these were just the ones the authorities knew about - on natural causes, everything from hot weather to bad fruit. She told reporters that she was sure that her trial would reveal the truth behind the various deaths attributed to her. "If there is any justice in Massachusetts, I will be cleared," she said. "I cannot see how I can be convicted of a crime I never committed.... All the deaths occurred in the summertime. The drinking water in Cataumet is bad. The land is low. The country is practically un-wooded, and conditions favor diseases that can be transmitted through drinking water... Each of the people who died I knew personally and was on friendly terms with."

That was what she told the press, and yet, she told her new lawyer exactly the opposite. On his first visit to the Barnstable jail, Jane admitted that she had killed everyone on the list.

Bixby was, not surprisingly, a little stunned by this. "Well, how did you kill them?" he asked.

"I gave them morphine and atropine in the mineral water and sometimes with a dilution of whiskey," she replied. "I also used injections, just as I did at Cataumet. I do not remember how I killed them all, but those that I do recall were poisoned by morphine and atropine. My memory is not good. I forget things."

Bixby had to be wondering what he had gotten himself into by taking the case. Jane likely knew how stunned he was.

"I know I am not a safe person to be at large," Jane added. "It would be better if I were locked up where I could do no one any harm. No one can tell when I am liable to have another paroxysm. I do not know myself, until it comes."

With Jane admitting to having sudden attacks of violent desires to murder, Bixby blurted out, "You must be insane."

Jane replied, "Insane? How can I be insane? When I killed those people, I knew I was doing wrong. I was perfectly conscious that I was not doing right. I never at any time failed to realize what I was doing. Now, how can a person be insane who knows what she is doing and is conscious of the fact that she isn't doing right? Insanity is a complete lack of mental responsibility, isn't it?"

"Yes," Bixby answered hesitantly, "but you have remorse, don't you?"

Jane sniffed. "No, I have absolutely no remorse. I have never felt sorry for what I have done. Even when I poisoned my dearest friends, as the Davises were, I did not feel any regret afterward. I do not feel any remorse now. I have thought it over and I cannot detect the slightest bit of sorrow for what I have done." But then Jane paused for a moment. "There is one thing that makes me think my mind is not right. I have great difficulty in remembering things. My memory is not good at times, but on other occasions I cannot recall what I have said or done."

Bixby then sat there stunned as Jane recounted the murders she had committed in detail. She spoke with a slight smirk on her face, unashamed of the chaos she had caused. By the time she'd finished, Bixby was deeply relieved that she had reached the end of her confession.

But as he stood to leave, she told him there was one more thing she needed to say. Once she told him what it was, he was sorry that he'd asked. Jane told him:

I will tell you how I killed the last member of the Davis family, Minnie, for which I was finally arrested.

Minnie Gibbs was my best friend. But we always go back to your best friends. I wanted to marry her husband, Captain Irving Gibbs. Minnie was jealous of me. It made a fuss in the family, and I cut up and flayed Minnie before her husband.

Still, they both thought a great deal of me. Minnie as well as Irving. This is just how I poisoned Minnie Gibbs. We all went driving to Woods Hole one day, when we came back Minnie was not feeling well - I had given her a morphia tablet dissolved in hot whiskey before we started, to brace her up for the drive, I said to her.

When they had returned, Jane had told Minnie that she needed to take some medicine that Dr. Latter had left for her. Minnie refused at first, but Jane managed to convince her it would help.

I gave her some, with morphia and atropia tablets dissolved in it, and she lay down on the lounge. The rest of the family ate their supper, and when it was bedtime Minnie was sleeping on the lounge. I told them she was tired out and was in a sleep of exhaustion. They tried to rouse Minnie but could not. She only made a groaning noise. So, I got a blanket and covered her up. Most of the others went to bed and I offered to sit up with Minnie. But Harry Gordon said he would look out for her that night, and he lay down on a lounge near her.

Harry, Genevieve's widowed husband, told Jane that he and Minnie planned to go into Barnstable the following day so that they could go to the Probate Court and look over papers and business matters. Jane continued:

That was just what I didn't want them to do, for I owed Minnie some money and had given her some notes. Several times during the night, I stole in while Mr. Gordon was asleep to give more doses to Minnie, for I was afraid she would come out of it. She was too far

gone to swallow, so I dissolved the morphia and atropia
tablets in water, filled my hypodermic syringe with it,
and made injections of the poison in her arm. I made
up my mind that she must die that night.

Around 3:00 a.m., Harry woke up and checked on Minnie. Again, he was unable to awaken her, and she seemed to be barely breathing. He called out and asked for help in getting her upstairs to her bedroom. They had to drag her upstairs, and the family - or what was left of them - wanted to send for a doctor. Jane insisted it was merely a fainting spell and she could care for her on her own. She was, after all, a trained nurse.

Minnie had not improved by dawn, so the family finally sent for Dr. Latter, who lived five miles away in Monument Beach. Jane's confession continued:

When the doctor arrived, Minnie Gibbs was almost
dead. He said it was heart failure. After she died, I did
not go near her. I did not even bathe her or lay her out.
When she died, I felt as if I had got through with her
and could not bear to go near her. I have a loathing of
dead bodies, but mind you, I'm not afraid of any
avenging spirits. I never saw any of the spirits of the
people I killed.

That was a statement that would come back to haunt her.

Finally, it seemed the horrific confession had ended. Bixby stared at Jane in shock. She had, in his presence, admitted to killing at least 31 men and women. She had started murdering in nursing school and continued doing so during her private nursing practice.

On the surface, Jane seemed to be a kind, caring, compassionate nurse and friend, but she had a secret desire to slowly murder the people she seemed to love the most.

"I do not know the feeling of fear and I do not know the feeling of remorse," she told Bixby, trying to explain what made her do the things that she did, "although I perfectly understand what those words mean. But I cannot sense them at all. I do not seem to be able to realize the awfulness of the things I've done, those I realize very well what those awful things are."

In early January 1902, Bixby met with District Attorney Holmes about Jane's case. Together, they went to Attorney General Parker with a proposal. Rather than prepare for a long and expensive trial, Bixby and Holmes proposed appointing a panel of "insanity experts" to diagnose Jane's mental condition "with reference to her legal responsibility."

After considering this for a few weeks, Parker agreed. By March 20, 1902, Dr. Henry Rust Stedman, one of Harvard's most distinguished alienists, Dr. George F. Jelly of Boston, and Hosea M. Quimby, superintendent of the Worcester Hospital for the Insane, had all come to an agreement - Jane Toppan was suffering from "moral insanity."

What those learned men failed to realize, though, was that Jane had her own plan "to avoid the gallows." She wrote:

> I have poisoned thirty-one people as far as I can count them up and recall them. But there are more that I can't name, just hospital patients. I was advised to confess and plead guilty to the murder of the thirty-one persons whom I have sent out of the world by poisoning. But I thought of a way better than that.
>
> When the famous insanity experts of Boston - Dr. Henry R. Stedman, Dr. George F. Jelly, and Dr. Hosea N. Quimby - came down to the Barnstable jail to see if I was insane, I knew how to fool them. I have been a trained nurse for fifteen years and know doctors and how to manage them. I know that people who are insane will always deny it.
>
> So, I said to the alienists: "I am not insane."
>
> I knew I could fool them all if I wanted to, and to make myself out insane. Dr. Jelly and the others raked me with hard questions. They tried to play on my woman's sympathy and asked me if I didn't think it was a terrible thing to take those mothers, Mrs. Gibb and Mrs. Gordon, away from their young children. But I

knew their game and said that I just up and killed them and didn't know why.

When I said that I killed four people in fifty-one days and set three fires, they said: 'Why, Jane Toppan, you must have been insane to have done such a thing.' But I still insisted that I was not insane. Then they went away and gave their verdict that I was insane, which is just what I wanted. I was too smart for the whole of them. I have the most spunk and grit of any person living.

People say I have no heart, but I have. While I have been in jail, a friend in Lowell sent me some forget-me-nots, and I cried. They were the flowers that my first lover used to send me when I was a schoolgirl. And a forget-me-not was engraved on that precious engagement ring.

I will never tell my girlhood lover's name that is still sacred to me, even though he went back on me, and it seemed that my whole lighthearted nature changed after that. I still laughed and was jolly, but I learned how to hate, too. If I had been a married woman, I probably would not have killed all these people. I would have had my husband, my children, and my home to take up my mind.

I could have worked for years longer at poisoning if I hadn't killed four people in one family almost all at once. That was the greatest mistake of my life. I've made up my mind to being sent to an insane asylum. But I have hopes of getting out in ten or fifteen years - when the doctors will say I am cured of insanity.

Even with the diagnosis of moral degenerative insanity, District Attorney Holmes moved ahead with the trial. The insanity hearing seemed more about newspaper headlines than a medical diagnosis. Jane's trial for the murder of Minnie Gibbs opened on June 23, 1902, with Judges Henry K. Braley of Fall River and Charles U. Bell of Lawrence hearing the case. A jury was empaneled, and, at the request of Attorney General Parker, all witnesses except for the witness on the stand and those expected to give expert testimony were asked to leave the courtroom.

Parker gave the opening address for the prosecution, promising their case would prove that Jane had poisoned and killed Minnie, then tried to cover up the crime by urging the undertaker to use great quantities of embalming fluid when taking care of Minnie's body. Since the fluid contained high levels of arsenic, Jane hoped it would hide the evidence of her crime.

He spent quite some time reviewing the case against Jane and then began calling witnesses, starting with Minnie's cousin, Beulah Jacobs. Mr. Swift, an attorney for the prosecution, then took over the actual questioning and led Beulah through the last days of Minnie's life. He started with Jane's trip to buy medicinal spring water and continued as Minnie fell ill after drinking it and finally died.

After the prosecution was finished with Beulah, Jane's attorney, Bixby, made a statement to the judge. "May it please, Your Honor. I think that in view of the nature of the defense which will be offered later, which perhaps, has been outlined somewhat by the learned Attorney General, that there will be no necessity of cross-examining this witness, or, perhaps, any of the witnesses offered by the Commonwealth."

The prosecution continued to call witnesses to the stand, even though, as Bixby had noted, the state's own experts had already ruled that Jane was insane. The trial now seemed to be more for the purpose of satisfying the public than for anything to do with the law. This became more apparent when the three alienists all testified:

> *Jane Toppan was insane and irresponsible for the crimes for which she was charged; that she was suffering from a form of degenerative insanity characterized by the absence of moral sense, by defective control and by an irresistible impulse to the commission of extreme crimes.*

Attorney James Murphy urged Dr. Stedman to emphasize the point that Jane was insane at the time of the murders by asking about her condition in August 1901.

"I consider that she was laboring under insanity," he testified.

"Are you of the opinion that the prisoner is incurably insane?"

"I am."

"And the opportunity offering for insanity to manifest itself might again be manifested in homicide if she was at large?"

"Unmistakably."

Once the prosecution and defense had rested, Braley cautioned the jurors before they left the courtroom to deliberate that they needed to decide if the defendant had given Minnie Gibbs poison to cause her death. If so, they needed to decide if the defendant was in a condition of mind that she could be held criminally responsible for the act. If she was not, then Jane would have to be found not guilty by reason of insanity.

The jury only deliberated for 27 minutes. When they returned, Jane was asked to stand and face the verdict of "not guilty, by reason of insanity." Judge Braley sentenced her to life at the State Lunatic Asylum in Taunton, Massachusetts.

The judge asked Jane if she had anything to say on her own behalf. She only grinned. "I have nothing to say," she replied.

Her transfer to the asylum was set to take place on June 27, but before she left the Barnstable jail, she couldn't resist hinting that her insanity would go away because her violent impulses were simply caused by a hormone imbalance. They would go away as soon as she entered menopause, she claimed.

But Jane couldn't know that she was soon to face a fate that was worse than death.

The State Lunatic Asylum in Taunton had been built in 1854 by the Boyden and Ball company of architects. It was their first project, but they had a standard pattern from which to work. The Neo-Classical campus of more than 154 acres (about twice the area of a large shopping mall) - and which would eventually include more than 40 buildings - was from a design proposed by Thomas Story Kirkbride. The psychiatrist suggested that the buildings of the asylums that were being built across the country could actually assist in the treatment of the inmates by exposing them to natural light and air circulation. This meant that the main buildings were laid out in what was called a "bat-wing" style, stepping back piece by piece to offer the most sunlight and the best air circulation for each wing of the structure.

The Taunton asylum was located on a tranquil farm that was just north of town, although the Mill River created a natural boundary line to keep the mentally ill separate from everyone else. In those days, the insane were mostly just locked away with the belief they were unlikely to be cured. In addition, the definition of insane varied greatly from what we would consider it to be today. Society generally wanted nothing to do with the inmates of the state hospitals. They wanted the mentally ill, children with birth defects, and those with learning disabilities to simply disappear. They shipped them off to lunatic asylum because having them out of sight meant also having them out of mind.

Behind the locked doors of the asylum the inmates were dehumanized and devalued. All manners of abuse and cruelty masqueraded as "treatment." Inmates faced a lifetime of beatings, solitary confinement, dietary neglect, being bound to shackles, held in chains, and confined to straitjackets. Later, "cures" would also include electrical shock therapy, lobotomies, cold water baths, insulin treatments, and mind-altering drugs.

During the nineteenth century, the asylums were filled with shell-shocked Civil War veterans, those with dementia, Parkinson's, Tourette's Syndrome, alcoholics, people with epilepsy, and eating disorders. There were women who suffered panic attacks, postpartum depression, anxiety, fatigue, and "disobedience" locked away in asylums, as well as men who engaged in "excessive masturbation."

By the time that Jane Toppan was committed to the asylum, ideas about the treatment of the mentally ill had slowly started to change, but there was still a long way to go before modern standards began to be applied.

When Jane arrived, she was taken to the administration building with its huge dome, expansive hallways, and wide windows, which offered a panoramic view of the countryside. The curved, enclosed breezeways were much different than the gloomy Barnstable jail cell where Jane had been confined for so long.

But she wouldn't enjoy what seemed to be the tranquil setting of the state asylum for long.

When the jury found her not guilty by reason of insanity, many people believed "the electric chair had been cheated of its rightful victim. No form of execution known to law could be torturesome enough for this inhuman woman," one newspaper editorial stated. Another added that the verdict was a "travesty of justice to allow such a tigress in human form to escape legal execution."

Jane was still grinning at the idea that she had escaped punishment. She shrugged off the hospital," In a few years, I'll be right. Then they will let me out."

She even handed the public one more shocking statement to tide them over until she could appear in the newspapers again. The statement claimed:

> *I have given the alienists the names of 31 persons I killed, but as a matter of fact I killed many more whose names I cannot recall. I think it would be safe to say that I killed at least 100 from the time I became a nurse at Boston Hospital, where I killed the first one, until I ended the lives of the Davis family.*

She even added how she rejoiced in holding "to her bosom a patient racked with the death struggles brought on by her poison, gloating in the convulsive quivers and twitches of the muscles, the moans of pain, the sweat of death."

There is no question that Jane Toppan was a monster. But, at this point, she truly believed that she was "playing the system," pretending to be insane so that she could beat the executioner. She expected to be free within a few years - but Jane was in for quite a surprise.

Soon, she was no longer just faking insanity.

The state asylum, she quickly realized, was not Barnstable jail. She found herself subjected to the hospital's "treatments," which mostly consisted of shock and water experiments in the basement. She spent days confined to her cramped cell or confined in a straitjacket.

It took two years, but the Taunton State Lunatic Asylum broke Jane Toppan. By 1904, her mind was gone. She began to believe that the avenging spirits of her victims were coming into her room at night, setting fire to her bed. Over and over, Jane would awaken the entire wing at night with piercing shrieks and the cry of "Fire, fire!"

Dr. J.P. Brown, the superintendent of the hospital, chronicled Jane's breakdown, watching her go from being a deceitful person with no pity or remorse for what she had done to a woman who was clearly insane. She soon began starving herself - because she was afraid that the ghosts were poisoning her food. She became abusive to the nurses, defying their authority and convincing the other inmates to do the same. This led to punishments and a further deterioration of her mental faculties.

By February 1904, Jane weighed only a skeletal 60 pounds and was so weak that she had to be force-fed through a tube. During a visit from Dr. Stedman, she went on a rant, insisting that all the food was "rotten" and the "meat was embalmed beef."

As her mind continued to fracture, she claimed: "not only that every article of food, every cup of tea or coffee, and every glass of water had been poisoned, but that she could see the specters of her victims hovering over her and dropping the poison into these things just as she used to do to them."

When Jane had first been admitted, she had been permitted to mingle with other patients, but as her delusions became more frequent, she was sent to the infirmary and then to isolation, where she would be "unable to hurt or injure anyone else."

One day one of Jane's nurses came in carrying a tray of bread and coffee, and Jane said to her, "I saw them all last night."

When she was asked what she meant, Jane replied, "Why, all the people I have killed. They all came and gathered round my bed in the night. There were the Davises, and Mr. and Mrs. Dunham, and Myra Connors, and Mrs. Brigham, and Mrs. Bannister, and Mrs. Gibbs, and Mrs. Harry Gordon - Oh, I'm sorry I killed her, she is so pretty."

Jane began to sob uncontrollably and only continued when she was able to compose herself a little. "But they're all after me now," she cried, "thirty-one of them. Some want to poison me, and some come at me with their skeletal hands as if they would choke me. See, they're coming for me now - help, murder!"

The newspapers used Jane's suffering to make a point, writing, "Jane Toppan is paying the penalty for her crimes by Nature's or God's own law in a way that is an appalling moral object lesson - that no one can take a human life, even if he escapes the punishment of human law, without suffering the most awful tortures to the end of his or her own wretched existence."

Jane Toppan died on August 17, 1938. She was 81 years old, and for the last three decades, she barely knew who she was. During her years at the hospital, she never received any visitors aside from Dr. Stedman and, once, her childhood friend, James Murphy.

When she died, no one came to claim her remains, so she was buried in an unmarked grave in the potter's field at the Mayflower Cemetery in Taunton.

"Don't blame me, blame my nature," Jane once said, "I can't change what was meant to be, can I?"

If she had been given a gravestone, it might have been a fitting epitaph for one of the most evil women in American history. In life, she never regretted the damage she caused, but in death, that might be another story.

Most everyone agreed that the old hospital was haunted. Such places almost always are - or so the stories say. As with any place where innocent people were tortured or died, a belief in lingering spirits usually follows. The tales always grow larger after people begin exploring the abandoned places and sharing their haunting experiences.

Locals began exploring the remains of the old hospital in 1975 when most of it was closed. It was a period when such places were being shuttered across the country. The asylum in Taunton was no exception. Most of the place was abandoned, and even the few sections that remained open struggled with outdated electricity, groaning pipes, peeling paint, and crumbling brick walls.

The next two decades brought the collapse of the administration building's dome, a devastating fire, and the complete destruction of the original Kirkbride buildings. Some of the existing buildings were slightly updated to keep them in use. Then, in 2012, the last of the patients were shipped out to other hospitals, and the remaining parts of the facility were turned into a recovery treatment center for women.

The old asylum was mostly gone, but the stories were still told about the buildings that remained. There were ghosts that walked those corridors and lingered in the cells. Stories still spread of ghostly screams, unexplained noises, bloodstained handprints, cries for help, and eerie apparitions. Some tales extended beyond the buildings to the woods surrounding the site, citing instances of occult activities taking place in the shadows.

The old hospital became known as one of the most haunted places in the state, and thanks to many hair-raising experiences, an often-used quote about the place claimed, "The Devil himself is still there..."

But in this case, the "Devil" was a woman.

More than any other person connected to the asylum was the belief that Jane Toppan had remained behind at her place of torment after her death. In her later years, Jane had come to believe that the spirits of her victims were following her and surrounding her bed at night, refusing to let her rest. It's believed that she remains unable to rest after death, too.

If the breaking of Jane's mind was her punishment in life, then perhaps being doomed to remain at the place that destroyed her is a fitting punishment for eternity.

THE "VEILED MURDERESS" HENRIETTA ROBINSON

Engraved by J. C. Smith

On May 15, 1905, an article appeared in newspapers about an elderly woman who had died at the Mattawan Hospital for the Criminally Insane in New York. She had spent the last 52 years in confinement for a crime she committed in 1853, but this wasn't what made her so unusual.

In criminal files, she was known simply as "Henrietta Robinson," but no one knew who she really was. Henrietta was an enigma. She had claimed to be many things in her life, from daughter of English lords to the wife of a wealthy man from Quebec. All of her stories were probably lies, but we'll never know for sure.

What we do know, however, is that she committed an inexplicable double murder and that all of those who helped bring about her downfall suffered from a "curse" that has never truly been explained.

When she came to Troy, New York, she was using the name "Henrietta Robinson." No one knows why she chose that name, any more than they knew where she came from, how old she was, or where she had obtained the money that she used to exist on.

Having both a maid and a gardener, she lived well, but not lavishly. She was polite to her neighbors and did not get involved in their business. When she first moved to Troy, she rarely went out during the day. She lived a very secret life, which, of course, added to her allure and mystery. Curiosity compelled her neighbors to imagine where the attractive woman had come from. The fact that she kept to herself created even more speculation, rumor, and gossip.

Later, there would be a number of people who attempted to learn about her background, connecting her families in Europe, to wealthy relatives, who spoke French, as Henrietta did. All the stories created to explain her identity were wrong. Her origins remain a mystery to this day.

Naturally, though, this didn't stop the rumors. According to one story, she was the illegitimate child of an Irish lord. Born and raised in her family's ancestral castle, she was seduced by a scoundrel at an early age. He carried her off to New York City and then abandoned her, taking all the money she had. After that, she moved upstate to Troy, where she became the mistress of "a certain well-known man in the city," who left her after a few years.

Another story claimed that she had been born in Quebec, the daughter of one of the city's oldest and most prominent families. Sent to the exclusive Emma Willard's female seminary in Troy at 16, she fell in love with a young man of lower social class. Fearing that their daughter might become married to a man beneath her station, she was removed from school, brought back to Canada, and married a wealthy British man who took her to London. Though the marriage produced two children, it was a cold and loveless one, and after a few years, she ran away and returned to her family in Quebec.

Her father was outraged by her return, who denounced her for bringing shame to their family. Thrown out of the house, she returned to Troy, where, for a time, she was the kept woman of a local politician. When that relationship ended, she became increasingly erratic and began to wander the streets, stopping passersby and telling them strange tales of burglars who were planning to pillage her home. She continually imagined that she was being followed by nameless individuals and started carrying a gun, threatening to "wash her hands in the blood of her enemies."

For the most part, however, Mrs. Robinson was a quiet, albeit eccentric, part of a neighborhood located on the north side of Troy. It was a predominantly Irish neighborhood, and Henrietta lived in a small cottage there. It was well-kept and, as mentioned, had a live-in gardener and maid.

The source of her money, like everything else about her, was a mystery to the community. Some wondered if there was a Mr. Robinson. If there was, none of the neighbors ever saw or spoke to him. Even more intriguing was that Henrietta never received a letter from him. When she did speak about him - and that was only on rare occasions - she said he was "upon the rails," implying that he worked for the railroad or traveled frequently.

Although the truth about Henrietta's background will never be established, there is no doubt about how she earned her national notoriety in the spring of 1853.

The story involved the Lanagan family, who owned a low, wooden building near Henrietta's cottage. One part of the building was the living quarters for the family, while the other half served as a grocery store and gathering place for the neighborhood. In addition to selling grocery items, the Lanagans sold beer and had a space for locals to play cards and spend time together. Occasionally, the Lanagans made some extra money by holding dances in the space on Saturday nights.

Timothy Lanagan was a former mill worker who had come to the industrial city of Troy from Ireland. At age 37, he bought the wooden building in the north end and opened it as a grocery in 1852. He lived there with his wife, Anna, and their four small children.

From the time the store opened, Henrietta had been one of the Lanagans' regular customers. She came in every day - as most women did at a time when refrigeration didn't exist, and families bought what they needed for the day - groceries, beer, and brandy. Like everyone else, Henrietta used credit when she shopped at the store. She paid her bill in a timely manner and was on good terms with the family. On several occasions, she had borrowed small amounts of money from the Lanagans when she ran low on funds, but always paid it back on time. Despite her often-odd behavior, the Lanagans considered her an excellent customer and even a friend.

And they weren't the only ones in the neighborhood with affection for Henrietta. In early 1853, she suddenly became a more active member of the community. Without explanation, she began leaving her cottage and seeking out the company of some of her neighbors.

One of the first people that Henrietta approached was a young seamstress named Mary Dillon. What started as a professional relationship between the two - Henrietta wanted to have some dresses altered - Henrietta tried to transform into a friendship. They were an odd pair. Henrietta spoke perfect English and French, and Mary was completely uneducated but eager to welcome the relationship.

Henrietta spent each day they were together spinning wild tales. Mary wasn't sure she believed them all, but the stories of parties and nobility were exciting to her. Henrietta claimed to be the daughter of a lord, recalling castles, balls, and parties. She once showed Mary a daguerreotype of a lady with a bouquet of flowers. She said it was her mother, and the image had been taken in the garden of the King of France. On another visit, Henrietta claimed to have been born in Vermont and had been thrown out of her house by her stepmother. Her father was stern and cold, she said, and the next day, he was described as forgiving and warm. On another occasion, she said her father gave her $150 to buy a dress that she could wear in court when she sued Oliver Boutwell - a wealthy neighbor and mill owner - for slander. There is no evidence that this lawsuit existed.

But the issue of slanderous comments became a recurring theme with Henrietta. Starting in March 1853, appparenty she first became aware that her neighbors were speculating about her. It had actually been going on for some time, but since Henrietta had finally started leaving her cottage, she now knew about the gossip. She said many times and to many people that Oliver Boutwell and his family had slandered her name. They lived immediately south of Henrietta, but if they ever discussed her behavior, it remains unknown. True or not, Henrietta couldn't stop talking about it.

The afternoons with Henrietta lasted for hours because whenever Mary started to leave, her host implored her to stay. She would sometimes beg her not to go, Mary said.

The daily visits lasted for two weeks. During this time, the visits always occurred at Henrietta's cottage. Mary would not go there on her own. Each time, Henrietta walked over to Mary's home to get her. The days spent together were pleasant, and Mary enjoyed the visits, regardless of how strange Henrietta sometimes behaved.

Many of her stories were laced with profanity, which was shocking to a young woman like Mary at the time. There was also her liberal use of a handgun. She liked to wave it around, and one night showed up at Mary's house wearing only her nightgown and carrying a pistol. She said that a group of ruffians were outside her home, threatening her and trying to get her to leave the neighborhood. She was so frightened, she said, that she'd run from her house in her nightclothes. Mary was able to calm her down, and she loaned her a plain dress to wear home.

After this incident, Mary's father - disturbed by the other woman's peculiar behavior - told his daughter that she could no longer be friends with Henrietta Robinson.

And then came the trouble at the dance.

It was an ordinary night for one of the "kitchen dances," as they were known. For a small admission, working-class folks could gather for some fun and, hopefully, a little romance, as well.

On this night, Anna Lanagan believed that she knew everyone who attended the dance except for a young man named David Smith. He was a boarder in a home just south of the store on River Street and was new to the area.

While the dance was going on, Henrietta came into the store for groceries. Hearing the noise and laughter, she decided to stay and socialize with her neighbors. David Smith came over to her and started a conversation. He then asked her to dance. Henrietta refused his offer. What he said to her next was unknown, but whatever it was, she became violently angry. Drawing a pistol that she kept in the bodice of her dress, she aimed it at the young man and threatened to "blow his brains out!"

Seeing the disturbance, Timothy Lanagan hurried over and told her that he would not tolerate "such a noise and that she should leave." Trying to quell the volatile situation, Anna joined her husband in telling Henrietta that it was best if she were to leave the dance. She even offered to accompany her home. When she resisted, Timothy firmly took her by the arm and escorted her outside. His wife kept her promise and walked Henrietta home.

But Henrietta didn't stay there. A little later that evening, she appeared at the door to the store but did not come inside. She asked the person collecting admission if David Smith would come outside. He was smart enough to duck out the back and not return to the store that night.

Two mornings later, Henrietta showed up at the Lanagans' front door and began to berate Anna, telling her that she was a "mean woman" who invited "rowdies to her house to insult me." She threatened to get the family evicted and to have their grocer's license revoked.

Anna rolled her eyes. "I want no trouble with you," she said. "Just go home."

Roused from his bed by the noise, Timothy went to the door. Less tolerant than his wife, he ordered her to leave the store at once.

Henrietta refused to leave. "Do you mean to throw out a good customer?" she cried. She had shopped there every day since the Lanagans had opened, and if he threw her out, she would find another place from which to buy her goods.

Timothy didn't care, replying that he "did not want her custom," he wanted her to leave his family alone.

Henrietta still refused. If he wanted her out, "he would have to call a constable to do it."

Once again, Anna stepped in to cool off the situation. She sent her husband back into the residence while she talked to Henrietta alone. Eventually, the woman left and did not return to the store for the next three weeks.

During her absence, she plotted and schemed.

On May 10, Henrietta visited a drug store on the corner of Federal and River Streets that William Ostrom owned. She came in to purchase arsenic, which she told the druggist to try and get rid of rats attracted to the neighborhood by a nearby mill. Ostrom sold her two ounces of the poison. He divided each ounce into a separate pile and wrapped it in a plain, white paper. A label that was clearly marked "poison" was placed on each wrapper.

Over the next two weeks, Henrietta slowly began to return to the Lanagans' store. Nothing was ever mentioned of their disagreement. Henrietta was largely silent, and the Lanagans never brought up what had occurred. Gradually, their relationship returned to its cordial status.

Or so the Lanagans believed.

Early in the morning on May 25, 1853, Henrietta came into the store and purchased a quart of beer and a pound of soda crackers. A few hours later, she returned and asked for a loan of $2. When Anna replied that she did not have the money on hand, Henrietta left.

She came back before noon. This time, she was highly agitated. She had just received a telegram with terrible news, she said. Her husband, who was traveling out west, had just been killed in a railway accident.

This would seem to truly be terrible news - but Anna and those in the neighborhood had heard this story before. They'd lost count of how many times her "husband" had been "killed."

A few neighbors were hanging around the store at the time, and one of the men joked that he didn't see what Henrietta was upset about. "I have a wife out west," he said, "and if she was dead, I wouldn't fret about it." The remark made the others laugh, but Henrietta was not amused. She started yelling at the men, and the scene became so heated that she was asked to leave.

Henrietta simmered. Less than two hours later, she was back at the store. Timothy and Anna were both at home entertaining a houseguest, Catherine Lubee. The 25-year-old was the sister of Anna's sister-in-law but was a close friend. The previous fall, her sister had passed away, and during the time of the illness, Catherine had lived with the Lanagans. She later moved to Albany, where she worked as a maid for a time but then, ran out of work and came back to Troy to visit. She spent her days with Timothy and Anna and slept at the home of James Lanagan, Timothy's cousin.

When Henrietta came into the store, she barged into the family's living quarters, where Catherine and the Lanagans were just finishing their noon meal at the kitchen table. Inviting herself to join them, she sat down and pointed to an uneaten hard-boiled egg. "Whose is that?" she asked.

"Yours if you want it," Timothy said, then left the table and went back into the store.

Henrietta sat down at the table while Anna good-naturedly peeled a potato for her. She put it on a plate and set it down in front of Henrietta. As she did, she noticed a piece of white paper folded into a small packet clutched in one of the other woman's hands. At the time, though, Anna thought nothing of it.

After finishing her egg and potato, Henrietta asked for a glass of beer and invited the other two women to join her. Both declined, but Anna did get up to fetch a glass for her unwelcome guest. As she did, Henrietta asked her if she had any sugar. Anna said she did but was surprised that Henrietta needed it. Hadn't she just bought several pounds of sugar last week?

Henrietta laughed. No, no, she didn't want to buy any. She only wanted a spoonful to mix into her beer to cut the bitterness of it.

Anna stepped into the grocery store and returned a few moments later with a quart jar of beer, and a saucer was filled with powdered sugar. Having decided to join Henrietta in a drink after all, she poured the beer into two glasses. While she was doing this, Henrietta stood up from the table with her back to Anna. In one hand she held the saucer, and in the other the folded packet of white paper.

When she turned back to the table, she complained that the glasses were only half-filled. With a sigh - better to do what she wanted than argue - Anna went back into the store for more beer. When she returned, Henrietta was stirring sugar into both glasses.

Anna filled the glasses the rest of the way and sat back down at the table. As she lifted her glass, she noticed a powdery film on the surface of the beer. Thinking, as she later testified, it was "some dust from the sugar," she picked up a spoon to skim it off. But Henrietta stopped her. She took the spoon from her hand, saying, "Don't do that! That's the best part."

Anna started to take a drink. She had just lifted the glass to her lips when Timothy called to her from the store. She put the glass down on the table and walked back into the grocery. Timothy had to run an errand downtown, he said, and needed her to watch the store while he was gone.

When Timothy was leaving, he crossed through the kitchen, and seeing his wife's untouched glass of beer, he stopped and drank it. As soon as he left, Henrietta - who had never touched her own beer - hurried from the house without a word to anyone.

Catherine Lubee was left alone at the table. She had turned down a drink earlier but now decided not to let Henrietta's beer go to waste. Though it tasted slightly peculiar, she drained the glass. Within minutes, she started to feel unwell.

A short time later, Henrietta returned to the Lanagans' home. When she walked in, she found Anna tending to Catherine, who was lying on a bed in the back room. She was groaning loudly in pain and gripping her stomach. Henrietta walked over to the bedside and asked the young woman how she felt.

"Very poorly," moaned Catherine. She said that she had started to feel sick just minutes after drinking the beer left on the table. In her pain, she accused Henrietta of putting "something in the beer that sickened her."

Henrietta, of course, denied the charge. She had put nothing in the beer, she said, "but what would do you good." She did admit to spiking the beer but had added "medicine" to it, which was advertised to restore a woman's health.

While the three women were in the back bedroom, they heard a commotion out front. Timothy Lanagan had stumbled through the door, banging into the kitchen table. His face was a corpse-like white. He staggered across the room and collapsed on the sofa. "Run for the doctor!" he told his horrified wife, "I'm done for!"

Turning to Henrietta, who stood watching the scene with little interest, Anna screamed at her, "What have you done? You have killed the father of my children!"

"I have done no such thing," Henrietta replied. She then walked over to the sofa as if to speak to Timothy as he convulsed in agony.

He raised his hands to defend himself. "Go, woman, go!" he shouted at her.

Anna could no longer stand to have Henrietta in her home. She pushed the other woman toward the door and begged her to leave. Reluctantly, Henrietta left the store.

Nearly a half-hour later, Dr. Henry Adams, the family physician, arrived, summoned by one of the Lanagan children. By then, Timothy was in excruciating pain and was vomiting uncontrollably. The doctor knew these were obvious signs of poisoning, and he did what he could to try and alleviate the suffering of both Timothy and Catherine. Timothy knew his ministrations were hopeless. "The villain has destroyed me," he said to Dr. Adams, "and I shall not recover."

Dr. Adams sent for a friend and colleague, Dr. A.J. Skilton, to ask his advice. He arrived around 5:00 p.m., but there was nothing he could do for either patient. They had been poisoned, he told his friend. It was too late to save them.

Around 6:00 p.m., Timothy's condition became much worse. He lost what little strength he had left and soon slipped into a coma. A short time later, with his family praying at his bedside, he died in the arms of his sobbing wife. His last whispered words to her were: "Do not grieve. You must make the best of it."

Catherine held on until around 5:00 the next morning before she too died from the poison. Her final hours, like those of Timothy Lanagan, were spent in agony.

Even before Timothy had died, the police had been notified of suspected poisoning. Based on the fact that they went immediately in search of Henrietta Robinson, it can be assumed Anna Lanagan filed the complaint.

Earlier in the afternoon, Henrietta had left home and walked downtown. At about 6:00 p.m., she stopped in at Clark's Drug Store - the same place she had purchased the arsenic a couple of weeks before. William Ostrom, the same druggist, was again on duty.

He later said that Henrietta paced nervously around the store, unable to stay in one place. Her hair was mussed, and her clothing was out of place. She anxiously told Ostrom that she was being charged with the attempted murder of Timothy Lanagan. When he asked her what her motive would be in trying to kill the grocer, Henrietta replied that it was because she had refused to loan the family $100. This made no sense to the druggist - it was another of Henrietta's nonsensical lies, of course - and he suggested that she go to the police to clear up the misunderstanding. Without saying anything else, Henrietta turned and left the shop.

She went next door into the furniture shop and asked a clerk about the cost of having a new bed made when the door opened, and Officer Charles Burns walked in.

"Are you a police officer?" Henrietta asked him.

Burns assured her that he was, and he took her into custody. It became one of the most bizarre arrests in the history of the Troy police department.

As they walked the two blocks to the jail, Henrietta behaved very casually. She seemed lighthearted, the officer later said, which seemed odd for someone who had just been arrested. She apologized for her disheveled appearance and laughed and joked with him. When she saw a group of men on the street by the corner outside the jail, she asked Burns if she could walk in on her own so that it didn't look as though she was being arrested. Strangely, he granted her wish, and Henrietta walked ahead of him into the building, where she was met by Sheriff John Price and Officer Nathan Camp. They relieved her of the two pistols that she kept in the bodice of her dress and locked her in a cell.

The strange arrest was a harbinger of the increasingly erratic behavior that Henrietta would display during her time in jail.

During an autopsy on Timothy Lanagan's body, it was discovered that he had ingested enough arsenic to kill ten men. During a search of Henrietta's cottage, the police found a packet of poison hidden under a carpet in the back parlor. Within a day, they had traced it to druggist William Ostrom, and he confirmed that Henrietta had purchased it from him a few weeks earlier, claiming that she was using it to kill rats. He had no reason not to believe her at the time. In hindsight, though, it's likely that he deeply regretted the sale.

Looking back, nearly everyone who knew her could now see that Henrietta's mania had been increasing since she began leaving her home and socializing in the neighborhood earlier in the year. In fact, that might have even been a symptom of the change that came over her. She had kept to herself since she moved into the neighborhood and then suddenly began mixing with others who lived nearby, telling outrageous stories, and verbally and physically confronting them. The past few weeks had also seen an increase in her paranoid stories of mysterious people who were out to get her.

Her insanity came to a full boil while locked behind bars. Even on her first night in jail she raved and screamed and called for someone to help her. Men who wanted to kill her were outside her cell, she cried throughout the night. Eventually, she was kept on the top floor of the jail, away from other prisoners.

Occasionally she would sit in a chair inside her cell and refuse to speak to anyone for hours at a time. Jailers and doctors who went to see her often described her eyes as "wild" or of an "unnatural appearance." All her clothing was brought to the jail. One day she would be finely dressed, and then she would refuse to change her clothing for days at a time, becoming dirty and unkempt.

She soon began to spin her paranoid stories. First, she claimed that she could hear men in the cell next to hers sharpening their knives all night because they were going to "destroy" her. The guards explained that the cells on either side of her were empty and dark, but Henrietta insisted they were there and asked for the return of her pistols to defend herself. The guard declined the request.

On another night, she became convinced that a mob was outside of the jail, trying to get in and kill her. She told one of the doctors who visited her that at least 200 people had tried to get inside. She also claimed that she was almost killed by a couple who had already been locked up in the jail when she arrived. They had filled a cauldron with boiling water, broke into her cell, and tried to force her into it so that she'd be burned alive. She made such a noise, she told the doctor, that they ran away.

In the months leading up to her trial, she grew worse. She often flew into uncontrolled rages and demolished all the furniture in her cell, including a washstand, wardrobe, a table, a mirror, and six chairs. These attacks were always followed by a period of deep melancholia, where she again refused to speak for days.

On July 21, 1853, a strange incident occurred that did almost lead to Henrietta's death. The details of what really happened remain a mystery to this day.

In his report of the incident, Sheriff Price stated that he visited Henrietta's cell around noon, bringing with him the noonday meal his wife had prepared. She appeared to be deeply asleep, so he left the tray and went on about his business. Later that afternoon, just before 4:00

p.m., one of the jail attendants was on his rounds and checked on Henrietta. She was still on her bunk, lying down, but he saw that she appeared to have vomited several times and the contents of her stomach had a bluish color to it. He immediately went looking for the sheriff.

When Price went into the cell, he managed to rouse Henrietta enough to ask her what had occurred. She said she had "taken a considerable quantity of vitriol" - this was sarcasm as "vitriol" is a word for hate. Price reported that she went on to say that she had taken enough to "end her life." She had, she told him, "seen trouble enough."

Price called for doctors. Ironically, one of them was Dr. Adams, who had cared for Timothy Lanagan. The doctors immediately treated her, and by evening, she was improving. By Sunday morning, she was weak but on her way to recovery.

The question was, however: how had Henrietta managed to get poison into her cell? It was suggested that she had hidden it somewhere on her person when she was first locked in her cell and waited until that point to attempt suicide.

Another suggestion was that she had not been poisoned at all - that her sickness was caused by spoiled food. It was the middle of summer, and there were few ways to preserve food in those days. It was possible that the sheriff's wife had "poisoned" her by mistake, accidentally serving her food that had gone bad.

And then there was the most ominous suggestion - that someone had tried to kill her. Henrietta had been ranting about people trying to murder her for months. So, what if someone really did? It would likely have been simple to have slipped something into Henrietta's food.

We'll never know for sure what happened, but it became one more strange incident in the life of Henrietta Robinson as she waited for her trial.

The grand jury finally got around to indicting Henrietta on two charges of first-degree murder on October 10, 1853. At this point, she had already been in jail for five months. She offered a plea of "not guilty" and gave the spectators a preview of what they could expect when the trial officially began. She appeared in court wearing a black dress with a low neckline, lace sleeves, and a lace collar. She was heavily adorned with jewelry - worth at least $400, which was more than an average family might earn in a year in those days. The last item she wore was one for which she would eventually become famous - a heavy, blue veil that completely hid her face.

At the arraignment, evidence was presented regarding Henrietta's mental state. She was violently opposed to this. Her attorneys - from the prominent firm of Pierson, Beach, and Smith - knew that this might be the only way to save her life, and yet Henrietta resisted the idea of anyone questioning her sanity. Even so, her attorneys asked that her trial be delayed until it was obvious that Henrietta was able to assist in her own defense. The judge granted the stay. The trial would be delayed again in February, then once more in April.

The trial finally opened on May 21, 1854, nearly a year since Timothy Lanagan had died. Hordes of curiosity-seekers showed up, eager to glimpse the madwoman who had become so notorious - and to catch a glimpse of her strange behavior. They would not be disappointed.

Henrietta arrived at the courthouse "magnificently attired in an elegant black dress, a white shirred bonnet ornamented with artificial flowers, white kid gloves, and a rich black mantilla lined with white satin." The most striking feature of her outfit again was the blue veil that shrouded her face. Despite demands, she refused to remove it for the entire six days of her trial. At one point, when the exasperated judge ordered her to lift her veil, she replied, "I am here, Your Honor, to undergo a painful trial - not to be gazed at."

Reporters sensationally dubbed Henrietta with the nickname by which she is still known: "The Veiled Murderess."

Despite abundant testimony from doctors, neighbors, and short-lived friends like Mary Dillon about Henrietta's mental derangement, the jury rejected the defense of insanity and returned a guilty verdict. They had deliberated for just a little more than two hours.

District Attorney Anson Bingham asked the judge to proceed to sentencing. One of Henrietta's attorneys, Job Pierson, stood to protest, but before he could speak, Henrietta was shouting at the judge and the jury. "Shame on you, Judge! Shame on you! There is corruption here! There is corruption in this court!" she wailed.

At first, Pierson tried to quiet his client, but then he gave up and asked the judge for a postponement of the sentencing, at least for a few days. The judge agreed, but before he could announce his ruling, Henrietta was back on her feet and screaming again.

Exasperated, Pierson gripped Henrietta by the arm and leaned in close so that he could speak to her forcefully but under his breath. "If you do not keep quiet, I will leave you," he hissed at her.

But his words meant nothing to her. "I will speak!" she cried. "Why should I not?"

In the middle of the fray, Martin Townsend, another of her attorneys, got to his feet. He was just as angry as Henrietta was, but not for the same reason. He exclaimed to the judge, "In finding a verdict of guilty, this jury has convicted the verist lunatic that ever lived!"

At that moment, there were many in court who certainly would have agreed with him - including members of the jury.

The sentencing was continued until the following Monday morning, and it took the sheriff and his wife several minutes to get Henrietta to sit down and be quiet. When she finally fell into her seat, she sat sullen, like a child. After things calmed down, she was out of the courtroom and returned to the jail.

She talked incessantly during the short carriage ride and as she climbed the steps to her cell. When the door clanged shut behind her, she turned to the guard and blurted out, "Well, you'll have a good time putting the rope around my neck!"

When Henrietta's breakfast was brought to her on Sunday, Sheriff Price found she had dressed all in white. She paced her cell, angry and vengeful, swearing against the prosecution and her own defense team. She said over and over again that the court would never pass sentence on her. Then, minutes later, she was laughing and joking and filled with merriment. Her changes in emotions were so sudden that the sheriff put her on suicide watch.

On Monday, Henrietta returned to the courtroom in a black silk dress. She looked as if she were in mourning. On her head was a white hat, and her face was shrouded once again by the thick blue veil.

The courtroom was still packed. There wasn't enough standing room, let alone seats, for everyone who wanted admission. The crowd was so large that the second-floor balcony seemed to sag under the weight of the onlookers. More than half of the crowd were women.

They brought their children with them and lifted them high so they could get a glimpse of The Veiled Murderess.

The stifling courtroom became an anxious place when the judge ruled that sentencing would again be postponed for arguments from the defense. They planned to appeal the guilty verdict.

Henrietta Robinson was returned to her cell.

It was not until May 1855 that the upper courts in Albany heard the appeal. On June 19, she was returned to the courtroom to learn that her appeal had been denied. Judge Harris - who had presided over her earlier trial - was now prepared to pass sentence upon her.

Judge Harris had expected to find the courtroom empty - the sentencing had not been publicized - so he was surprised to find all the seats filled and all the standing room taken by an unruly crowd.

Again, perhaps for the final time, he asked the prisoner, "Mrs. Robinson, have you any objecting to removing the veil?"

Henrietta had been talking quietly to her attorney. When the judge's words finally registered in her mind, she threw the veil back over her bonnet and revealed her face for the first time during all the proceedings. A gasp went through the crowd who could see her. Those who didn't know her personally were stunned to discover that she didn't look like a madwoman. Henrietta was very pretty and was in her late 20s, perhaps only as old as 30. Seeing the effect the sight of her face had on the crowd, Henrietta laughed.

Before he pronounced sentence, Judge Harris asked her if she had anything to say. "Yes," she answered, "I have much to say, but I know I will be interrupted."

Assuming this meant she did not want to make a statement, the judge continued, "You have been convicted of the wilful murder of Timothy Lanagan." Only Timothy's murder had been prosecuted. The death of Catherine Lubee had been held back in the event anything went wrong with the case.

Henrietta immediately spoke up. "Yes, but it was upon false evidence," she blurted out. "You have all conspired against me! Shame, judge!"

But Judge Harris was not interested in trying to shout down the defendant. Instead, he calmly lectured her to accept her punishment.

Henrietta spelled out her answer to the judge, "p-o-o-h!" she said.

Judge Harris just shook his head in dismay. "I am aware that you would listen to nothing from me. I shall, therefore, with no further remark, proceed to pass sentence upon you," he said firmly. "The sentence of the court is that you, Henrietta Robinson, be detained in the county prison until the third day of August next, and that on that day between the hours of 10 o'clock in the forenoon and 2 in the afternoon, you will be hanged by the neck until you be dead. May God in his infinite mercy save your soul."

Henrietta shrieked at him. "You had better pray for your own soul, sir!"

Attorney Pierson rose from his seat and tried to get her to be quiet, but Henrietta refused. "Why should I remain silent?" she cried. "I am a victim of a political conspiracy. All have deserted me!"

As Henrietta continued to cry out about injustice, the audience in the courtroom began to stir. Voices were raised, even as Judge Harris banged his gavel and tried to restore order to the proceedings.

Finally, Henrietta turned her attention back to the judge, pointed her finger at him, and screamed, "May the Judge of Judges be your Judge!"

This moment would begin the legend of the curse that would follow Henrietta for years. It would be a few years before strange things began to happen, but many lives would be shattered once they did.

As it turned out, Henrietta did not hang. On July 27 - just one week before the scheduled execution -- the governor commuted her sentence to life behind bars. Most of Henrietta's possessions were given away but wearing what little she still owned, she was taken by train to Sing Sing. With Sheriff Price as her only escort, they left the jail late at night. Even so, a crowd of people lined the streets to watch her go. They hoped to get one last look at her face, but to their disappointment, she was wearing the heavy blue veil.

Henrietta Robinson died on May 15, 1905. It had been 15 years since she was transferred from the penitentiary to the Mattawan State

Hospital for the Criminally Insane. She was a quiet patient at the asylum, spending most of her time making lace.

Toward the end, when it was clear that she was dying, she was urged to reveal her true identity. But Henrietta refused. She said that she had "kept the secret for half a century and intended to die with it."

No one ever came forward to claim her body, and she was buried in the hospital's cemetery - a veiled mystery to the very end.

That was not really the end. Henrietta Robinson - or whoever she was - had died. However, the story of the curse that followed her to a prison cell lived on. In fact, it didn't merely live - it thrived and grew.

From the beginning of the trial, it was clear to District Attorney Anson Bingham that he was outgunned by the skill of his defense attorney opponents. To offset this, he hired a local attorney named George Van Santvoord and an out-of-town man named Henry Hogeboom. Those two men handled most of the actual prosecution in the case. Bingham played a very small role.

During the trial, the only person who really testified against Henrietta was Anna Lanagan. The only other person with whom Henrietta seemed to have a serious problem was Sheriff Price.

Henrietta's defense involved the attorneys William Beach, Martin Townsend, and Job Pierson. It was Pierson who did most of the work. He argued with his partners about the case because he believed no defense should have been offered. The prosecution, he felt, had failed to prove their case. He didn't want to make an insanity argument because he believed it would fail, and he was right.

Henrietta was grateful that he stood by her, and perhaps, for this reason, Pierson was never affected by the string of bad luck associated with the curse. Pierson led the fight for Henrietta's appeal and stood beside her when her death sentenced was imposed by the judge. He always believed that his closing arguments would have swayed the jury if not for the slanted way that the judge influenced them.

He went on to lead a prosperous and acclaimed life and died from natural causes in April 1860.

Others would not be so lucky.

The only defense witness who cast aspersions on Henrietta was an attorney named Richard C. Jennyss. He was used as someone who had encounters with Henrietta that could show that she was clearly insane. She was not happy about what he had to say about her.

The other person that drew Henrietta's anger during the case was Judge Ira Harris. During the trial, he was considered to be generally fair, but many later criticized his charge to the jury as being biased in favor of the prosecution.

Henrietta's sentence may have been commuted from death to life in prison, but she never forgot what happened to her and never stopped blaming the men she felt were responsible for her fate.

Anson Bingham married Laura McClellan a decade before Henrietta's trial. Between 1841 and 1851, they had five children together. In the wake of the trial, all but two of them died in childhood, and the other two died at 21 and 22-years-old.

Bingham outlived the two oldest children and his beloved wife, dying alone in 1882.

George Van Santvoord was the local attorney who Anson Bingham had recruited to assist in the prosecution. He was a bit of a legend in Troy. He was the son of a minister from one of the old Dutch families that first settled in the area. He attended Union College and studied law at Kinderhook. After marrying into a wealthy family, he and his young wife moved to Indiana, where he earned acclaim for writing and publishing a book on Indiana law. A few years later, he returned to farm in upstate New York and commuted each day by rail to his law office in Troy.

Before the trial began, in addition to numerous articles, he wrote a second book, a collection of biographies of several Chief Justices of the U.S. Supreme Court. He went on to write several more books on law and history, and in the election after the trial, he replaced Bingham as the county's district attorney.

But Henrietta wasn't through with him.

In April 1863, Van Santvoord was waiting for a train at the depot in South Albany. He didn't see a second train that backed into the yard and struck him from behind. He was knocked onto the tracks, and the wheels severed his right arm. He was immediately carried into the station, but he was bleeding badly. A doctor was summoned, but it was too late. He died before help could arrive.

Henry Hogeboom was another attorney that Bingham had asked to assist in the case. His family was Dutch and had been involved in law and order for generations. His grandfather and father were both sheriffs in Columbia County, and his grandfather had died in the line of duty. Henry chose to become an attorney and had been a judge before his involvement in the Robinson case.

In 1832, he had married Jane Eliza Riverington, the granddaughter of a Revolutionary War officer and the daughter of a major landowner in the region. They had four children together, although one of them died in childhood.

He was utterly devoted to his wife, which is why what happened after Henrietta's trial was so heartbreaking. In May 1858, Jane died from a "lung inflammation."

Henry was destroyed by her death and was known to have written that "all the joy and light in his life" was gone. He never socialized after that, and he never remarried.

Anna Lanagan mostly disappeared from history after the trial. By the late 1860s, she was still alive and running the grocery store with her daughter-in-law. What happened to her after that is unknown, but she seems to have escaped from the curse.

Sheriff John Price wasn't as lucky. He lost the next election and watched as his life fell apart. The records of the following years in Troy include a notice for his arrest for stealing chickens. He was locked up in the same jail that he once was in charge of.

Richard Jennyss was called as a witness for the defense during the trial and upset Henrietta with his testimony. He was a young lawyer at the time and was used to bolster the suggestion that she was insane.

In 1860, six years after the trial, Jennyss married. He had six children, five daughters, and a son. The boy was named Richard after his father, but to avoid confusion, he was referred to as Louis, which was his middle name. As he grew older, Louis also became a lawyer - which would lead to his downfall.

In the late 1880s, Louis took on a divorce case, representing Minnie Nelligan, wife of Thomas Nelligan. Minnie was the rebellious daughter of a wealthy mill owner from Cohoes named William Moore. The beautiful young woman had a wild streak and had first scandalized the family by eloping with Thomas Nelligan, who her family believed was below her station. She soon became bored, but Nelligan was cooperative and granted her a divorce in an unusual gesture for the time.

Soon after, Minnie eloped again - with Louis Jennyss.

Shortly after they were married, Louis realized that Minnie's many scandals had turned the couple into an item of gossip. They left town in 1889 and moved to a rugged logging town called Murphy, North Carolina.

It wasn't long before Minnie was bored again. She started an affair with a lumber dealer named Will Wilkinson, but Louis soon found out. It was a small town, after all.

In early July 1895, Louis and Wilkinson met by accident at the train depot. During a conversation, Wilkinson asked Louis when he planned to be home. He was taking an overnight trip, Louis said. The men parted on good terms, taking separate trains, but when Wilkinson's train slowed down on the edge of town, he hopped off and walked to Louis and Minnie's house. When he arrived, he told her that Louis would be away overnight, so they were free to be together for the evening. Wilkinson had to catch an early train, though, so Minnie would have to take him to the station in the morning.

Apparently, Louis wasn't as clueless as he seemed. He finished his business in Ashville early and took the late train back home. When he neared his house, he tied up his horse and approached on foot. It was about 2.30 a.m. when Minnie and Wilkinson left the house, heading to the train station.

Then, a gunshot rang out, and Minnie slumped forward. The horses, startled by the sound of the gun, bolted, pulling the wagon at breakneck speed. Louis cut across an open field to try and catch them, and as he approached the carriage, he fired four more shots.

About a mile down the road, Wilkinson met a farmer in a buggy. Wilkinson switched vehicles with him, telling him to take the wagon and to get a doctor. He drove Minnie to a nearby farmhouse, placed her across two chairs on the porch, and tried to wake up the owners.

In the meantime, Louis had retrieved his horse and was in pursuit of his wife and her lover. When he arrived at the farmhouse, he found Minnie alone, dead, on the porch. Wilkinson had fled. He was found later in a neighboring town, where he claimed he went for "legal advice." The feeling in the community was that he was a coward who had left a woman alone to die.

Louis was never punished for what he had done. In those days, the killing had been what was known as the "unspoken law." But it did ruin his life. Two years later, he was alone in California, where he vanished from history.

William A. Beach was an ineffectual member of the defense team. Henrietta blamed Beach and Martin Townsend for the insanity defense they had attempted and failed during her trial.

Beach was born into a family of lawyers with an uncle who was on the U.S. Supreme Court. He was raised to be an attorney, and all his sons - Miles, John., William, Jr., and Warren -- followed suit.

By the time he was in his late 20s, Miles was a partner in his father's office. He went on to be the mayor of Troy for one term and two decades later was a justice on the State Supreme Court. He also amassed a fortune in the stock market, but he lost everything during the great financial crash of 1893. One of his stockbrokers, who Miles was unable to pay, sued him. Unable to get money from him, the stockbroker maliciously got him on the witness stand and forced him to admit that he had a mistress in New Jersey with whom he'd had two children. In the aftermath, Beach kept his position on the court but lost his wife. He later died in his suite at the Waldorf Astoria, abandoned by everyone but his brother, Warren.

It was William Beach's third son, though, who showed the greatest promise in the family, but who paid the highest cost from the alleged curse.

Named for his father, William, Jr. was an intelligent, handsome scholar and a champion debater. He was so gifted that he entered Williams College as a sophomore. He was a member of the Literary

Society and also played on the baseball team. After finishing college in 1863, he served in the Civil War and was wounded on the wrist.

At the end of the war, he returned to Troy, studied law, and also became a partner in his father's firm. He became an esteemed attorney, winning more than his share of cases.

In November 1864, he married Isabella Ellis, the daughter of an attorney from Syracuse. A son was born the following year.

In the summer of 1866, William and Isabella decided to spend the summer season in Saratoga. William's birthday was August 25, and with the season winding down, he decided to spend the morning shooting game birds with a childhood friend named Lowery on a farm west of the city. They didn't have much luck and by 9:00 a.m. decided to return to the city.

According to newspaper reports, their carriage hit a rock on the way into town, and William's gun fell out of the carriage. The gun was cocked, and in a freak accident, the hammer hit the wheel, and it discharged. The gun was less than two feet away from William when it went off, blasting him in the side of the head. Lowery rushed the wagon toward town, but William knew he was dying and dictated notes for his wife, father, and a friend. By the time the carriage was back at his grandmother's house, where the family had been staying, William was failing fast. They sent for a doctor immediately, but by the time he arrived, it was too late.

The funeral was held at his grandmother's home, and so many people wanted to attend that arrangements were made for a special train to get everyone to the service. William, Jr. was a beloved member of the community, and everyone who knew him was shattered by the loss.

Or were they?

There seems to be one problem with the story told about the gun that accidentally slipped out of the carriage. William had been driving when the accident occurred, which meant that he would have been sitting on the left side of the seat. However, the gunshot that killed him was fired so that the wound appeared on the right side of his head.

No questions were ever asked about his death, and no investigation was conducted by the police. What actually happened that day remains, even after all these years, a mystery.

Martin Townsend was one of Henrietta's other attorneys during the trial. Like Beach, he had done little to help her defense, and, in fact, Henrietta once stated that she felt that Townsend had abandoned her at the time of the sentencing.

Townsend had not had a lucky life, at least when it came to his family. He and his wife only had one child who lived to be an adult, a daughter named Frances. When she was older, Frances married Henry Nason, one of the leading chemists in the country.

Sadly, though, Townsend had little respect for his daughter. In 1899, he was given a silver cup in recognition of his lifetime of achievements as an attorney. In his speech, he remarked that he had not been blessed by sons but hoped the many men that he had mentored and his grandson would carry on his tradition of hard work and community service.

Frances did have one son, a boy named Henry, Jr. He was raised in a modestly wealthy family with servants and the opportunity to attend the best schools. He excelled at Williston Academy, a preparatory school, and won an academic scholarship to Yale University. After Yale, he studied at Columbia Law School and, in 1888, formed a partnership with his grandfather. Eight years later, he became a judge on the New York Supreme Court. He was one of the youngest to ever serve. He seemed to have everything - but he was not married and had no child to carry on his name.

Even so, the Townsend and Nason families were doing well. Anyone who thought there was a curse attached to those involved in Henrietta's trial had to reconsider the idea when it was pointed out how this family had thrived.

Until December of 1902, at least.

First came the death of Henry's mother, Frances Nason, followed by his grandfather, Martin, just four months later. Suddenly, Henry found himself a very wealthy man with the burden of carrying on the family alone. Although no one knew it at the time, Henry had already struggled with mental illness and had taken off the preceding summer in seclusion so he could "rest."

Late in the morning on March 30, 1903, Henry stopped by his office in Troy to sign some papers. He visited briefly with his secretary and clerk. He told them that a college classmate from Albany was in town, and the two of them were having dinner together. When he left, the clerk noticed that Henry was not wearing an overcoat. Henry waved away his concern. It was only raining a little; he didn't need a coat.

A few hours later, Henry was leaving a local drug store and ran into a fellow judge. Like his clerk, his colleague noted that he was not wearing a coat. He was concerned that Henry might catch a cold. Henry replied, "It might be well if I take cold, for then it would take my mind off the troubles I have had with the loss of my devoted mother and grandfather."

The next day Henry did not show up at the office. His law clerk and secretary were unable to reach him, so they made some inquiries. To their surprise, they learned that his college classmate had never planned to come to the city at all. They spent the day searching for Henry among his friends. No one had seen or heard from him. By the following day, it was clear that something was wrong. The police were alerted, and a $500 reward was offered for information.

On Friday, April 3, a man who lived south of town took his new hound out to continue his training as a hunting dog. As he crossed an open field that led into some woods, the dog ran into the brush and began to bark. Thinking the dog had found some rabbits, the man walked over and was startled to find a man's body instead.

Henry was found with his face covered in cloth and three empty bottles lying next to him. One of the bottles had contained liquor, and the others had held laudanum and chloroform. His money, watch, and a diamond pin were still on him. He had not been robbed - it appeared he'd committed suicide.

It was eventually determined that he had used an assumed name to purchase the laudanum at one drug store and the chloroform at another. It was at the second store where he met the judge he was acquainted with. Henry had apparently taken the laudanum to dull the pain of the chloroform, which could burn the skin. He had pressed the cloth to his face and poured the chloroform over it. He went to sleep, and he never woke up.

Judge Ira Harris, in most ways, suffered the worst of Henrietta's curse. She had, perhaps, despised him the most. According to all accounts, Harris had presided over a fair trial and managed not to let himself be too bothered by Henrietta's antics, like refusing to remove her veil. However, during his charge to the jury, Harris told the jurors that the defense had failed to claim that Henrietta was not guilty. He said they had only presented a case based on insanity. This wasn't true, but the jury was swayed by it.

And Henrietta never forgot it.

Harris was an unusual man. He was known as an intellectual and was an avid reader with a collection of more than 3,500 books. He never sought a position as a judge; it happened by accident. But he served for a number of years until fate sent him in another direction.

Harris was a friend of a political operative named Thurlow Weed, and in 1860, Weed had put his support behind William Seward in the presidential race. When the Republicans nominated Abraham Lincoln, Lincoln needed the support of New York, so he named Seward as his Secretary of State. That opened a position as a New York senator. At that time, senators were elected by state legislatures, not by the public. A fierce battle followed. Horace Greely, a sworn enemy of Thurlow Weed, vied for the seat. Weed initially supported a candidate from New York City - anyone but Greeley, he thought.

In the meantime, Ira Harris had decided to accept a position at the newly formed Albany Law School. As a show of respect, Harris' name and five others were placed on the senate nomination list. A group of 20 legislators - who didn't want Greeley or Weed's handpicked choice - decided that Harris was a good compromise, and he stayed in the race on ballot after ballot. After six ballots, Weed realized that his man couldn't win, so he threw his support behind Harris. After two more ballots, Harris won the seat.

Harris turned out to be a better friend than legislator. While in Washington, he accomplished very little in the Senate, but he did become a close friend and ally of President Lincoln. The Harris and Lincoln families became so close that on the evening of April 14, 1865, as the Civil War was coming to a close, the Lincolns decided to attend a play at Ford's Theater in Washington and asked Senator Harris and his wife to accompany them.

Harris was unable to attend but suggested that his daughter, Clara, and her fiancée, Major Henry Rathbone, go in their place.

Judge Harris barely avoided a brush with death that night. If he had been at Ford's Theater, many believe that Henrietta's curse would have killed him.

But the Harris family did not come through the night unscathed.

When assassin John Wilkes Booth broke into the theater's Presidential Box that night and shot Abraham Lincoln in the back of the head, it was Major Rathbone who attempted to keep him from escaping. He was both stabbed and slashed with a knife in the skirmish that followed.

After Booth had escaped, Henry and Clara tried to care for the First Lady while her husband was being examined, but then, quite unexpectedly, Henry fainted from a loss of blood. When he awakened, he was taken to his fiancée's home so that his wound could be treated. He didn't respond well to the doctor's efforts. Henry became delirious, talking about the shooting and his failure to apprehend Booth. He would be haunted by the assassination for the rest of his life because, unlike President Lincoln, Henry recovered from his physical wounds. He and Clara both had a very difficult time dealing with the memories of the tragedy in the years to come.

For instance, Clara made the peculiar decision to pose for photographer Matthew Brady while wearing the dress that she had on the night of the assassination. It was still crusted with Henry's dried blood. She could never throw the dress away or even bear to have it cleaned. Later, she took the dress to Judge Harris' home in Albany, New York, placed it in the back of her closet, and never planned to look at it again.

And then came the horrific dream.

On April 14, 1866 - the anniversary of the assassination - Clara was staying at her parents' home in Albany and woke to see the ghost of Abraham Lincoln, sitting in a chair, facing the closet. He was laughing to himself as though watching a humorous play. He vanished when the clock struck midnight, and Clara ran screaming to tell her family what she had seen. Of course, they told her it had just been a dream, but she was so terrified that she had the door to the closet bricked over so that it could never be used again. The dress linked to that tragic night, she believed, would stay entombed forever.

In 1867, Henry and Clara were married, and he retired from the Army a few years later. The marriage turned out to be a volatile one -- largely due to the post-traumatic stress that Henry suffered from. As the years passed, he became increasingly unstable, plagued by health problems, including chronic heart palpitations.

After Henry's retirement, he moved his family to Germany. If they were hoping that a fresh start would help their marriage -- or Henry's precarious mental health -- they were tragically mistaken.

Two days before Christmas, in 1883, Henry went into a rage and, gripping a revolver and knife in his hands, made his way to the bedroom of his children. He had become convinced that they needed to die. Clara tried to stop him, but he shot her and then stabbed her to death. When he saw what he had done, Henry stabbed himself in the chest five times. The wounds did not prove fatal.

The broken man never stood trial for his wife's murder. He was declared insane and was sent to the Provincial Insane Asylum, where he died in 1911, at age 74.

Perhaps Henrietta Robinson had her revenge after all.

Women and elephants never forget an injury.
H.H. Munro

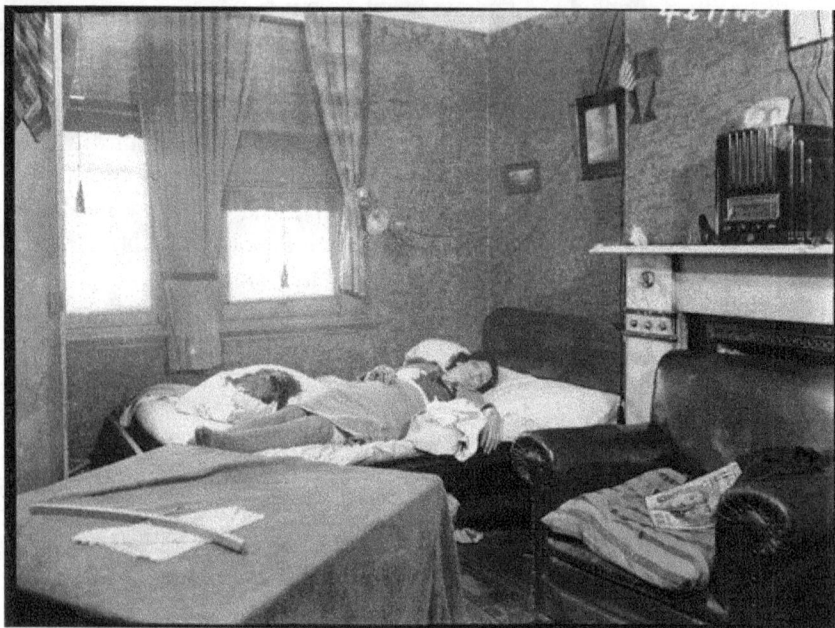

PART TWO:

THE WRONGED

"I'LL MEET MY SISTER IN HEAVEN, WHERE I'LL FIND HER MISSING HEAD"

PEARL BRYAN

When a young woman named Pearl Bryan boarded a train in Central Indiana bound for Cincinnati, she undoubtedly believed that her troubles were almost at an end. She simply needed a problem to go away - never realizing the fate that awaited her.

Pearl was desperate. Unmarried and pregnant, she was on her way to a far away city where the father of her unborn child promised that he had arranged for an illegal abortion.

But there would be no salvation for Pearl. She would be betrayed and gruesomely murdered by the man she trusted.

In most cases, a story like Pearl's would have long faded into obscurity by now. It would have ended after her killer kept his date with the hangman. But this crime was different for several reasons. Mostly, it was tailor-made for the popular culture of the era. The horror of the crime, its characters, and its cause created a melodrama that could only be found in the yellow back novels of the time - a villain deflowers a pretty young girl and then murders her to cover up her unplanned pregnancy so that he can continue to live a life of debauchery. To make matters even more lurid, he cuts off her head to keep her from being identified, and her head is never found.

Such a tragedy understandably resonated with the public, prompting stories, legends, and even a folk ballad that was meant to encourage young ladies to embrace chastity.

And then there were the ghost stories.

Most of these chilling tales are linked to a small Kentucky nightclub near where Pearl's body was found. It marks the site where a grisly piece of evidence in the murder allegedly vanished. If there is any truth to that tale, then the club may be one of the most haunted - and most sinister - locations in the region.

Pearl Bryan was the attractive young daughter of a wealthy dairy farmer named Alexander Bryan from Greencastle, Indiana. The family was well-respected in the area, known for their upright character. The Bryans had been in Central Indiana for nearly a century, dating back to the days before statehood.

Pearl was the youngest of 12 children, one of the most popular young women in the area, and considered to be beautiful and delicate. She graduated near the top of her high school class in 1892 but did not pursue further education. She lived with her parents and was a skilled seamstress who made most of her own clothes. That commitment to sewing would be readily identifiable by the callouses unique to practitioners of the trade. This later proved useful to homicide investigators.

Pearl was courted by a number of young men but was in no hurry to settle down. According to a newspaper report, "none of her ardent admirers had made a deeper impression upon her, and her heart was still her own. Money and position did not have any effect upon her favors, the young man, struggling hard to make his way in life, was as graciously received and as well treated by her as the young swell, rolling in luxury and wealth."

The only man that Pearl was close with was her cousin, William Wood, a medical student at DePauw College. He was her nearest relative in age, and the two were more like brother and sister than cousins. Pearl considered him to be her closest friend. So, when Will introduced her to his friend, Scott Jackson, a dental student, Pearl was immediately taken with him. Her family was impressed with the young man, as well. He came from a good family and was always polite and courteous when he called on Pearl.

But all was not what it seemed. Even though Will's intentions had been completely honorable when he introduced Jackson to Pearl, he did leave out the fact that the two of them often frequented some of the region's more questionable saloons and gambling joints together. But like many others involved in this story, Will was overwhelmed by the strength of Jackson's personality. Will was the son of a Methodist minister, attending a religious college with hopes of becoming a doctor, and he undoubtedly would have never arranged a meeting between Jackson and his cousin if he had ever suspected his friend's intentions toward Pearl. By the time he'd realized what he'd done, though, it was too late.

But William Wood eventually paid for his "sin." After the notoriety surrounding Pearl's murder, and the role he would play in the trials that followed, Will found his plans for medical school in ruins. Whatever became of him is unknown, but he never became a physician.

And of course, so did Scott Jackson, the handsome, blond-haired, mustached man who went by the nickname of "Dusty." Jackson was a short, domineering man who had a talent for finding companions who couldn't stand up to his forceful personality. They went along with his schemes - as Will Wood did - and were quick to follow him, no matter how disreputable of a path he might choose.

The *Cincinnati Enquirer* described Jackson:

Belonging to an excellent family, he was outwardly a man whom any father would be proud to have his daughter associate with. With dimples on his chin and cheeks, a childish smile on his lips, frank, beautiful, pale violet-blue eyes, he had a most winsome countenance. But behind the angelic front was hidden a very demon...

To those not knowing his habits, a handsome, affable, pleasing man of fine form and features; to those who knew him truly, a villain of the deepest dye, a very demon in human shape.

Like Pearl and Will, Jackson also came from a good family, but this seemed to have little effect on his character. His father had been a merchant marine fleet commodore and was highly respected. Jackson apparently inherited few of his father's attributes.

In the fall of 1894, Jackson and his widowed mother moved from Jersey City to Greencastle so that Mrs. Jackson could be closer to one of her daughters, the wife of a DePauw College professor.

Or at least that's what she said publicly.

The truth was that the family had fled New Jersey after Scott narrowly dodged a long prison term for grand larceny. He had been working in the mailroom of the Jersey City office of the Pennsylvania Railroad and was tasked with opening all correspondence. This gave him access to checks and lots of cash. He had stolen more than $32,000 before he was caught. He only avoided prosecution because he cooperated with the police. Another man in the office, Alexander Letts, was also part of the scheme and had forged the signatures on many of the checks. Jackson was presented with a deal that let him avoid prosecution if he testified against Letts, which, of course, he took.

The crime ruined the family name on the East Coast, and when it became clear that there was no future for them in New Jersey, Jackson and his mother moved to Central Indiana.

Because the Jacksons were not native to Greencastle and had few acquaintances there besides the sister, news of Jackson's criminal past didn't reach the city. Will Wood was a neighbor to Jackson, and once he was introduced to Jackson's lifestyle of drinking and gambling, the two young men became fast friends.

Jackson enrolled in the Indianapolis Dental College and frequently met Will in the city for a night of drinking since it was only a short interurban train ride away. As the *Cincinnati Enquirer* noted, "Both being fond of ladies' company, they spent much of their time together in the company of women of loose moral character and were in several very unsavory escapades, escaping notoriety however under assumed names, which prevented their families and friends at Greencastle from hearing of them."

Will introduced Jackson to Pearl in the spring of 1895, and it was love at first sight. The smooth-talking Jackson quickly seduced the young woman. Her parents never suspected that anything was wrong. Without hesitation, they permitted their youngest daughter to accept the attentions of Jackson, to go out with him when he was home, and to remain alone with him in their parlor until the late hours of the night. They had every confidence in Pearl and no suspicions about the attentions of Jackson.

Pearl was like putty in his hands, and he twisted and molded her into what he wanted. Older, more experienced, and with a plan that ended her innocence, Jackson knew all the things Pearl wanted to hear and how to manipulate her. Unknown to her friends and the polite members of Greencastle society, Pearl became pregnant.

In a panic, Pearl turned to her trusted cousin, Will Wood, who took the news to Jackson. He was angry at first, but he suggested that they wait and see what happens. But Will told him that the baby was healthy and was likely to stay that way, so Jackson began making plans to remedy the situation providing some recipes for homeopathic tinctures and oils that would produce a miscarriage. The concoctions were tried without success, and Will reported to his friend that Pearl was starting to show signs of her condition. Her mental state, he added, was bordering on hysteria.

Jackson - who had transferred from the dental school in Indianapolis to one in Cincinnati - told Wood that he was going to procure an abortion. He needed Will to get Pearl to agree to it. It didn't take much to convince her.

In addition to sharing his troubles with Will Wood, Jackson also confided everything to his roommate, Alonzo Walling, a 19-year-old fellow student at the Ohio Dental College.

Pearl left her parents' home on January 27, 1896, telling them that she was going to Indianapolis. Instead, she made plans to meet Jackson in Cincinnati.

It was the last time her parents would see her alive.

At the train depot, Pearl met Will Wood, although this meeting was mere chance. He was there to pick up his father, who was returning from a church conference. Will was the only relative who knew where she was really going that day.

Pearl arrived in Cincinnati later that afternoon, where she was met by Jackson and taken to the Indiana House. After that, her activities until the night of her murder are unknown. Most likely, she remained in her room or close by during the day. Jackson managed to keep her in limbo for nearly a week, waiting for the date of the abortion.

Early on Saturday morning, February 1, 1896, near Fort Thomas, Kentucky, 16-year-old Jack Hewling, a hired hand for a farmer named James Lock, was cutting across his employer's property when he saw a woman sprawled out in the grass beneath some apple trees. The orchard was about 200 feet from the Alexandria Turnpike and less than two miles from an abandoned slaughterhouse. Hewling was not especially startled by the sight - at least not at first. After a night on the town, carousing soldiers from the fort often brought their girls out into the fields for a tumble, and on more than one occasion, Hewling had come across a female sleeping off the effects of too many drinks from the night before.

But this time was different.

As he got closer, he realized, to his shock, that the woman's head was missing. It was obvious from the blood that had been spattered on the grass that a furious struggle had taken place. A man's torn and bloody shirtsleeve was lying nearby. Hewling ran to the nearby house of Wilbert Lock and, along with a man named Mike Noonan, returned to the orchard. After viewing the bloody scene, they went immediately to the fort and notified the commander, Colonel Cochran, who called the Newport police headquarters. The call brought Sheriff Jule Plummer, Coroner Robert Tingley, and several other county and city officials to the blood-soaked spot.

Tingley examined the scene. The coroner later stated that the woman's head had been "cleanly" cut off and, horribly, that she had been alive at the time the beheading occurred, based on the presence of blood on the underside of some leaves at the murder scene. When he turned the body over, he found that her outer clothing had been ripped open and her corset torn off, exposing her breasts. The palm and fingers of her left hand had been sliced nearly to the bone. A large pool of blood had soaked the ground beneath the body.

While Tingley was inspecting the body, Sheriff Plummer and one of his deputies examined the crime scene. They soon discovered several sets of footprints. From these markings and other physical evidence - the scattered clothing trampled ground, and widely sprayed blood - they deduced that the dead woman had a male companion and that they "had walked side by side for a short distance when, for some reason, the woman had attempted to flee." Overtaking her, the murderer had "choked her into silence and dragged her toward a bushy bank. She struggled desperately, and he tore handfuls of clothing from her dress. He threw her to the ground and slid over the bank with her." Drawing a knife, he "slashed her throat." Fighting for her life, she clutched the blade with her left hand, and it "laid her palm and fingers open to the bone. Her struggles were useless, and in a moment her lifeblood was pouring from the gaping wound in her throat." Afterward, the killer had sawn through her neck below the fifth vertebra and carried off her head.

While the body was being loaded onto a wagon and driven to an undertaker's establishment in Newport, police officers set to work trying to identify the dead woman. Two detectives from Cincinnati, Cal Crim and John McDermott, were assigned to help with the case and soon arrived at the murder scene. By the time they arrived, though, they were stunned to find hundreds of souvenir hunters, curiosity-seekers, and soldiers from the nearby fort roaming around and picking up everything that had blood on it. The crowd, along with heavy rains that fell later that afternoon, wreaked havoc on the crime scene.

The scene outside of W.H. White's undertaking parlor in Newport was equally frenzied. The *Enquirer* reported, "All day long and up to a late hour at night, the place was besieged with people anxious to get a look at the remains of the unfortunate woman."

With Coroner Tingley and several other physicians in attendance, Dr. Robert Carothers conducted a postmortem examination, which revealed that the victim was between four and five months pregnant. The fetus, which had been alive when the victim was butchered, was removed and taken to a nearby pharmacy, where it was placed in alcohol for preservation. The stomach was also excised and turned over to Dr. W.H. Crane of the Ohio Medical College, who was able to ascertain that the victim had ingested 17 grams of cocaine shortly before her death. All the victim's blood loss had occurred through her open neck -- there was not a single drop remaining in her veins, arteries, or heart.

Following the autopsy, Dr. Carothers issued a statement that proved to be uncannily accurate: "I judge that it was a premeditated and cold-blooded murder. The girl, in my opinion, was from the country and comparatively innocent. She was brought to Cincinnati to submit to a criminal operation. Once here, she was taken to Fort Thomas and murdered. Her head was taken away, horrible as it may seem, merely to prevent the identification of her body."

News of the gruesome murder made newspaper headlines across the country. "The awful deed struck horror to the hearts of the people, and they were worked up to a pitch that had never been witnessed," one observer wrote. "The entire country was startled from center to circumference and aroused as it never had been before. Telephones and telegraph were called into service, and the finding of the headless body of a young and doubtless beautiful woman in a sequestered spot near Fort Thomas was flashed around the world."

With forensic science still in its early stages - even the use of fingerprints was still more than a decade away in America - detectives resorted to the only means at their disposal. They contacted Arthur Carter of Seymour, Indiana, who owned a set of bloodhounds named Jack, Wheeler, and Stonewall that other investigators across the Midwest had used. The dogs had helped to capture 20 fugitives who were then spending time in various penitentiaries. The dogs were given the scent of the murdered woman's clothing and then released at the crime scene - where they found nothing useful. The thousands of visitors to the site had ruined any chance of a good trail.

The only hope the detectives had was to find someone who could identify the body. Every woman missing in the entire region was considered and then ruled out. They decided to open the doors of the undertaker's establishment in Newport and allow people to view the corpse in hopes that someone might recognize her. This, of course, created another circus-like scene as the morbid curious formed lines to look at the nude, headless body. Several times the body was identified, but each time the "identified" person was found to be alive and well.

In the end, it was the victim's shoes that broke the case open. They bore the imprint of Louis and Hays, a shoe company in Greencastle, Indiana. Detectives found that only a dozen pairs of the same shoes had been sold and quickly accounted for all but two of them. This information made the newspapers and caused concern for Pearl's mother. She mentioned it to her son, Fred, and he went to the Western Union office and telegraphed some of Pearl's friends in Indianapolis to ask if she was all right. The manager of the telegraph office, A. W. Early, read the telegraph and the reply stating that Pearl had never arrived in Indianapolis. Early was shocked and became suspicious. He hurried to the hotel where the detectives were staying and told them what he knew.

Early had only been living in Greencastle for a few months but had become close friends with Will Wood. He recalled seeing a letter that Will had received from a man named Scott Jackson. In the letter, Jackson admitted that he got Pearl pregnant, and she was supposed to travel to Cincinnati for an illegal abortion. Normally, Early would have kept this embarrassing information to himself, but he felt compelled to reveal it based on the discovery of the murdered woman.

By this time, it was midnight, but the detectives left their hotel and went to the home of the manager of Louis and Hayes. They traveled to the store to check its records and discovered that Pearl Bryan had indeed purchased a pair of the company's shoes. The next morning, the men arrived at the Bryan house with the clothing taken from the unidentified woman's body. Mrs. Bryan began to sob when she recognized her daughter's dress. Her description of her daughter, including a scar on her right hand, provided proof of the dead woman's identity.

A telegram was sent at once to Cincinnati, ordering the police to arrest Scott Jackson. The detectives left Greencastle and departed for South Bend, Indiana, where Will Wood was supposed to be staying with his uncle.

Meanwhile, officers were sent to Jackson's home in Cincinnati, which was located on Ninth Street next to Robinson's Opera House. They staked out the apartment and a nearby saloon for almost seven hours before getting word that Jackson had been seen at the Palace Hotel. They followed a man who matched Jackson's description back to Ninth Street, but he stood on the street, not going up to his room. Finally, one of the officers approached him and asked if he was Scott Jackson. The man said that he was, and the policeman told him that he had been looking for him. Jackson turned pale and began to tremble as he was taken into custody. Chief Dietsch of the Cincinnati Police Department greeted Jackson when he arrived at headquarters.

"Well, we have got you," Dietsch said.

"Yes, it looks like it," Jackson replied.

He was then ushered into a room filled with police detectives, city officials, and newspaper reporters to be questioned. He admitted that he knew Pearl Bryan but claimed that he had last seen her during the holidays. He also knew Will Wood and said he had last seen him around January 6. Chief Dietsch then read the arrest warrant aloud and asked him for a response. Jackson claimed that the accusations were all false rumors and that he knew nothing about Pearl being murdered except what he had read in the newspaper. On Friday night, when the murder occurred, he said he had eaten supper and studied in his apartment. On Saturday, he had gone to the theater with a friend. He was shocked and sickened when he read about the murder, but he claimed that he did not know that Pearl was even in Cincinnati.

Chief Dietsch listened to Jackson's story and then surprised him with a strange question, "Do you remember leaving a valise in Legner's Saloon on Saturday night?"

Jackson stated that he did but thought it was empty or did not know what was in it. He claimed that he loaned it to another student named Hackleman, but later admitted to lying about that. Witnesses remembered him having the case, but it was not found when Jackson's home was searched.

Jackson was booked on suspicion of murder. Detective Bill Bulmer held his arm as he took him into the Newport police station's booking room. A number of employees of the waterworks and a group of janitors followed them up the steps, and soon, the receiving room was filled with curious onlookers.

Jackson was booked and then searched. His pockets revealed two carriage tickets that proved that he had crossed the Central Newport Bridge into Kentucky. After that, he was taken back to his cell, where Bulmer ordered that he be strip-searched. This provided more damning evidence. On Jackson's right arm were two scratches. One of them ran from his elbow to the wrist, and the other was about three inches long. Jackson claimed that he had scratched some insect bites, but the detectives knew that Pearl had been found with blood and skin under her nails after she struggled with her killer.

Even with this evidence, there was nothing to prove that Jackson had killed anyone. But this all changed on Thursday morning at 3.30 a.m. when his roommate, Alonzo Walling, was arrested. The police did not initially believe that Walling had anything to do with the murder, but Jackson revealed otherwise around 2:00 a.m. that morning. After a restless night of trying to sleep, he asked the guard outside of his cell if Walling had been arrested yet.

The guard asked, "Why should he be arrested?"

Jackson immediately went silent, realizing that he had made a mistake. Detectives roused Walling out of bed and peppered him with questions. He admitted that he had been with Jackson at a saloon on Friday night, but he claimed to know nothing about the murder. They arrested him anyway and took him down to the station.

That same morning, a telegram arrived in Newport stating that Will Wood had been arrested in South Bend, Indiana. He confessed that he had arranged for Pearl to go to Cincinnati for an abortion. He believed that the operation caused her death and that her head must have been removed to prevent her from being identified. He named Jackson and Walling as the perpetrators of the crime.

When word spread that arrests had been made in the murder of the headless woman, hundreds of people flocked to the police station. Additional officers had to be called in to handle the crowds as Walling was taken to the chief of police's office for interrogation. Walling startled the police by admitting to his role in the crime. He recounted a conversation on Christmas Day between himself and Jackson when his friend confessed to getting Pearl pregnant. He went on to tell of the botched abortion and the plan to get rid of the girl.

Walling said that Jackson had purchased cocaine and had injected the girl with it. He said he took Pearl Bryan to Fountain Square on Friday night and was instructed to wait until Jackson came back. In 10 to 15 minutes, Jackson arrived and then left again. Jackson later brought him a valise and asked him to take it, but Walling refused. Walling also confessed that Jackson told him, just hours before he was arrested, that he would go to the Palace Hotel and write to Will Wood, sending him a fake letter that was supposed to be from Pearl. Wood was to mail the letter in Indianapolis on his way home from South Bend. That way, it would look as though Pearl was still alive when her family received the letter.

The authorities immediately telegraphed the postmaster in South Bend and instructed him to seize all of Will Wood's letters and send them to Newport. Unfortunately, Will had already received the letter and destroyed it, a fact that would not become known until later.

Chief Dietsch then decided to try and trick more information out of the dental student. He told Walling that he knew he was lying, that Jackson had already told them that Walling had performed the abortion on Pearl. Walling became enraged that Jackson was supposedly blaming him for everything. He swore that it was Jackson who was guilty.

The following day, the chief brought Jackson into the interrogation room and asked him if he wanted to make a confession. He told him that Walling had shifted all the blame onto him. Jackson became upset by this and tried first to blame Will Wood, then Walling, for the crime. He also claimed that it had been Will who had gotten Pearl pregnant and that Will had asked for his help because he was studying medicine. Dietsch then told him that he had been seen near Fort Thomas with Walling on Friday night, but Jackson swore this was not true. He then asked Jackson who he believed had committed the murder and the young man now blamed it on Alonzo Walling. Jackson even went as far as to say that Walling had taken Jackson's trousers with him when he butchered Pearl.

Crowds continued to descend on the police station. By 9:00 p.m., detectives had arrived with Will Wood in custody. He was questioned, and after his side of the story was recorded, he was sent to the Grand

Hotel with his father. The mob outside was in a volatile state. There were angry suggestions made that Jackson and Walling should hang in the streets, and plans were formed to lynch them. Inside the station, the police feared the worst, and they closely guarded the prisoners. Eventually, the mob settled down and slowly dispersed.

A short time later, the case took another turn. John Kugel, a saloon keeper, walked into the station, claiming to have Jackson's mysterious leather valise. The police knew about the case but did not know what had become of it. Kugel turned it over to the detectives. They found it was empty but was stained with blood. Jackson was brought in and questioned about the valise. He pretended not to know that the interior was soaked with gore but looked extremely nervous and upset when Kugel identified him and said that Jackson told him that he wanted to get rid of the case. Kugel had taken it and then was shocked to find the blood inside.

Jackson was seen with the case on Friday evening by a porter named Allen Johnson. He had seen Jackson with Pearl and Walling on Friday evening, leaving Wallingford's saloon in a carriage. The case had been with them at the time, and it was thought to belong to Pearl. On Saturday, Jackson returned with the valise, and Kugel took it when Jackson left it behind.

On Saturday, February 8, more evidence against Jackson was discovered when his blood-stained coat was removed from a sewer at the corner of Richmond and John Streets. A detective found tansy flower seeds in the pockets, which were reported to cause miscarriages. Alonzo Walling had placed the coat in the sewer at the request of Scott Jackson, he said. Further evidence was found in Jackson's locker at the Ohio Dental College. When detectives opened it, they found muddy trousers with bloodstains on the legs. Jackson and Walling each claimed that the pants were the property of the other.

Later that evening, Jackson provided directions to where Pearl's clothing could be found in a sewer on Richmond Street. Jackson claimed that Walling had been the one who put it there.

Naturally, Walling had a different story. He told the police how he believed Jackson had killed Pearl. He said Jackson had been reading medical books for several days, looking for the best poison. Jackson chose four grams of cocaine mixed with 16 drops of water. If he made her drink it, her vocal cords would be impaired, and she could not scream. He then said Jackson told him that he was going to cut off her head.

Confronted with this story, Jackson admitted that he had purchased the cocaine but swore he had given it to Walling. The two men were brought together at this point, and they continued to blame one another for the murder.

But, bizarrely, when the two were asked what had become of Pearl's head, neither of them would say.

With both men shifting the blame back and forth, it was realized that without a confession, or more evidence, no one could be definitively charged with the crime. Keeping that in mind, the authorities devised a rather dramatic plan that they believed would force a confession out of one -- or both -- of the men.

Jackson and Walling were brought into a room where the body of Pearl Bryan was put on display. They were stationed at each end of the coffin and forced to face Pearl's brother and sister. Jackson was terribly excited and nervous, but Walling remained calm and cool, except for the quiet tapping of his foot. Chief Dietsch asked Walling if he recognized the body. He said that it was Pearl Bryan but that he only knew that because Jackson had told him. Jackson called him a liar, and Walling began to shout at him. The grotesque scene erupted with cries and accusations. The two men both continued to insist that the other had committed the murder. Finally, when she could stand it no more, Pearl's sister demanded to know what had become of Pearl's head. She wept as both refused to answer her. The attempt to force a confession had failed.

Eventually, Walling and Jackson were moved to the Hamilton County Jail for their safety, and on Tuesday, February 11, a jury was selected for a formal inquest. Police detectives and officials testified as to how the dead woman's identity had been determined, and doctors gave their opinions on the cause and manner of Pearl's death. Detective Crim told of how he had been assigned to the case and what he had learned from the crime scene. They had come to the conclusion, the detective stated, that the victim had been murdered at the spot and that she had been alive when her throat was cut. Blood had soaked the surrounding trees and bushes and had seeped into the ground to a depth of eight or nine inches. Crim was then asked, to the best of his knowledge, who he believed had committed the crime. There was a deep silence in the courtroom.

Finally, Detective Crim answered: "Scott Jackson and Alonzo Walling."

The detective went on to testify as to how the men had been accounted for on Friday evening up until the time that Pearl accompanied them in the carriage from Wallingford's Saloon. Neither of them was seen again until 3:00 a.m. on Saturday morning, and they could not account for their whereabouts during that time. He also described the situation with the blood-stained valise before he was excused from the witness stand.

Dr. Robert Carothers followed with his postmortem report, and the chemist who tested the contents of Pearl's stomach, Dr. W.H. Crane, testified to the presence of cocaine. After a few other witnesses testified about the state and condition of the corpse, the inquest was completed. The jury debated for less than an hour and unanimously determined that the remains were those of Pearl Bryan. They also found that Pearl had been given cocaine, had been decapitated while she was still alive and that she was last seen in the company of Scott Jackson and Alonzo Walling. The jury asked that these conclusions be filed with their verdict.

On Wednesday, February 12, a Campbell County grand jury, in session in Newport, returned an indictment against Jackson and Walling, charging the two men with Pearl Bryan's murder. The state of Kentucky had to obtain the proper papers to extradite the pair from Cincinnati, where they were being jailed, and authorities in Ohio granted several continuances in the case to allow them the time to do so. The men were basically being kept away from Newport for fear of another lynch mob. When Kentucky came through with the indictment, papers were approved by the Ohio governor to grant the release of the two men to Kentucky. When the papers were served on the authorities in Hamilton County, the attorneys for Jackson and Walling began a bitter fight to keep their clients in Ohio. Kentucky was the only place that the men could be put on trial since the murder took place in that state, but the lawyers hoped to prove that Kentucky was not safe for their clients. Governor William O'Connell Bradley offered the full command of the state militia to Sheriff Plummer in Newport to protect the men from any lynch mobs, but this was not enough. The attorneys fought the extradition, tying up the courts and causing delay after delay.

The defense had chosen Judge M.L. Buchwalter of the Hamilton County Court of Common Pleas to hear their case because they knew that the judge had recently refused to turn over a prisoner in another murder case. At this point, one of Kentucky's most acclaimed lawyers, Colonel Robert T. Nelson, volunteered his service for the prosecution. The judge's bias against Kentucky was no match for the skills of Colonel Nelson and the public sentiment in the case.

It took until March 17, but Jackson and Walling were finally turned over to the authorities in Newport. That afternoon, a patrol wagon backed up to the door of the Hamilton County Jail, and the two men were hustled inside. They were each handcuffed to either Detective Crim or Detective McDermott. Crowds of people followed the wagon down Sycamore Street to Eighth, and the sheriff had the wagon stop at Cincinnati's Central Police Station for their safety. The men were kept there for a few hours, and then the detectives and their prisoners slipped away in another wagon to cross Central Bridge and end up at the Newport Jail.

On that same day, Pearl's body was placed in a temporary vault at the Forest Hill Cemetery in Greencastle, Indiana. Her white casket had been followed to the cemetery by a long procession of her classmates, grieving family members, and sympathetic townspeople. It was one of the largest funerals in the history of the town. She wasn't buried, however.

Her family was still hoping that her head would be found.

On March 23, Jackson and Walling were both arraigned on charges of murder and asked for a plea. The attorneys for both men entered pleas of not guilty. Colonel George Washington, Walling's lawyer, asked the court for separate trials and L.J. Crawford, the attorney of record for Jackson, agreed. Jackson's trial was set for April 21 and Walling's for May 5.

M.R. Lockhart prosecuted Jackson, and he immediately began calling witnesses, starting with Jack Hewling, who told of finding the body. The second witness, Coroner Tingley, provided damaging forensic testimony, detailing how Pearl had been alive when she was beheaded. He also identified the clothing that belonged to the victim.

Lockhart stumbled on the second day when he brought a headless dummy into the courtroom, dressed in Pearl's blood-soaked clothing. Along with the spectators in the courtroom, the jury was offended by this gruesome sight, and the defense attorney petitioned to have it removed. The judge ordered it taken out of the courtroom.

Pearl's sister, Mary Stanley, was the next witness called. She identified Pearl's clothing and her valise. Pearl's mother also took the stand to identify Pearl's clothing and evoke sympathy from the jury.

Lockhart then called the bartender from Wallingford's Saloon, who recognized Pearl's clothing as that worn by the young woman who accompanied Jackson and Walling on the Friday night of the murder. Next, George Jackson testified to driving the carriage out of Cincinnati while Walling gave him directions. He further testified that he heard what sounded like a woman crying out in pain coming from the back and a struggle that caused a window to break. George Jackson said he went to hand the reins over to Walling so that he could see what was going on, but when he turned, Walling was pointing a gun in his face. He threatened the driver, ordering him to stop the carriage, climb down from the seat, and turn around. Jackson said he climbed down and ran away because he feared that he would be shot.

The next important witnesses were detectives Crim and McDermott. They gave testimony about the crime scene and the investigation, noting that some of Pearl's clothing had been found in Jackson's possession. John Kugel, the saloonkeeper from Wallingford's, was presented next, and he testified about the valise that Jackson had left behind in the tavern.

Will Wood was the next witness called to the witness stand. All the charges filed against Wood as an accessory to the crime had been dropped on the condition that he testified against his friend. He said that Jackson and Pearl were intimate and that she had become "sick," meaning that she was pregnant. Jackson suggested remedies that failed to cause her to miscarry, followed by suggesting she have an abortion. Will was told to arrange to get Pearl to Cincinnati but claimed that he did not make the arrangements. He also testified that he had received a letter from Jackson that warned him to stick by him and Walling or there would be trouble.

The last prosecution witness was Cincinnati Police Chief Colonel Dietsch, who testified about his interrogations of Walling and Jackson.

He also told of a phone conversation between the two defendants, but this conversation, because it was illegally obtained, was ruled inadmissible. No record of what was said during this conversation exists today.

After Colonel Dietsch, the defense took over, and Scott Jackson was put on the stand. Jackson calmly answered all the questions that were put to him without hesitation. He continued to place all the blame for the murder on Alonzo Walling and Will Wood for sending Pearl to Cincinnati in the first place. Jackson claimed that he ran into Pearl on the street and offered to help her find a place to live. He said that this was the only reason that he had some of her clothing. Jackson was followed on the stand by his landlord, Rose McNevin, who claimed that Jackson was home at the time of the murder. She was his only defense witness, and apparently, the jury didn't believe either one of them. On May 14, the jury deliberated for only a few minutes before finding Jackson guilty of murder in the first degree.

Alonzo Walling's trial, which had originally been scheduled for May 5, finally began on May 29. The events in this case almost exactly mirrored those of Jackson's trial, including the verdict. Walling was also found guilty of first-degree murder. The prisoners were remanded to the Newport Jail during their appeal process, but all the appeals were turned down. They were sentenced to hang on March 20, 1897. Because of the temper of the public, the prisoners were first transferred to the Covington jail and then were finally housed in Alexandria, which was considered safer. They would be returned to Newport for the hanging.

Legends persist, claiming that Jackson and Walling were both offered life sentences instead of execution if they revealed the location of Pearl's head.

Both men again refused.

On the night before they went to the gallows, Jackson and Walling were lodged together in the death house and spent their final hours writing letters to family and friends, eating hearty meals, and talking with the jailers who watched over them and the newspapermen who crowded into the cellblock, hoping for one last sensational comment.

By now, both men were resigned to their fates, but Walling seemed to be more accepting. He ate a steak dinner and then decided to go to sleep around 1:00 a.m. A reporter wrote that he was "soon sleeping like a baby."

Jackson, on the other hand, did not sleep. He talked with his jailers well past 2:00 a.m. when Sheriff Jule Plummer visited him. The sheriff interrupted Jackson in his letter writing and asked if he planned on making a statement. "If you are, I would appreciate knowing that in advance," the sheriff said. Jackson replied that he would not make a statement. Plummer then asked if Jackson would exonerate Walling and perhaps save his life.

Jackson shook his head and pronounced his companion a villain to the end. "I cannot save Walling without lying, and I will not do that," he said.

Shortly after dawn the next morning, Jackson and Walling were dressed in black cutaway coats, black pants, and white shirts.

Then, just minutes before the executions were to take place, Jackson announced that Walling was innocent of the crime. An appeal was sent to the governor, who stated that if Jackson were to confess to everything, Walling would be released. Jackson refused to do it. He was still maintaining his own innocence, and to admit that he had committed the murder and not Walling, would be the same as a confession. He told the county officials that he had nothing else to say.

The two men were marched to the gallows just before 11.30 a.m., and Sheriff Plummer asked Jackson if he had any last words. Jackson replied, "I have only this to say: that I am not guilty of the crime for which I will pay the penalty with my life."

When it came to be Walling's turn, he stated, "I have nothing to say, only that you are taking the life of an innocent man, and I call upon my God to witness the truth of what I say."

At 11:40 a.m., the trap was sprung beneath the gallows, but the drop was too short. The men's necks did not break. Instead, they slowly strangled to death. The crowd that had gathered to witness the execution began to stir, and cries of horror went up from the women in the audience. It took three minutes for Jackson's fingers to stop twitching and four minutes for Walling to stop struggling for air. Finally, both men died.

Stories and rumors ran rampant after the hangings, and while many stated that they felt Jackson and Walling got what they deserved, others were not so sure. They had nagging doubts brought on by Jackson's last-minute claims of Walling's innocence. Walling's possible innocence started more stories. One newspaper reporter commented later that Walling, as the noose was being slipped over his head, threatened to come back and haunt the area after his death. The same writer also stated a few days later, in an article in the *Kentucky Post*, that an "evil eye" had fallen on many of the people connected to the Pearl Bryan case. Legend has it that many of the police officials and attorneys involved in the case later met with bad luck and tragic ends.

Less fanciful - but more gruesome - stories were written about the aftermath of the hanging. In one account, it was reported that Walling's face was almost peaceful when the black hoods were removed from the corpses, but Jackson, as he slowly strangled, died hard. The *Cincinnati Enquirer* described how Jackson's head had swollen to three times its normal size and caused an undertaker's assistant to nearly faint with fright.

The greatest mystery that lingered in the region for years after the hangings was the location of Pearl Bryan's missing head. Nearly everyone speculated about it, and stories ranged from the head being dumped into the sewers under Cincinnati, thrown into the river, or buried somewhere in the woods. In the end, it was never found despite the efforts of the police and the public to reunite it with her body.

Alonzo Walling claimed that he didn't know where it was, putting the whole thing on Jackson. A reporter with the *Enquirer* asked him, "Did you do it or did Jackson? He says you did it."

Walling replied, "He's putting it all on me now, is he? Well, he's the one who is guilty. I know nothing of it."

"What did he tell you had become of the head?" the reporter now asked.

"I understand he threw it in the Ohio River."

The reporter shook his head. "Jackson says that you threw the head into the river, and the next day you told him to get rid of anything lying loose at the boarding house by throwing it into the river."

"I never saw the head," Walling replied. "And he told he that he threw it into a sewer."

Walling's stories - like Jackson's - changed repeatedly, making it impossible to know if either of them was offering the authorities anything resembling the truth. He would later again suggest that Jackson had thrown the head off a bridge into the river. He offered this story with another - that Jackson not only brought Pearl's head back to the rooming house quarters they shared but that he was excited to have it. "He came in with a valise," Walling said, "and I saw him open it and say, 'You are a beaut, you are.' He thought I was asleep."

After Walling eventually admitted that he knew about Pearl's murder, he told the police that he believed Jackson had disposed of the head near the murder site. Extensive digging around the area revealed nothing, but for several decades after, each time a human skull was unearthed in Northern Kentucky, it was suspected of being poor Pearl's head. Each time, though, the skull was ruled out.

Pearl's father, Alexander, eventually reconciled himself to the idea that Pearl's head would never be found and allowed his daughter's remains to be buried without it. Her coffin was removed from the temporary vault by the same pallbearers from her high school class who had placed it there and carried it to her final resting place at the highest point in the cemetery.

Pearl's sad and tragic journey had finally come to an end.

If there was ever a ghost who was doomed to spend eternity searching for something, it would be the spirit of Pearl Bryan. And if the stories are to be believed, that's exactly what she continues to do well over a century after her death.

Just a short distance away from the orchard where Pearl was murdered and beheaded was an abandoned slaughterhouse that had been built in the 1850s. For years, it was one of the largest in the reason. At the time of Pearl's death, it was empty, and today only a well in the basement where blood from the slaughtered animals was drained remains.

One persistent rumor around the area was that Pearl's head had been thrown into the depths of this well and, of course, was never recovered. Why neither Jackson nor Walling would admit this is unclear. More recent stories claim that the old slaughterhouse was used for occult rituals and that Jackson might have been involved with those who frequented it. This might explain how he knew the well was there in the first place. It's further been claimed that he was afraid of what might happen to him if he revealed the location of Pearl's head. Whether or not these stories have any truth to them, the simple fact remains that Pearl's head was never found - and many people believe that it vanished into the slaughterhouse.

If true, it might explain the haunting that had been occurring there for decades. But it seems that if Pearl's spirit lingers here, she may not do so alone.

After the trials and the hangings, the old slaughterhouse was silent and empty for many years. It was eventually torn down, and a roadhouse was constructed on the site. During the 1920s, the place became known as a speakeasy and as a popular gambling joint. Local lore has it that during this period, several murders took place in the building. None of them were ever solved, and they weren't linked to the roadhouse because the bodies were normally dumped elsewhere to keep attention away from the illegal gambling and liquor operation.

After Prohibition ended in 1933, the building was purchased by E.A. Brady, better known to his friends and enemies alike as "Buck." Brady turned the building into a thriving tavern and casino called the Primrose. He enjoyed success for a decade or so, but eventually, the operation came to the attention of syndicate mobsters in Cincinnati. They moved in on Brady, looking for a piece of the action. Brady turned away the new "partners" and ignored demands to buy him out of the Primrose. Soon, the tavern was being vandalized, and customers were being threatened and beaten up in the parking lot. The violence escalated, and Brady was involved in a shooting in August 1946. He was charged and then released in the attempted murder of a small-time hood named Albert "Red" Masterson. This was the last straw for Buck, and he gave in and sold out to the gangsters. It was said that when he left, he swore the place would never thrive again as a casino. Brady committed suicide in September 1965.

After Brady sold out, the building re-opened as a nightclub called the Latin Quarter. It was during this period that the legends about the building gained another vengeful female ghost. According to the stories, the daughter of the club's owner, a young woman named Johanna, fell in love with one of the singers who was performing there. Her resulting pregnancy made her father furious. Thanks to his criminal connections, he had the singer killed. Johanna became so distraught that she attempted to poison her father and failed. She then took her own life. Her body was later discovered in the basement of the club. According to the autopsy report, she was five months pregnant at the time.

Business did not fare well after this. During the early 1950s, new owners of the bar were arrested several times on gambling charges. In 1955, Campbell County deputies broke into the building with sledgehammers and confiscated slot machines and gambling tables. Apparently, Brady's prediction had come true.

Bad luck continued to plague the owners of the tavern. In the 1970s, it became known as the Hard Rock Café, but authorities closed it down in early 1978 because of a fatal shooting on the premises.

Finally, the building was turned into the bar and dance club that it is today. Bobby and Janet Mackey became the new owners in the spring of 1978 with the intention of turning it into a country-western bar. Mackey was well-known as a singer in Northern Kentucky and had recorded several albums. He scrapped his plans to record in Nashville to renovate the old tavern. Once the bar was opened, it immediately began to attract a crowd. It's been largely successful ever since, but the stain of tragedy and death has never gone away from the location.

Carl Lawson was the first employee hired by Bobby Mackey. He was a loner who worked as a caretaker and handyman. He lived alone in an apartment upstairs and spent a lot of time in the sprawling building after hours. When he began reporting that he was seeing and hearing bizarre things in the empty building, people around town first assumed that he was simply crazy. Later, though, when others started to see and hear the same things, Lawson didn't seem quite so strange after all.

He later reported, "I'd double-check at the end of the night and make sure that everything was turned off. Then I'd come back down hours later, and the bar lights would be on. The front doors would be unlocked when I knew that I'd locked them. The jukebox would be playing the 'Anniversary Waltz' even though I'd unplugged it and the power was turned off."

Soon, the odd events went from strange to downright frightening. The first ghost that Lawson spotted in the place was that of a dark, terribly angry man behind the bar. Even though others were present at the time of the sighting, they saw nothing. A short time later, Lawson began to experience visions of a woman. She would often speak to Lawson, and he was able to answer her and carry on conversations. The rumors quickly started that Lawson was "talking to himself." Lawson claimed the woman was a tangible presence, though, often leaving the scent of roses in her wake.

Odd sounds and noises often accompanied the sightings, and Lawson soon realized that the spirits seemed to be the strongest in the basement, near an old-sealed up well that had been left from the days when there was a slaughterhouse at the location. The lore of the area, Carl knew, stated that the well had once been used for occult rituals. Some of the local folks referred to it as "Hell's Gate." Although he wasn't a particularly religious man, Lawson decided to sprinkle some holy water on the old well one night, thinking that it might bring some relief from the spirits. Instead, it seemed to provoke them, and the activity in the building began to escalate.

Soon, other employees and patrons began to have their own weird experiences. They began to tell of objects that moved around on their own, lights that turned on and off by themselves, disembodied voices and laughter, and other strange events. Bobby Mackey was not happy about the ghostly rumors that were starting to spread around town. He said, "Carl started telling stories, and I told him to keep quiet about it. I didn't want it getting around because I had everything I owned stuck in this place. I had to make a success of it."

Mackey was not one to believe in ghosts or the supernatural, and he didn't want his customers thinking that his staff was crazy. He was sure there was nothing more to the stories than wild imaginations. However, when his wife, Janet, revealed that she had also encountered the club's resident spirits, Mackey was no longer sure what to think. Janet told him that she had seen the ghosts, felt their overwhelming presence, and even smelled the woman's rose perfume. She also had a very frightening encounter in the basement. While she was there, she was suddenly overcome by the scent of roses and felt something unseen swirl around her. She later recalled, "Something grabbed me by the waist. It picked me up and threw me back down. I got away from it, and when I got to the top of the stairs, there was pressure behind me, pushing me down the steps. I looked back up and a voice was screaming 'Get Out! Get Out!'"

Once Janet admitted that she had seen the ghosts in the building, other people began to come forward with their own tales. Roger Heath, who often worked odd jobs in the club, remembered a summer morning when he and Carl Lawson were working in the building. Heath was removing some light fixtures from the dance floor, and Lawson was carrying them down to the basement. Lawson came up the stairs just before lunch, and Heath noticed that he had small handprints on the back of his shirt. It looked just like a woman had pressed her hands onto his back.

Erin Fey, a hostess at the club, also confessed to encountering the female phantom. She had laughed one day at Lawson when he was talking to the ghost. But she stopped laughing when she got a strong whiff of the rose perfume.

Once the stories began making the rounds, they caught the attention of a writer named Doug Hensley. He decided to investigate and started hanging around the club, striking up conversations with the regular customers. No one was anxious at first to talk about ghosts. Hensley said, "When I first talked to these people, almost every one of them refused to be interviewed." After he talked to Janet Mackey, though, other people came forward. Soon, Hensley had 30 sworn affidavits from people who said they had experienced supernatural events at the club.

He continued to collect stories and reports of sightings, intrigued by the various spirits who had been seen -- including a headless ghost who was dressed in turn-of-the-century woman's clothing. Strangely, independent witnesses provided matching descriptions of the phantom, never knowing that others had seen her. That was when Hensley turned to historic records to shed some light on the building's history. In old newspaper accounts, he found the story of Pearl Bryan and heard the rumors about her head being tossed down the well in the basement. None of the witnesses to the haunting activity were even vaguely aware of the Pearl Bryan case or what connection it might have to the building.

And neither was a psychic whom Hensley brought in to get her impressions of the club. The psychic later reported that the nightclub was one of the scariest places she had ever been to. She claimed to have seen a vision of a woman named Pearl, who was holding her head in her hands, as well as a male ghost named Scott, who kept repeatedly yelling at her that it was her fault that he was dead. The psychic swore that she knew nothing about the history of the place when she reported these visions to Hensley.

Strange activity continues to occur at Bobby Mackey's Music World, despite several attempted exorcisms. It's as though this place's dark and bloody history refuses to let go of its hold on the present. And that bloody past will likely continue reaching out from the grave for many, many years to come.

TESTIMONY FROM A GHOST
ZONA HEASTER SHUE

January 1897, in Greenbrier County, West Virginia, a bride of only three months was found dead by a neighbor boy. Within a month, her ghost had appeared on four successive nights and told her mother that her husband had killed her and described exactly how he'd done it. At the mother's insistence, the young woman's body was exhumed, her cause of death determined, and her husband was tried, convicted, and sentenced to a life behind bars.

It is a story unlike any other in American history - a legal case in which the word of a ghost helped solve a crime and convict a killer.

But there is much more to this story than meets the eye. It's a case where the prey returned to avenge herself on the predator - or did she? Who was the young bride? Why did people believe her mother's story? And what happened to make the story of the "Greenbrier Ghost" one of the strangest in the annals of the supernatural?

Zona Heaster, a pretty girl with dark hair, was born in Greenbrier County, West Virginia, in 1873. Little is known about her early life other than she grew up in the Richlands region of the county, an area of rolling hills, limestone bluffs, natural springs, and neatly tended farms.

In October 1896, she met a man named Erasmus Stribbling Trout Shue, who would eventually be her husband. He had arrived in Greenbrier County just that fall, a drifter working as a blacksmith and trying to start a new life for himself. He began working in the shop of James Crookshanks, located just off the old Midland Trail. A blacksmith could find plenty of work along this rough, unpaved trail, and throughout the county, and Shue became well-known for his work.

Zona's mother, Mary Jane, would always regret the day that her daughter met Trout Shue. She never liked him, not at all, and that was even before she found out that Shue had been married three times before.

Mother and daughter had stopped into the blacksmith shop at a place called Livesay's Mill. It was a small cluster of buildings - mill, store, a handful of houses, and the blacksmith shop - that happened to be on the way to Lewisburg, which was the Heasters' destination. Zona took one look at the new handsome and muscular blacksmith, and she was smitten. From the start, Mary Jane believed, Shue had her daughter twisted around his finger. She often told Zona that she felt there was something the otherwise amiable man was hiding.

But Zona, of course, didn't listen.

The couple had a whirlwind courtship and on October 22, 1896 - just a week after they met - the local newspaper announced that the two of them were married by Reverend T.W. Brown at the church parsonage in Lewisburg.

Mary Jane probably attended, although Zona's father, Jacob, was ill at the time. It's unlikely that anyone from the groom's family was in attendance. No mention was made in the newspaper of a reception or celebration, though these were commonly reported in detail at the time. The marriage records of Greenbrier County show that Zona was 22 years old when they married, and Shue was listed as being 29, although he was really six years older than that.

Just a few days after the wedding, a "grand barbecue" was held in the "grove near Big Clear Creek," and it's likely that just about everyone in the area attended, including Trout and Zona. There were both Republican and Democrat speakers on hand and food enough for 5,000 people. It was probably their first public event as husband and wife, and it's easy to imagine them greeting friends and neighbors, feasting on barbecued beef, roast corn, bread, fruit preserves, and drinking apple cider and homemade whiskey.

Gifts may have been given to the happy couple, like dishware, the promise of a cord of wood for the winter, or a spice box - a treasured gift with which to begin housekeeping. These boxes were made from tin and contained little jars of cloves, cinnamon, pepper, and nutmeg, which were hard to obtain at the time and costly even when available.

Whatever happened in the days and weeks after the wedding, they were apparently happy. Trout Shue took his new wife to live at Livesay's Mill, where the blacksmith shop was located.

The mill was next to the shop. Here, corn and wheat were milled for the farmers who lived within several miles in each direction. Across Milligan Creek was the small general store, which stocked groceries and dry goods.

At the top of the hill to the south from the store was a white frame house that served as the home and office for the local physician, Dr. George W. Knapp. To the northeast of the mill and blacksmith shop was the house that Shue rented from the estate of Will Livesay, who had recently died.

Between those two homes was the schoolhouse where Charlie Tabscott taught the area children, all eight grades in the same room.

Scattered about were prosperous farms and well-built houses. The Tuckwillers, the area's richest family, lived in one. John Alfred Preston, the prosecuting attorney of Greenbrier County, lived in another. Colonel Sam McClung's farm was also nearby. He had a stillhouse and made whiskey.

It was a peaceful and quiet area, and there is no record of anything out of the ordinary happening until January 23, 1897 - the day that Zona's body was found inside of the Shue home.

The boy's name was Andy Jones, and he didn't just find Zona's body by accident. He had been sent to the house by Trout Shue himself. He was supposed to ask Zona if there was anything that she wanted from the store.

He knocked lightly on the kitchen door. Then, he tapped a little harder when no one answered. Finally, after several loud raps and a call for Mrs. Shue, Andy stepped inside. The kitchen was dark and cold. The next room is the dining room, from which stairs lead to the second floor.

Andy was not prepared for what he found in the dining room. Zona was lying on the floor at the bottom of the stairs. She was stretched out, with her feet together. One hand was on her abdomen, and the other was lying next to her. Her head was turned slightly to one side, and her eyes were wide open and staring. Even to this inexperienced young boy, Zona Shue was obviously dead. Andy, not surprisingly, ran home to tell his mother.

Andy and his mother, Martha, rushed to the blacksmith shop to tell Shue what had happened. Andy was nearly in hysterics, and Martha wasn't feeling much better. It took several minutes before Shue understood what they were trying to say, and then he grabbed his coat and ran toward home. Andy, Martha, and schoolteacher Charlie Tabscott - who was having a horse fitted with a new shoe - followed quickly behind. When they reached the house, they saw Shue inside, kneeling on the floor with his wife's lifeless form in his arms. He was crying loudly and angrily shouted at Andy, "Why didn't you get Dr. Knapp?" he demanded.

The boy tried to explain, but Shue cut him off, telling him to bring the doctor. Andy and Martha ran for the doctor's house and found him in the middle of his noontime meal. It took them several minutes to explain what was going on, but Dr. Knapp then retrieved his medical bag, put on his coat, and followed them back to the Shue house.

By the time Dr. Knapp arrived - by most accounts, an hour after Zona's body was found - Shue had carried his wife's body upstairs and had laid her out on the bed. Contrary to local custom, he dressed the corpse himself. Typically, it was the proper thing for ladies of the community to wash and dress a body in preparation for burial. However, Shue took it upon himself to dress Zona in her best clothing.

A high-necked, stiff-collared dress covered her neck, and a veil was placed over her face.

While Dr. Knapp examined her and tried to determine a cause of death, Shue stayed by his wife's side, cradling her head and sobbing. Because of Shue's obvious grief, Knapp gave the body only a cursory examination, although he did notice some bruising on her neck.

A newspaper account in the *Pocahontas Times* reported on what Dr. Knapp found when he tried to examine Zona's body: "There were slight discolorations on the right side of the neck and right cheek. The doctor unfastened the collar and examined the front of the neck and right cheek and was about to examine the back of her neck when Shue protested so vigorously that he desisted from further examination and left the house."

Initially, he listed her cause of death as "everlasting faint" and then as "childbirth." It is unknown whether Zona was pregnant or not, but for two weeks prior to her death, Knapp had treated her for "female trouble."

Dr. Knapp sent someone out to notify Zona's parents, but word of the young woman's death quickly spread through the community. By late afternoon, two young men who were friends of Zona's - Dick Watts and Lewis Stuart -- volunteered to ride out an area called Meadow Bluff and tell the Heaster family what had happened. The Heasters lived in an isolated area, about 15 miles away, where a small scattering of homes and farms were nestled against the side of Little Sewell Mountain. When she was informed of the news of her daughter's death, Mary Heaster's face grew dark. She reportedly said, "The devil has killed her!"

On Saturday, January 24, Zona's body was taken by carriage to her parents' home. She had been placed in a plain, unfinished coffin from the Handley Undertaking Establishment in Lewisburg. A handful of neighbors presided over the funeral entourage, and they brought Trout Shue along with them to the mountain farm. He showed extraordinary devotion toward the body, keeping a vigil at the head of the open coffin as the wagon traveled over the rutted and bumpy roads.

The body was displayed in the Heaster's house for the wake, an event that lasted all day Sunday. It gave neighbors and friends an opportunity to pay their last respects to the dead woman, visit with one another, give solace to the bereaved, and bring food for the family. A few local ladies sat up with the body throughout the night and until the time of the burial on Monday.

Those who came to pay their respects during the wake pointed out the bizarre behavior of Trout Shue. His grief swung back and forth between overwhelming sadness and manic energy. He allowed no one to get too close to the coffin, especially while he was placing a pillow on one side of her head and a rolled-up cloth on the other. He explained that these items were to help Zona "rest easier." He was agitated and distracted, telling everyone that he had dressed her himself. In addition, he tied a large scarf around her neck and explained tearfully that it "had been Zona's favorite."

When it came time to move the corpse to the cemetery, though, several people noticed that there seemed to be a strange looseness to Zona's head. Needless to say, people started to talk, and speculation began about how Zona had really met her untimely demise.

But Mary Jane Heaster did not need to speculate about whether or not Trout Shue had some part in her daughter's death -- she was convinced that he had. She was sure that he had murdered her, but there was no way that she could prove it.

After the wake, Mary Jane took the sheet from inside the coffin and tried to return it to Shue, but he refused it. Folding it back up to put it away, she noticed that it had a peculiar odor, so she washed it out. She came to believe that what happened next was some sort of strange omen.

Mary Jane dropped the sheet into the washbasin, and when she did, the water inside turned red. Strangely, a few moments later, the sheet turned pink, and the color in the water disappeared. Mary Jane then boiled the sheet and hung it outside for several days, but the stain could not be removed. She interpreted the eerie "bloodstains" as a sign that Zona had been murdered.

After this strange incident, she began to pray. Every night for the next four weeks, Mary Jane prayed fervently that her daughter would return to her and reveal the truth about how she had died.

And then, as she would testify to the authorities and tell anyone who would listen, her prayers were answered.

Over the course of four dark nights, the spirit of Zona Shue appeared at her mother's bedside. On the first night, Mary Jane felt a cold chill sweep across the room, followed by what sounded like a sigh and a small, shifting movement, like a cat across a wooden floor. When the sound came again, Mary Jane tried very hard to peer into the inky darkness but could see nothing. She waited, almost afraid to breathe, and then she saw a figure start to take shape in the shadows; it moved very slowly toward the bed.

Mary Jane elbowed her husband, who was sleeping next to her, but he only groaned and turned away from her, still asleep.

As the shadow detached from the darkness and neared the bed, Mary Jane saw that it was Zona. She was wearing a blue homespun dress that her mother had made for her just a year before. Mary Jane trembled and yet, reached out a hand to touch her daughter. She later said that it was as though she had dipped her fingers into ice-cold water.

Mary Jane called out to her, but Zona only stood there, looking sad on that first night. She seemed to want to speak but was unable to form the words. She turned to walk away and vanish back into the dark corner of the room, and when she did, she turned her head to look at her mother. Most terrifying, though, was that she didn't look back over her shoulder - she turned her head all the way around!

Mary Jane was horrified and pulled the covers over her head in fright. She reached out for her husband, she later said, just to have something to touch so that she could feel warm again.

Her daughter had returned from the dead, and then she was gone.

Zona returned to Mary Jane's bedroom on each of the following three nights. Every time she left, she turned her head all the way around to look at her mother. Her head was just as loose as it had been in the coffin.

On the second visit, Zona started to speak. She told Mary Jane over and over that her husband had murdered her. Trout Shue had been abusive and cruel and had attacked her in a fit of rage because he thought she had not cooked any meat for supper. He had savagely broken her neck.

Mary Jane had been right. Shue had killed her daughter, and, as far as she was concerned, the word of her spirit proved it.

A short time later, Mary Jane went to the local prosecutor, John Alfred Preston, to try and convince him to re-open the investigation into Zona's death. She offered the visitations from her daughter's spirit as evidence that a miscarriage of justice was taking place. By all accounts, Preston was both polite and sympathetic to Mrs. Heaster. The two spoke together for "several hours," and Preston agreed to dispatch deputies to speak with Dr. Knapp and a few others involved in the case at the end of the meeting. While it seems unlikely that he was willing to take another look at the case because of the statement of a ghost, the investigation did get re-opened. Local newspapers reported that Mrs. Heaster was not the only one in the community who was suspicious about Zona's death. There were also "certain citizens" who had started to ask questions, as well as the growing "rumors in the community."

Preston himself went to see Dr. Knapp, and the physician admitted that his examination of the dead woman had been cursory and incomplete. The two of them agreed that an autopsy was needed to answer the questions about Zona's death once and for all. If Trout Shue were innocent of any wrongdoing, this would clear his name.

A few days later, an exhumation was ordered, and an inquest jury was assembled. The autopsy was performed in the Nickell School House, which was just a short distance away from the Soule Methodist Church graveyard, where Zona had been buried. The schoolchildren were dismissed on the day of February 22, 1897, and Zona Shue's grave was opened. It was reported in the local newspaper that Trout Shue "vigorously complained" about the exhumation, but it was made clear to him that he would be forced to attend the inquest if he did not attend willingly.

On his way to the cemetery, he said that he knew that he would come back from the inquest under arrest. Then he added, "But they will not be able to prove I did it." This was a rather odd and careless statement for a man who claimed to be innocent.

Shue was surly when he arrived at the schoolhouse, accompanied by Constable Shawver. He had little to contribute to the proceedings other than to stare angrily at the others gathered there, especially Mary Jane Heaster. He snarled at her as he walked toward the door to the schoolhouse. "You're a pretty thing, having your daughter brought up and cut up like this," he said. Shawver jerked him by the arm, and Shue stumbled over the threshold, muttering a curse.

Shue took his place inside and heard Shue say aloud, "I don't know what they are taking her up for. They aren't going to find anything."

But that prediction turned out to be wrong.

The autopsy lasted for three hours under the uncertain light of kerosene lanterns. The dead woman's body was "in a near state of perfect preservation," thanks to the cold temperatures of February, making the work of the doctors much easier to complete. A jury of five men had been assembled to watch the proceedings, and they huddled together in the cold building with officers of the court, Trout Shue, Andy Jones, who had found the body, Mary Jane Heaster, and other witnesses and spectators.

The autopsy was carried out by the standard methods, which meant that an examination of the vital organs came first. The physicians were initially looking for poison. At that time, such a test could only be carried out by smell. Most poisons available to those not in the medical field, like cyanide, had a characteristic smell. Since Zona had been ill for a month prior to her death, it had been suggested that the doctors try and determine if she had been poisoned. They checked her stomach contents but found nothing out of the ordinary.

After that, the doctors would have normally cut an incision along the back of the skull so that the brain could be removed, but this step was not taken in the case of Zona Shue. There was no need -- the doctors quickly found what they were looking for. One of the doctors turned to Trout Shue, "We have found your wife's neck to have been broken."

Shue's head dropped, and an expression of despair crossed his face. He whispered, "They cannot prove that I did it."

The autopsy findings were quite damning to Shue. A report on March 9 stated, "The discovery was made that the neck was broken, and the windpipe mashed. On the throat were the marks of fingers indicating that she had been choken ffisicffl. The neck was dislocated between the first and second vertebrae. The ligaments were torn and ruptured. The windpipe had been crushed at a point in front of the neck."

The findings were made public at once, upsetting many in the community. Shue was arrested and charged with murder. He was locked up in the small stone jail on Washington Street in Lewisburg. Even though the evidence against him was circumstantial, at best, he was indicted by a grand jury and was formally arraigned for murder. He immediately entered a plea of "not guilty."

While he was in jail, waiting for his trial to begin, information about Shue's unsavory past began to surface.

He had been born Erasmus Stribbling Trout Shue in 1861 in Augustus County, Virginia. After the Civil War, his parents, Jacob and Elizah, moved to West Virginia and settled near the border of Greenbrier and Pocahontas Counties. The Shues were fairly wealthy and owned a large amount of land in the area. Trout Shue was a handsome man, skilled in both woodworking and blacksmithing.

Shue was married the first time to a young woman named Allie Estelline Cutlip. Her parents did not approve of the match, but Shue managed to lure her away from home to visit one of his uncles. Once he got her away from the influence of her parents, he talked her into marrying him. They had one child together in 1887 - Girta Lucretia Shue - but two years later, Shue was arrested and convicted for horse stealing. He was sent to the West Virginia Penitentiary in Moundsville and served a little less than two years.

While he was in prison, Allie divorced him. In the divorce decree, she alleged that he had been violent and had frequently beaten her.

In 1894, Shue married again, this time to Lucy Ann Tritt. Lucy died just eight months later under circumstances that were described as "mysterious." There are a number of versions of the story of Lucy's death.

One story claimed that Shue was fixing a chimney, and he asked Lucy for a drink of water. She went and got it, and when she came back, he dropped - or threw - a brick on her head and killed her. There were enough people in the area who believed that he'd done it on purpose that his life was soon in danger. A group of neighbors chased him, and he hid in a barn. They shot at him several times through the door, but he escaped.

Another story claims that Shue was away from home, and Lucy, heavily pregnant, slipped and fell on some ice while on the way to the outhouse. She bled for two days before she told anyone about her fall and eventually died during early childbirth.

Another story claimed that she died when she was poisoned by a mountain laurel tea that Shue gave her. Another tale claimed that Shue and Lucy were working in a hay field, and he pulled her off a haystack, causing her to fall and break her neck.

No one really knows what happened. In the *Pocahontas Times* of February 15, 1895, a report states, "Mrs. E.S. Shue, wife of 'Trout' Shue, died very suddenly at her home near here on last Monday morning the 11th. We haven't been able to learn the particulars of her death." It seemed to be an unfinished story, but it was never followed up.

Most of the stories about Lucy's death make no sense. It was wintertime, which makes working in a hayfield and fixing a chimney unlikely. It was cold, so it's possible that Lucy had some sort of respiratory infection, which might have seemed like poisoning.

All we know for sure is that Shue later left the area and moved to Greenbrier County, where he had his fateful meeting with Zona and her mother in a blacksmith shop - a meeting that eventually led to Zona's death.

In jail, Shue was in remarkably good spirits and reported that his grieving for Zona had ended. In fact, he announced that he had a lifelong goal of having seven wives. Since Zona had been his third, he said, and he was still a young man, he believed he had a good chance of realizing such a worthwhile ambition.

He was also convinced that he would be out of jail after his trial. He repeatedly told reporters that his guilt in the matter could not be proved. He also had, he announced, two exceptional attorneys. He either obtained them, or they were assigned to him - no one knows - but he began to be represented by William Parkes Rucker and James P.D. Gardner. In a serious case, the court would appoint an older experienced lawyer and a younger one so that the defendant received full legal representation. In this case, Rucker was well-known in Greenbrier County and had been an attorney for many years. Gardner was new in the area and was African American. In the years after the Civil War, many black attorneys offered to represent poor defendants in capital cases. He likely volunteered to represent Shue, and Gardner was appointed to assist him.

During the next four months, Prosecuting Attorney Preston gathered all the evidence he could against Shue. They believed he had killed his wife but had to prove it. At the same time, Gardner and Rucker worked to try and establish their client's innocence, seeking out character witnesses and, if worse came to worse, looking for ways to get Shue to confess and get a lighter sentence if the trial didn't go his way.

It's easy to imagine that the quest for character witnesses for Trout Shue didn't go well. The gossip in the community must have been discouraging to the defense team, especially in light of newspaper stories like one that ran in the *Greenbrier Independent* that noted, shortly before the trial, "Trout Shue, who is now in jail awaiting trial for the murder of his wife, has threatened to kill himself."

Even so, the attorneys managed to allegedly line up 120 witnesses to testify on Shue's behalf. They were mainly people he had worked for or with who could speak to his good character. They also included family members, preachers, and teachers who knew him. Not all of them were quick to respond to the summons, though. According to the *Greenbrier Independent,* one witness was so intent on not appearing at trial that he went into hiding. A deputy had to be paid expenses to go and find him and bring him in.

That witness? Shue's brother - John Patrick Shue.

In a report in the *Pocahontas Times,* it was remarked, "On the issue of his trial depends the question of whether Shue will reach his seventh wife, as he has boasted he would have seven. The passing of the third endangers his neck or is liable to send him to the penitentiary where there is no marrying or giving in marriage."

The trial began on June 22, 1897, before Judge J.S. McWhorter, who was described as a "staunch Republican." He had spent most of his life in public office. He had been an attorney, served as mayor of Lewisburg, and spent eight years on the judicial bench. After the jury was sworn in, the trial began with opening statements from both sides. District Attorney Preston explained to the jury that the case against

Shue was a circumstantial one but was compelling, nevertheless. In fact, it would offer evidence "such as had never been presented in any court before." This may have been referring to the testimony of the ghost, but there's no way to know for sure. There is no transcript of the trial, and Preston never referred to the ghost story in his opening.

In all honesty, Preston might have never mentioned the ghost at all. It would be an attorney for the defense who made the fatal mistake of bringing it up.

For the next several days, numerous people from the community testified against Shue. There were doctors, neighbors, Andy Jones and his mother, and many others.

The first witness for the state was Dr. Knapp, who had revised his initial conclusions about Zona's death following the autopsy that had been conducted.

Zona Shue had been murdered.

The other doctors present at the autopsy were called and agreed with his findings. It was clear that someone had dislocated her neck, which caused her death.

Andy Jones testified next, recounting what he had seen on the morning he found Zona's body. Under some circumstances, the boy might have been a suspect himself - but only because he was African American. Shue may have hoped that this would be enough for suspicion to fall on the boy, but it didn't work. His mother, Martha, was well-respected in the community, and she followed her son to the stand. When she testified, she stated that Shue had asked her four times on the day of Zona's murder to send Andy to "help his wife."

The state's witnesses that followed testified to Shue's behavior around Zona's body and those that "observed the head to be very loose on the neck and would drop from side to side when not supported." Some spoke of Shue's stated intention of having seven wives. Other bragging that he had done in the community came back to haunt him, while close neighbors declared "that they did not think Shue, from his actions and words, was regretful of the death of his young wife."

Others recounted the things he did and said at the autopsy, like when he said, "that he knew he would come back under arrest." And finally, it was noted by several that, in the preceding months, "in speaking to a number of witnesses on the subject, he always said that he knew that they could not prove he did the killing."

The highlight of the trial, of course, came with the appearance of Mary Jane Heaster. By that time, just about everyone in the community had heard some version of her ghost story. They packed into the courtroom, anxious to hear her talk about it, so they must have been surprised when District Attorney Preston avoided the subject altogether.

Preston put her on the stand as both the mother of the dead woman and as the first person to notice the unusual circumstances of Zona's death. He wanted to make sure that she appeared both sane and reliable. For this reason, he skirted the issue of the ghost because it was bound to make her appear irrational and because it was inadmissible evidence. The teller of the story, in this case, Zona Shue, could obviously not be cross-examined by the defense, and so her testimony would be hearsay under the law.

Unfortunately for Shue, his attorney, William Rucker, decided to ask Mrs. Heaster about her ghostly sighting. It seemed obvious that he was doing it to try and make Mary Jane look ridiculous to the jury. He characterized her "visions" as a mother's ravings and worked hard to admit that she might have been mistaken about what she allegedly saw.

Rucker asked, "Now, Mrs. Heaster, this sad affair was very particularly impressed upon your mind and there was not a moment during your waking hours that you did not dwell upon it?"

"No, sir," Mary Jane replied, "and there is not yet either."

"And this was not a dream founded upon your distressed condition of mind?"

"No sir. It was not a dream, for I was as wide awake as I ever was."

"Then, if not a dream or dreams, what do you call it?"

"I prayed to the Lord that she might come back and tell me what happened; and I prayed that she might come herself and tell on him."

Rucker rolled his eyes at the jury. "Do you think you actually saw her in flesh and blood?" he now asked.

"Yes sir, I do," Mary Jane answered him. "I told them the very dress she was killed in, and when she went to leave me, she turned her head completely around and looked at me like she wanted me to know all about it. And the very next time she came back to me, she told me all about it. The first time she came, she seemed that she did not want to tell me as much about it as she did afterwards. The last night she was there she told me she did everything she could do, and I am satisfied that she did do all that, too."

Rucker was exasperated by her story, putting on a show for the jury to show them that he didn't believe a word that Mary Jane was telling the court. "Now, Mrs. Heaster," he said, "don't you know that these visions, as you term or describe them, were nothing more or less than four dreams founded upon your distress?"

But Mary Jane disagreed. She shook her head at the attorney. "No, I don't know it," she said. "The Lord sent her to tell it. I was the only friend that she knew she could tell and put any confidence in. I was the nearest one to her."

He continued to badger her for quite some time, but Mary Jane never wavered in her descriptions of Zona's ghost - nor about what the specter had told her about Shue's guilt. He continued to try to get her to admit that she had merely dreamed about her daughter, but Mary Jane refused. "I am not going to say that," she told him. "For I am not going to lie."

Rucker continued his line of questioning, trying to get Mary Jane to admit that she could have imagined things, or that she was mistaken about what she had heard - or at the very least, prejudiced against the man she believed killed her daughter, even though she had no proof of it.

He wanted her to say anything other than that a ghost had told her of Trout Shue's guilt - but she refused. When Rucker realized that the testimony was not going the way that he wanted, he dismissed her.

By that time, though, the damage was done. Because the defense and not the prosecution had introduced the testimony about the spirit, the judge had a hard time telling the jury to exclude it. It was apparent that most of the people in the community believed that Mary Jane had seen her daughter's ghost.

Even after the defense counsel offered a long string of witnesses in support of Shue and after Shue offered eloquent testimony in his own defense, the jury quickly found him guilty. There were even 10 of them who voted that he be hanged, which spoke volumes about

Mrs. Heaster's believability as a witness. Without a unanimous verdict of death, though, Shue was sentenced to life in prison.

In the wake of the trial, the *Pocahontas Times* declared that Mary Jane's story of Zona's visits was instrumental in bringing about the autopsy and the inquest, which then led to Shue's arraignment for murder. The article read:

> *Trout Shue was found guilty of murder in the first degree, in the Greenbrier Court, the jury recommending a life sentence. The evidence was convincing that Shue murdered his wife by breaking her neck, and the case presented this aspect, that the woman died of a broken neck, and that it was impossible for her to break it herself, and that no one could have done it except her husband. What was the closing scene of the woman's life will probably never be known, but the explanation of the "vision" of the woman's mother gives a very striking suggestion of the last quarrel which ended in the death of the woman. She said that her daughter appeared to her and said that on the last evening she had gotten a good supper except there was no meat on the table, and that her husband had become enraged on account of it. Shue is a bad man and he has no sympathy from the neighborhood in which he was raised.*

Trout Shue's life sentence didn't satisfy everyone in Greenbrier County. On July 11, 1897, a citizen's group of anywhere from 15 to 30 men assembled eight miles west of Lewisburg to form a lynching party. They had purchased a new rope and were well-armed when they started towards the jail. If not for a man named George M. Harrah, who alerted the sheriff, Shue would have surely been lynched. Harrah contacted Deputy Sheriff Dwyer at the jail. It was said that when Shue was informed of this threat against his life, he became "greatly agitated" and was unable to tie his own shoes. Dwyer hid him in the woods a mile or so from town until deputies were able to disband the mob and return them to their homes.

Shue was moved to the West Virginia State Penitentiary in Moundsville on July 14, where he lived only for the next three years. On March 13, 1900, he died during one of the epidemics that swept through the prison that spring. At that time, the prison commonly buried unclaimed remains in the nearby Tom's Run Cemetery, for which no records were kept until the 1930s. Thanks to this, no trace of Trout Shue can be found today.

Mary Jane Robinson Heaster lived to tell her tale to all who would listen. She died in September 1916 without ever recanting her story about her daughter's ghost.

And as for Zona, her ghost was never seen again, but she has left a haunting mark on Greenbrier County. It is one that is still being felt today. In fact, a roadside marker along Route 60 still commemorates the case. It reads:

Interred in nearby cemetery is Zona Heaster Shue. Her death in 1897 was presumed natural until her spirit appeared to her mother to describe how she was killed by her husband Edward. Autopsy on the exhumed body verified the apparition's account. Edward, found guilty of murder, was sentenced to the state prison. Only known case in which testimony from ghost helped convict a murderer.

The dead don't always rest in peace.

"CAPTIVE OF A JEALOUS SUITOR"
MARY JANE REED

On a dark night in June 1948, a young girl named Mary Jane Reed went out on a date and never came home. Her death, along with the death of the man who was with her, shocked the small town of Oregon, Illinois. That night was the beginning of a curious, macabre series of events, which included a hushed conspiracy, a purported ghost, and a crime that remains unsolved to this day.

Oregon, Illinois, is a quiet community located along the Rock River, about 100 miles west of Chicago. Founded in 1838, it has seen its share of infamy and oddity over the years. Outlaws Jesse and Frank

James tried their hand at horse racing at the local fairgrounds. Renowned sculptor Lorado Taft created a massive monolith of a Native American on a river bluff while living at a nearby art colony founded by an eccentric group of artists and writers after the 1893 World's Columbian Exposition. It was once the scene of a battle between an outlaw gang called the Prairie Pirates and a group of vigilantes and lawmen. A local pizza joint was revealed to be part of a Mafia cocaine trafficking ring in the 1980s. And in 1974, Ogle State's Attorney Richard Caldwell snapped when he lost the chance to become a judge and saw his marriage collapse. He compiled a hit list of everyone he believed had wronged him, killed his ex-wife and son, and went on a rampage that ended with a sheriff's deputy shot and Caldwell committing suicide.

But even after all that, there is only one crime that continues to haunt the town of Oregon today - an unsolved double murder that occurred in 1948.

Mary Jane Reed was a 17-year-old telephone switchboard operator who had grown up in the small town. Her father, Clifford, was a machine repairman and her mother, Ruth, was a housewife with serious health problems. She suffered from rheumatoid arthritis, and it became so debilitating that Mary Jane left Oregon High School in her senior year to care for her mother and home.

The Reed family lived on Hastings Road, just east of the Rock River. The area was known as "Sandtown" since most residents worked at the nearby silica plant. Sandtown was considered the wrong side of the tracks, but it didn't matter to Mary Jane, a headstrong and independent girl who was determined never to let her circumstances get in the way of what she hoped to accomplish in life. She did all she could to wring whatever joy she could while growing up in a small town in post-World War II America. She sometimes escaped from her needy, hectic household with friends and even with her job, which connected her to the outside world in what was then a very modern way.

She was tied to Oregon, though, through her family - her mother and father, siblings, and especially her younger brother, Warren. And while she may have wanted to leave, like so many young people in small towns, there was much that held her there.

A date with a sailor, who'd likely seen the world, seemed like an exotic adventure to Mary Jane. Stanley Skridla was a 28-year-old Navy veteran who worked as a lineman for the Dekalb/Ogle Telephone Company, where Mary Jane also worked.

Stan was born in Rockford, Illinois, in 1920 and was raised there, one of five children. He attended Saints Peter and Paul School, then high school in Rockford. He began working as a cabinetmaker in 1938 but was a machinist at Mattison Machine Shop when he enlisted in the U.S. Navy in 1943. He served aboard the USS *Ormsby*, a troop transport ship, as a machinist's mate during the war. He was honorably discharged in 1945 and began working as a telephone lineman the following year. He had been living with his widowed mother, Amelia, in Rockford in 1948. Around 8.00 p.m. on June 24, Stan got into his relatively new Buick and left for his first - and last - date with Mary Jane.

Various reports later had the couple at taverns on both the east side and south side of Oregon that night. It's believed that their last stop was the Stenhouse -- now known as the Roadhouse -- and after that, they drove out to a popular lover's lane on County Farm Road in Stan's Buick. They were never seen alive again.

The following day around 6.00 a.m., a state highway department employee named John Eckerd was driving to work on County Farm Road and noticed a shoe lying alongside the roadway. He stopped to take a look and discovered Stan's bullet-ridden body lying face-down in a grassy ditch. Police later found five .32-caliber bullet casings at the scene. A pool of blood found on the edge of the road showed where the killer had dragged the young man's body into the grass. His Buick was found abandoned about an hour later, about one mile north of the lover's lane, where Illinois Route 2 and Pine Road intersected.

Sheriff Joseph Mass initially said the killing had the earmarks of a crime of passion, a love triangle. The sheriff's theory was that one of Mary Jane's former boyfriends surprised the couple and pumped five bullets into his rival.

Other than a lipstick-stained cigarette on the car's floorboard, there was no sign of Mary Jane. One early theory was that the jealous lover kidnapped her and was holding her captive. On the day after

Stan's body was found, a newspaper headline announced, "Girl Companion Hunted in Lovers' Lane Slaying."

Back in Sandtown, Mary Jane's parents were already worried about their daughter when they got the news about Stan's death. Before this, she had always called home if she was going to be late or spend the night at a friend's house. She had never telephoned.

The police still believed she might have been kidnapped. Worried, two of the older children in the family went to see a psychic, who told them that their sister was still alive and was being held prisoner in a shack by an older man.

The psychic's "vision" turned out to be badly flawed.

Stan Skridla was buried at Calvary Cemetery in Rockford on June 28. The next day brought terrible news for the Reeds.

On June 29, two policemen came to the door and told them that they had news. Mary Jane's brother, Warren Reed, was just six years old at the time, but he never forgot that day.

He had been very close with his big sister; she cared for him in ways that his mother was too ill to do. She took him to the movies, made picnic lunches for them to enjoy near the river, or simply took long walks together. She took him shopping and to Sunday services at the Church of God, where Mary Jane taught Sunday School.

"I was her baby," Warren later recalled. "She loved me, watched over me because there were times when Ma didn't feel good. They were good times. I can remember falling asleep lots of times, listening to the radio or something, and she'd carry me up and put me to bed."

During the few days before the detectives came to the door of the Reeds' house, Warren asked his mother many times when Mary Jane would be coming home. She assured him it would be soon. She'll be coming home, Ruth said.

Warren was standing next to his mother when she opened the door for the detectives that day. They asked if she was Mrs. Reed, then they said they had bad news. Her daughter had been found.

"Well, when is she coming home?" Ruth asked. "When are you going to bring her home?" Warren was holding his mother's hand at that moment when the detectives replied that she would not be coming home - Mary Jane was dead.

"I'll never forget that feeling," Warren said, decades later. "I could feel vibes going through my mother's body. I don't know how to explain it, but I could feel the energy just drain out of her."

The detectives told Ruth that Mary Jane's body had been found in a patch of weeds along Silica Road. She had been shot in the back of the head with what appeared to be the same caliber gun that had been used to kill Stan Skridla.

She was wearing only her underwear when they found her. The rest of her clothing - brown slacks, a white blouse, shoes, and socks - had been tossed onto her body.

Ironically, the police had checked the area along Silica Road, now known as Devil's Backbone Road, several times after Mary Jane disappeared. Her father had even passed that way several times on his way to work at the silica plant. Her body was found by Harold Sigler, a truck driver who was on his way to the plant. The height of the truck's cab allowed him to see over the weeds and catch a glimpse of the pale body that had been hidden among them. The police recovered a bullet casing at the scene.

The Reed family was devastated. Mary Jane's older brother, Donald, was supposed to be married on June 26 and Mary Jane was to be one of the bridesmaids. The wedding was postponed until after the funeral, which was held on June 30. Mary Jane was laid to rest at Daysville Cemetery in Oregon, but she would not rest there in peace.

And the Reed family would have little peace themselves in the days, months, and years that followed. In time, the slaying vanished from the front pages of the newspapers, but they never stopped haunting the Reeds.

Ruth Reed was never the same after Mary Jane's murder. From the day she learned of her daughter's death, she became terrified that whoever had killed Mary Jane was going to do the same to Warren or the entire family. Warren later recalled that his mother started keeping all the curtains in the house closed all the time. She moved the family's couch out a few feet from the living room wall and started hiding him there, convinced that his sister's killer was coming after all of them. A pillow and blanket were kept for him behind the couch, and he was forced to use it as a play and nap area. If he wanted a toy or a book, she brought it to him.

Ruth stopped sending him to first grade. Even when the school principal came to the house, Ruth insisted that he wasn't safe. When Warren finally did return, months later, he was so far behind that he had to repeat the first grade.

About a year after Mary Jane's murder, Ruth had a mental breakdown. She continued to believe that her daughter was going to come home. Clifford had no choice but to place her in a state mental institution in East Moline, about 80 miles away.

Warren, the only child at home, went to stay with a sister while his father buried his grief in work. Ruth returned home a year later, but she wasn't the same. She had been given electroshock therapy at the state hospital, and any mention of Mary Jane would send her into a panic. The family avoided the subject altogether unless Ruth brought it up. When she did, she constantly spoke of Mary Jane walking through the front door. Warren, dealing with his own grief, corrected his mother, but she refused to listen.

Warren continued in school but dropped out of high school his junior year to work at a printing company.

A few years later, an ambulance came for Ruth. On the day she left, as she was taken out on a gurney, she grabbed Warren's hand and told him that she wouldn't be coming back. "But there's one thing I want you to do for me," she said. "Will you please find out who killed Mary Jane for me?"

He told her that he would try as they took her away. Ruth died the next day. She was 64 years old. Warren always believed that Mary Jane's murder took at least 15 years off his mother's life.

And tragically, he has been unable to keep the promise of finding out who killed his sister.

In the wake of the murders in 1948, the Ogle County Sheriff's office enlisted the help of the state and local police. There were very few clues to go on but Chief Deputy Willard "Jiggs" Burright, the lead investigator, ruled out robbery as a motive. Stan still had his wallet, containing cash and his paycheck, and Mary Jane was still wearing her mother's wedding ring.

Authorities returned to the original theory - a love triangle gone bad - believing that jealousy may have been a motive for the killings. Detectives interviewed Stan's family and Mary Jane's friends. The investigation extended to Dixon, Rockford, Freeport, and Chicago. Police looked for a couple that Stan and Mary Jane had reportedly been seen arguing with before they went to Country Farm Road. A witness interviewed at the inquest said that he saw two suspicious men outside one of the taverns the couple had visited. They also looked for two railroad employees who had disappeared after the murder: a 19-year-old Navy veteran who used to date Mary Jane and for a dark blue-and-gray Pontiac in which Mary Jane had allegedly claimed to see a gun two months earlier. They arrested a "Negro" who was speeding in a Pontiac similar to that one but had to let him go. All of the leads turned out to be dead ends.

Investigators rounded up Mary Jane's boyfriends, including one former mental patient and another who allegedly threatened to kill her "unless she was true to him alone."

Detectives also questioned a few of the "numerous girlfriends squired by Skridla in his romantic roamings about the countryside," noted the *Chicago Tribune*. They found four such women - not exactly "numerous" - but they had nothing to do with the crime.

The police then started to theorize that the wife of one of Mary Jane's boyfriends might have killed her. Rumors were going around that Mary Jane might not be the innocent "Sunday School teacher" that her family made her out to be. In fact, the *Tribune* reported, "Close friends told the police, 'Mary Jane didn't care whether a man was married or not.' Authorities in both Oregon and nearby Rockford admitted the murders would be hard to unravel because Mary Jane Reed, the beautiful telephone operator, led such a complicated life."

Calling her "the comely, blue-eyed girl with the reddish-brown thatch of hair," the article added that police were questioning her "male friends," but that "it is still anybody's guess who perpetrated the crime."

Within a few days, authorities were talking about having hit a "blank wall" in the investigation. In November, a roofer from Wisconsin confessed to the killing, but that lead also fizzled. The story of the lover's lane murders made an appearance in year-end newspaper roundups of memorable events of 1948; then, slowly, it was forgotten and remained so for many years.

The Skridla-Reed murder case was briefly re-opened in the 1950s but with no success. As years went by, evidence disappeared from the original case files, including the bullet casings, photographs, and investigation reports. Jerry Brooks became the Ogle County sheriff in 1970, and he re-opened the case again. He re-interviewed witnesses and wrote new reports from scratch because the case file was almost empty. Many of the original interviews could not be re-created as many witnesses had died, and too much time had passed for the ones still around to remember specific details.

His most intriguing lead was the report of the two men outside the tavern, and he theorized that they might have followed the couple to the lover's lane. Brooks worked the case for almost two decades but was no closer to solving it than the detectives were back in 1948. Brooks left office in 1990, but he refused to give up on the case. He always believed that a solution was possible.

And he was not the only one. Warren Reed came to believe there was much more about the case still to be revealed.

Warren's life had not been easy. Over the decades, he found work as a welder, then at a factory that made automobile coils, where he worked until he retired in 2000. His personal life was much less stable. He was married four times and had five children. Two of his wives, he said, had drinking problems, and the other two cheated on him. There had been fights with brothers-in-law and confrontations in bars. But by the time he turned 50, that was behind him. He met his next wife at the automobile coil factory, and they were married in 1997. Although they were happy together, an easy life still eluded them both. His wife was a diabetic and in poor health, and then, his stepdaughter was murdered in Central Illinois. She was shoved off a bridge by her boyfriend, hit her head, and drowned.

In 2005, Warren's attentions returned to Mary Jane. He pressed for an exhumation order for his sister's body, wondering if clues might be found that were beyond the forensic skills of investigators at the time of the murder. In August, an Ogle County judge approved guidelines for exhuming the body that would allow pathologists to examine Mary Jane's remains. Warren was thrilled with the outcome of the hearing. "I want to wake up the community. People just kind of hushed things up when they shouldn't have. This crime should have been solved. It probably took 20 years off my parents' life," he told reporters at the time.

Joining Reed in his fight for answers was Mike Arians, a former insurance fraud investigator. Arians owned a restaurant in Oregon and was elected the town's mayor in April 1999. He was drawn to the mystery surrounding the murders because he became convinced that certain aspects of the case were covered up after some investigating of his own. At first, he would speak at length about his investigation but was more uncomfortable about the other thing that led him to the case -- namely Mary Jane's ghost.

Mike Arians was born in 1949 and was raised by his grandparents on a farm about 40 miles northwest of Chicago. His life was a mixture of stability and neglect, and it was rooted in the belief that he had always been unwanted. His mother was abusive and worked as a secretary at a large manufacturing company. His stepfather was a traumatized World War II veteran who drank too much and would disappear for days. Mike missed kindergarten because no one would drive him to school. When he did join in a few activities, he was occasionally stranded afterward. At a few Christmas celebrations for extended family, he was the only child who didn't receive a present.

What could have turned Mike Arians into a resentful, troubled young man instead made him independent and resourceful. In school, he worked at the student newspaper and yearbook, was in the library club, Future Farmers of America, and the AV club. He was the Chess Club president, but he also played football, baseball, and performed in theater.

Yet, he had a hard time getting away from the farm life where he'd spent his childhood. He gravitated toward auto shop and woodworking. After graduating in 1967, he enrolled in a vocational school in Southern Illinois. Poor and far away from home, he developed stomach ulcers. He left school before earning his degree, returned home, married his college roommate's sister, and began working in an auto shop in Elgin, Illinois. After he and his wife had a daughter, he moved closer to the old farm.

Around this time, Mike's career began to change. He became a body shop manager, which led to him testifying in several insurance cases. He liked that side of things and soon began working as an insurance adjustor on the side. After cracking several fraud cases for the insurance company, he became intrigued by the law. He enrolled in paralegal classes. Not long after that, he hit a rough patch.

His marriage fell apart. He got divorced and married again. That one didn't work out either. The insurance job soured on him, too. After he uncovered a fraud scheme involving an insurance company attorney, he was forced out of the business in the late 1980s.

Around this same time, Mike opened a playhouse in a barn on his family farm. The Oak Dell Farm Theatre staged a handful of performances that earned rave reviews and brought in crowds. Mike appeared in many of the shows himself.

He met a new woman, a schoolteacher named June, who stabilized his life and helped raise his daughter. They were married and stayed together until June later passed away. Oak Dell, meanwhile, ran afoul of the zoning boards and was forced to close in 1991. Mike was so irritated by how he'd been treated by officials from the local government that he ran for County Board. He lost the first time around but won in the next election.

He only served one term, and near the end of it, an attorney acquaintance told him about a vacant restaurant in Oregon. Mike was intrigued, visited, found a different vacant restaurant, and bought it in 1998.

That was also the same year that he read a series of stories in the local newspaper about the 50th anniversary of the unsolved murders of a local girl and her Navy veteran date. He was interested but didn't put much thought into it at the time. He had decided to run for the office of Mayor of Oregon, and his campaign took most of his time.

In April 1999, he beat the 20-year-incumbent mayor, and, shortly after, people began coming to him and telling him about the murders of Mary Jane Reed and Stan Skridla. He would later recall a waitress telling him about overhearing local law enforcement officers and businessmen talking about it quietly in her diner. She couldn't hear precisely what they said, but Mike would remember that she was upset by their demeanor.

The case began to gnaw at him. Mary Jane was from Sandtown, a section of Oregon on the east side of the river where residents were seen as lower-class troublemakers and viewed as disposable. Mike was personally bothered by this, and when Sandtown residents asked him to look into the case, his own life gave him the motivation to start digging. He started paying closer attention to what he heard, found background on the murders, and talked with people - many of whom told him that a law enforcement official had been involved. Soon after that, he got in touch with Warren Reed, and they started the ball rolling on an actual investigation.

And then the strange events began to happen.

You see, the restaurant that Mike purchased was the former Stenhouse in Oregon - allegedly Mary Jane and Stan's last stop before they drove out to the lover's lane and were never seen alive again. When Mike bought it, he renamed it the Roadhouse, and right away, employees assured him that it was haunted. Even as a non-believer - at that point anyway - he grudgingly admitted that he "perceived an energy" in the place.

Mike admitted that he had not come to Oregon in the late 1990s to see the Roadhouse. He initially looked at another building. But there was something about this building that drew him to it. At the time, it was a closed-up place called the Seven Seas, and it "was in shambles." It would take a lot of work to fix it up, but Mike decided it was the place he wanted. It had potential, he said, "and it just kind of grabbed me."

He bought the building and started to sleep there overnight when it was being remodeled. He slept just fine most of the time, but on other nights, he would hear the creak and groan of "peculiar noises." Once or twice, a stack of plates or a collection of pots and pans would collapse in the middle of the night, startling him from his sleep.

After the Roadhouse opened, the disturbances continued. He and the staff shrugged it off, joking that it must be the ghost of Esther Stenhouse, the no-nonsense woman who had owned the establishment with her husband in the 1930s and 1940s. Legends claimed that she died of a heart attack in a bathtub upstairs and that her ghost returned to haunt the place.

But then things became more disturbing. The same haunting acoustic song, Sergio Mendes and Brasil '66's "After Sunrise," would play spontaneously and repeatedly on the jukebox. Employees began to see the apparitions of Mary Jane and an older woman, believed to be her mother, Ruth. Without explanation, drafts of cold air and the overwhelming scent of flowers would fill the room.

Mike started to see connections to Mary Jane in his daily life. He admitted that he might have been looking for them, but it was still "crazy." An Illinois EPA letter sent to him about storm water management was signed by Mary Reed. A fax from an equipment manufacturer included the name of the woman who sent it - Mary Reed. A flower delivery came to the restaurant for Mary Jane. No one could trace where the arrangement came from, and the Roadhouse was closed that day. He later learned that it had been Mary Jane's birthday.

He later stated, "It was getting to the point where myself, my wife, June, and our help were experiencing these incidents and they were so abundant that we just kind of accepted it and in a jovial way said that it was never Esther - it was Mary Jane."

But one bartender quit, saying she was freaked out by the vibe of the place at night. One of his waitresses saw a figure in a hallway near the restrooms after closing, and Mike reached his limits. Finally, encouraged by others - mostly Warren Reed - he accepted the fact that the Roadhouse was truly haunted.

"There was no way I could explain what they saw," he said about his employees. "I was starting to question my own sanity."

In the summer of 2002, he contacted a psychic who visited the restaurant. The woman said that one of the spirits in the Roadhouse was named Ruth - the same as Mary Jane's mother - but the psychic had difficulty digging any deeper than that. `

It didn't matter. Mike was convinced, and from that point on, he was dedicated to the investigation into Mary Jane's death. He knew that most people would not believe that she haunted his restaurant, but Mike knew they were there and stated that he did not believe the ghosts would rest in peace "until this thing is resolved."

Mike's assistance was instrumental in helping Warren Reed obtain an exhumation order for Mary Jane's body. As a result, the grave was opened on August 23, 2005. While it did not immediately point out her killer, the exhumation did manage to dispel some of the rumors that had circulated for decades. Like those that claimed her head was not buried with her body or that a gun had been placed in the casket.

Officials were surprised to find that her corpse was mostly intact. She had been buried with all her organs and skin still covered her body. Authorities kept the undergarments that she was wearing when she was buried, and oddly, some additional clothing was found inside the vault. A dress and a slip were found wrapped in newspapers dated June 25, 1948, blaring headlines about her murder. These added artifacts had no explanation.

A few months after the exhumation, officials seemed optimistic when opening the grave yielded a few clues and pointed detectives in the direction of two "people of interest," but that optimism soon faded. According to a 24-page report that was written by Captain Rick Wilkinson --with certain names and details blacked out -- in February 2006,

Wilkinson followed up on several original leads from 1948 and leads from the 1950s when the case was opened again. According to the scenario he laid out, he believed that two local brothers had seen Stan flashing money around town on the night of his date with Mary Jane - including at the Stenhouse. They planned to take it from him, followed the couple to the lover's lane, and confronted Stan. One of them pulled a gun and shot him dead. Unfortunately, both brothers were deceased by 2006.

The story was a mess but so was the case - and had been from the beginning. Captain Wilkinson noted a number of inconsistencies in early police reports on the case, including the number of shell casings found on the lover's lane, references to different guns used as the murder weapon, confusion over the wounds on the bodies, missing interview records with a key person, and no contact made with a man who "appeared to have been a very strong lead."

In the middle of the report were four very troubling sentences. In that section, he stated, "I did find suggestions throughout the report and during the investigation that pointed to political, as well as social connections, appearing to have some influences on this investigation. It also appears as if the information that had developed in the case was not documented and passed on between administrations. Evidence also appears to have been either lost or been destroyed over the years."

At the end of the report was this final sentence: "This investigation, in my opinion, was corrupt and mishandled from the start, and nothing that I am aware of can possibly change those facts," Wilkinson wrote.

In other words, the crime had been covered up, and the perpetrators had been protected for unknown reasons - and he wasn't the only one who thought so.

The exhumation provided little new evidence, but it got people talking as Warren Reed had wanted. However, the story of the exhumation wasn't over yet.

In December 2007, something very strange came to light when a forensic anthropologist who Warren Reed and Mike Arians had hired to examine Mary Jane's remains revealed that the bones in her casket came from *two different bodies*. The skeletal analysis was conducted by Lisa Klepinger, a board-certified forensic anthropologist at the University of Illinois. She was assisted by John Moore, professor of anatomy, pathophysiology, and forensics at Parkland College in Champaign. They jointly wrote that the skull and part of the top portion of the spine found in Mary Jane's casket belonged to someone else. Had the rumors that Mary Jane's head was not buried with her body turned out to be true?

Apparently so. There was a skull, but it wasn't Mary Jane's, according to the scientists. Could it have been a mistake? Could the skull and backbones have been accidentally switched during an examination at the police lab after the exhumation? This seemed the most likely explanation to police officials. Others said that Klepinger's findings were a mistake, merely an opinion open for debate. Still, others said that none of it mattered because, although the case will never "officially" be closed since it's an open homicide, it will certainly never be solved.

Regardless, it seemed to be a case of a dead person telling a tale; it just wasn't the story that anyone expected to hear.

Warren Reed and Mike Arians were not as surprised to hear that Mary Jane's skull was missing as you might think. Rumors had circulated that Mary Jane's head had been carried away by a lovesick killer because he couldn't stand to let her go. And perhaps the rumors were correct.

They believed the killer kept Mary Jane's head as a trophy. And they believed they knew the identity of the killer, too.

Mike has long conceded that Mary Jane had a lot of boyfriends. One of them was a man named Vince Varco, a chief deputy sheriff. He had a brief fling with Mary Jane that ended before Vince wanted it to. The deputy showed up at Mary Jane's house the afternoon before her disappearance, pulled her outside, and tried to persuade her - with threats - that they should keep seeing each other. There are other accounts that say Vince ran into Mary Jane in a bar a few hours before the shooting. It's also possible that both incidents occurred. Vince was known in town as an arrogant bully who threw his weight around as a deputy sheriff to get what he wanted.

Mary Jane's relationship with Vince had been awkward. He was married, and while he was a little forbidden fun for her, she didn't see any reason for them to continue. Besides, she had started flirting with Stan, the handsome former Navy man from the big town of Rockford, and he was more her type.

Vince didn't appreciate being tossed aside, and Mike learned that he roughed her up that day. He grabbed her arm and slapped her a few times, but she wanted nothing more to do with him.

The next night, Mary Jane's date was shot five times. Three of the bullets struck him in the "lower abdomen" - a likely target for a spurned lover who was angry about someone taking his place.

Mary Jane was abducted, probably raped, murdered, and dumped in the weeds near the silica plant.

Mike discovered that on the morning of the murder, Vince showed up for work without his .32-caliber service revolver - the same caliber of the weapon used in the killings. As a law enforcement officer, he was in a position to switch Mary Jane's head for another before the body was buried. Did he? Who knows? But it's been suggested that he wanted to keep a part of her as a souvenir.

Vince Varco died in the mid-1980s. His involvement in the murders seemed plausible, and if correct, Ogle County officials had reason to be nervous. They could be on the hook for a conspiracy that could result in a huge court judgment. Covering up a double homicide could be worth millions of dollars to the surviving family members. Was this the kind of corruption Captain Wilkinson hinted at in his report?

We'll never know that either. I think it's highly unlikely that this case will ever be solved. And that is the reason why Mary Jane's ghost will continue to walk.

Mike Arians continues to find ways to keep the memory of the ill-fated young woman alive. He started a foundation in Mary Jane's name, and the Roadhouse - restaurant, bar, museum, and tourist attraction for ghost hunters - features photographs of the slain young woman on its walls.

Her pretty eyes and half-smile serve as a reminder that, in many cases, absolute answers will elude us, and all we'll have left are the memories that haunt us as ghosts.

"THE ICE CREAM BLONDE" THELMA TODD

The ghost of actress Thelma Todd still walks in Los Angeles, or at least that's what the owners of a building on the famous Pacific Coast Highway have been saying for many years. This building was once home to Thelma's glamorous "Roadside Café," and it's not far from the house where she met her mysterious end.

What killed Thelma Todd? Official statements say it was accidental carbon monoxide poisoning, but the true story of what happened that night may never be known.

And this is likely why Thelma still lingers there, looking for someone to finally reveal what really happened to her on the cold night of December 16, 1935.

Thelma Todd - the woman that Hollywood would know as the "Ice Cream Blonde," who made 69 films during her too-short career - was born on July 29, 1905, in Lawrence, Massachusetts. Her father was a former police officer who became one of the leading politicians in the state, and he had little time for his family. Her frustrated mother turned all her energy toward raising her children - Thelma and her younger brother, William -- to be exceptional. It worked.

Thelma was an excellent student, earning high marks in school. She was also considered to be one of the most beautiful young women in the city. After high school, she enrolled at the Lowell State Normal School and became a teacher. She supplemented her modest salary from teaching sixth-graders by taking a few modeling jobs. She never expected that part of her life to lead anywhere, but in 1925 her brother was killed in an accident. Overwhelmed by this family tragedy, Thelma began dreaming of moving and making a life away from her grief-stricken home.

It's possible she would never have made it had it not been for a family friend who submitted her photograph in a contest held by Jesse Lasky from Famous Players-Lasky, which later became Paramount Studios. He invited Thelma to a screen test for the studio's first film school, where she studied for six months.

During her training, Thelma fell in love with a classmate, Robert Andrews, but the studio nipped the romance in the bud, fearing gossip would somehow taint the new school. This led the always-rebellious Thelma to seek revenge by being extra sexy and flirty around studio executives from that time on. With her classmates from the film school, Thelma made her screen debut in the silent feature *Fascinating Youth* in 1926. It launched her career.

Initially, Thelma's mother had been thrilled by her daughter's career opportunities, but she had doubts when she saw a publicity photo of the pretty girl in a flimsy costume. Alice Todd rushed to New York to voice her moral objections to studio executives. Already at wit's end with Thelma's rebellious behavior, Paramount gave her an ultimatum -

relocate to Paramount's studio in Hollywood or go home. Thelma packed up and moved to California.

Thelma went to work under a five-year, $75-per-week contract with Paramount, and throughout 1927 she was given small parts in several feature films like *Rubber Heels* with Ed Wynn and *Nevada*, a western with Gary Cooper. Then, Al Jolson spoke a few words onscreen in *The Jazz Singer*, and motion pictures were changed forever.

The industry went through a terrifying series of changes as the "Talkies" became the new medium of choice. The old silent films were gone for good and with them went some of the biggest stars of the era. The careers of screen legends like John Gilbert, Clara Bow, Norma Talmadge, and many others were suddenly over. They were forced into retirement when the public did not respond to the sound of their voices. For Thelma, the coming of sound motion pictures could not have occurred at a better time. She had a wonderfully throaty voice which helped her to make a swift transition to talking pictures. She was also now able to develop a wisecracking persona, and the demise of many screen veterans made room for newcomers and little-known actors like Thelma. A new generation of screen stars was born. However, Paramount failed to renew her contract in 1929. Her career seemed over before it really began.

And then along came Hal Roach, the maker of some of Hollywood's most popular comedies. He offered her a movie deal and even allowed her to freelance for other studios.

A former director at Essanay Studios, Roach persuaded another company, Pathe, to sponsor him in his own studio. He soon emerged as a comedic talent, envisioning hilarious situations and translating them to film. Roach concentrated more on story than slapstick, and audiences loved him at the box office. His biggest stars became Laurel and Hardy and Thelma Todd. She proved to be a real asset to Roach, not only appearing in her own films but as a female foil to Stan and Ollie and others. Roach had big plans to feature Thelma with another comedic actress, Zasu Pitts, in a series of two-reel comic shorts.

At first, Thelma was reluctant to take the deal with Roach because the obligation came with conditions. The first was that she had to bleach her hair platinum blonde and the second required her to abide by the "potato clause." This meant that she was being signed at a certain weight, and if she gained more than five pounds, it was cause for instant dismissal. Thelma's mother, widowed since 1925, was in Hollywood for one of her frequent visits, and she urged Thelma to take the deal. Before reporting to the Roach lot for her first shoot, Alice Todd supervised the bleaching of her daughter's hair and helped her to plan a stringent diet.

In addition to Thelma's comedies for Hal Roach, Thelma also played major roles in films for other studios. They were primarily comedies in which she portrayed the sarcastic and wisecracking blonde role that most suited her. She appeared in two different films with the Marx Brothers, *Monkey Business* and the classic *Horse Feathers*. Stan Laurel always wanted Thelma as the female lead in the Laurel and Hardy films, but her personality didn't always mesh with the two comedians on screen. She and Laurel became close friends, and he often found work for her in other films when she wasn't working for Roach. He loved her bawdy sense of humor, and when she suffered from boyfriend problems, she always confided in Stan.

Thelma was always up for partying when she was not at work and found it difficult to avoid liquor and foods, both of which "made her fat." Friends on the Roach lot introduced her to diet pills - essentially amphetamines -- and she soon became hooked on the tablets.

By 1930, Zasu Pitts had moved on to other work, and Thelma was often joined on screen by Patsy Kelly. They were still going strong in 1935, and her professional career was filled with high spots. Always restless in her personal life, though, Thelma was pleased when director Roland West started showing an interest in her, even though the unattractive older man was already married to silent screen actress Jewel Carmen.

West was a respected director in Hollywood during the 1920s and early 1930s. While his output of films was small, his work was appreciated by studios and audiences alike. His greatest success came in 1926 with *The Bat*, an atmospheric thriller starring Jack Pickford and Jewel Carmen. His visually astounding 1928 film, *The Dove*, won an Academy Award for art direction. In 1931, he created one of the most extraordinary chillers of the time, *The Bat Whispers* with Chester Morris. West and Thelma began a romance, with West promising her the lead in Howard Hughes' *Hell's Angels*, but that role went to Jean Harlow instead.

To make amends, West cast Thelma as the lead in *Corsair*, a new film that he was producing and directing for United Artists. Unfortunately, when released, the film bombed, and Thelma returned to her usual heavy work schedule making comedy shorts.

The romance between Thelma and West faded, and while they remained friends and were still sleeping together occasionally, Thelma had other lovers. When West came to her and suggested they open a restaurant that catered to the film colony, Thelma promised to consider the idea.

Around this same time, Thelma met Pasquale "Pat" DiCicco, a handsome New York playboy who associated with gangsters for the thrill of it. Pat was suave and new to Hollywood, promoting himself as a talent agent and began making the L.A. restaurant and nightclub circuit rounds. Movie industry people knew that he associated with Charles "Lucky" Luciano, the Syndicate gangster based out of New York, which, of course, made him an intriguing character. Thelma was also amused by DiCicco, and dating him gave her life a touch of danger - although it would prove to be more dangerous than she ever wanted.

Thelma and DiCicco had a whirlwind romance, and, despite his violent temper and a number of beatings, the couple eloped on July 10, 1932, to Prescott, Arizona. The happy marriage didn't last long. DiCicco refused to settle into married life and often left his new wife alone at their Brentwood home while he was out on the town. Frustrated, Thelma began drinking heavily, always relying on her faithful diet pills to keep the weight off.

One night, when Thelma convinced Pat to take her out with him to the clubs, DiCicco introduced her to Lucky Luciano, who was in town for a visit. Thelma was excited to be in the presence of the famous mobster, although DiCicco was unnerved by the gangster's obvious interest in his wife.

By 1933, DiCicco was frequently away on business in New York, and Thelma continued to churn out films, including her popular shorts with Patsy Kelly. She was out on the town with several other men while he was away. Finally, enough was enough, and Thelma filed for divorce.

In August, right after turning 30, Thelma came to the realization that her stardom couldn't last forever. So she put her money into bonds and real estate and took top billing and a half interest in the swank new beachside roadhouse that had been proposed to her by Roland West. With funding from West's wife, Jewel Carmen, supervision by West himself, and Thelma's name to lure in the film crowd, Thelma Todd's Sidewalk Café opened for business. Many of West's and Thelma's famous friends began frequenting the place, and it became popular with actors and star-struck fans alike.

Located under the palisades of what is now the Pacific Coast Highway -- then known as Roosevelt Highway -- the restaurant occupied the ground floor along with a drug store. On the second level were a bar, lounge, and West's business office, as well as two apartments, one of which Thelma and West often shared. They parked their cars high about the roadhouse in a large garage with a loft above it. The garage was located next to 17531 Posetano Road, a grand house where Jewel Carmen lived, along with her brother, who managed the café, and his wife. The only access from the roadhouse to the garage and bungalow atop the palisades was a flight of 270 stone steps that had been cut into the steep cliff behind the restaurant.

In mid-1935, Thelma was spending much of her spare time operating the café. She was still working hard, drinking, and keeping up her steady doses of diet pills. Her hectic life was further complicated by several threatening letters demanding a sizable blackmail fee. They proved to be the work of a deranged stalker in New York, and while this bit of strangeness worked itself out, it was not the most frightening thing that Thelma had to deal with that summer.

Her most disconcerting problem was the pressure that she was receiving from Lucky Luciano to turn over the café's third-story storage room -- used unofficially as a gambling parlor for wealthy customers -- to him as a Syndicate operation.

At that time, organized crime was starting to thrive in California, moving west from places like New York and Chicago. Bootlegging and drug trafficking had long been a part of Hollywood, but in the middle 1930s, Luciano was trying to penetrate California with his illegal gambling enterprise. He already had casinos all over the country, and with so much money flowing in and out of Hollywood, he was looking for a way to get a piece of the action. Thelma kept refusing Luciano's request, and he eventually became violent, causing her to break off all contact with him.

Their final confrontation came one night in late November at the Brown Derby in Beverly Hills. According to witnesses, the pair had a brief exchange in the restaurant:

Thelma Todd: "You'll open a gambling casino in my restaurant over my dead body!"
Luciano:" That can be arranged."

Thelma threatened to take her problems with Luciano to L.A. District Attorney Buron Fitts and made an appointment at his office for December 17, 1935. To spite Luciano, she began converting the third-floor café space into a steakhouse. Meanwhile, Pat DiCicco showed up at the restaurant one day and asked her about the possibility of managing the place. Thelma didn't know if he was trying to get back into her life - or if he was on a mission from Luciano. She had a feeling that it was the latter.

Thelma's film work continued to thrive. In 1935, she appeared with Bing Crosby in the Paramount musical *Two for Tonight.* In November, she began working with Laurel and Hardy again in the feature-length musical *The Bohemian Girl.* This film was also based on an operetta, and Stan found an unusual part for Thelma to play. She appeared as a gypsy's daughter, wearing a black wig to cover her blond curls. She continued to work on the film well into December.

On December 14, Thelma received an invitation to a Hollywood party. A few years earlier, she had made a film with Stanley Lupino, the British stage comedian, and father of actress Ida Lupino. Stanley and his wife were in town, and Ida was hosting a dinner party for him at the Café Trocadero. When Thelma informed West about the party, he was irritated with her that she would not be at their own restaurant on such a busy night before the holidays. But this was not the worst thing to come that night. A few days earlier, Pat DiCicco had run into Ida Lupino at the Trocadero, and she had unknowingly invited him to the party.

On the afternoon of December 14, Thelma and her mother went out Christmas shopping, driven by her chauffeur, Ernest Peters. Later, she returned home to change clothes while her mother continued with her errands. At 7.30 p.m., Peters, along with Mrs. Todd, picked up Thelma. The actress was wearing a blue satin evening gown with lace and sequins, expensive jewelry, and a luxurious mink coat. Before leaving, she and West argued again about the café, but the still-rebellious Thelma slammed the door in his face and walked out. After dropping Thelma off at the Trocadero, Peters took Mrs. Todd home and then made himself available to drive Thelma home after the party.

It was a small gathering by Hollywood standards, about a dozen people, but it was not without drama. Thelma arrived alone, but DiCicco did not. He had two companions, the lovely actress Margaret Lindsay and one of her equally attractive starlet friends. Thelma dined next to a vacant seat while Pat made a show of enjoying himself at another table. Thelma was not amused and stopped by DiCicco's table and told him so.

A little later, she left her seat to make a telephone call and use the restroom. When she returned, she seemed moody but did not say why. Around midnight, DiCicco also made a mysterious phone call, which left him jittery. He refused to comment on it and left with Margaret and her friend at about 1.15 a.m. without saying good night to anyone.

While Thelma waited for her driver to arrive, she asked her friend, theater owner Sid Grauman, to call Roland West and tell him that she was on her way home. Sid made the call, telling West that Thelma should be back at the apartment by 2.30 a.m., although she was still waiting on her car at the restaurant a half-hour after that.

When Peters finally arrived with the car, Thelma's friends escorted her out, and before getting in, she turned back to them with a theatrically grand flourish and a grin. "Goodbye!" she called.

In the car, she told Peters to take her out to the roadhouse, and they drove for a bit in silence. Then, Thelma began to urge him to drive faster. They were being followed, she said, by gangsters. After her recent brushes with mob boss Luciano, she was worried about being kidnapped or murdered. Peters hit the gas. At speeds of up to 70 mph, the car careened westward around the curves of Sunset Boulevard until the ocean and Thelma's café finally came into view.

It was 3.30 a.m. Sunday morning when they arrived at the roadhouse. As usual, Peters offered to escort Thelma to the door, but she told him that it wasn't necessary. She gathered her coat around her and walked off into the dark - and this was the last time that Thelma Todd was ever seen alive.

On Monday morning, December 16, Thelma's housekeeper, Mae Whitehead, reported for work around 10.00 a.m. She looked around, but oddly, Thelma was nowhere to be found. She wasn't in the apartment above the roadhouse or the café. She looked around for Thelma's new Packard convertible and thought she could see it through the partially open doors of the garage atop the cliff, where it was usually parked. An older man named Smith, who kept the books for the roadhouse, lived in the loft above the garage.

Mae assumed Thelma was visiting with the bookkeeper because there was no one else around that morning. After a while, though, it began to nag at her. Finally, around 10.30 a.m., she climbed the 270 steps up the cliff, entered the garage, and turned on the light.

And she found Thelma Todd.

She was lying face down on the front seat of her Packard. Her blond hair was matted, and her skin was pale. She was still wearing her clothes from Saturday night. A porcelain replacement tooth had been knocked out of her mouth, and blood was spattered on her skin, her evening gown, and on the mink coat. There was also blood all over the car's interior, on the floor, and in the garage.

Thelma was dead at the age of only 30.

Her death launched one of the strangest investigations in the history of Los Angeles. It was strange because of the contradictory clues, the leads that were never followed, and the suspects never questioned, or at least not questioned seriously. It's no wonder that her death is still considered one the most mysterious in Hollywood history and that the investigation is seen more as a cover-up than as a real search for clues and suspects.

A coroner's jury would insist that Thelma died by her own hand, perhaps intentionally. The official cause of death was carbon monoxide asphyxiation. The official version was that Thelma, finding herself locked out of her apartment, climbed the stone steps from the street to the garage and had tried to stay warm in her Packard by starting the engine. The exhaust then suffocated her.

This was a neat and tidy solution to a potentially large problem. Thelma was dead, and nothing could bring her back. An official finding of death by her own hand, accidental or otherwise, put an end to speculation about murder. It got Thelma Todd, her studio, and the whole film industry off the front pages with very little fuss. If Thelma had been murdered, the most obvious suspects were her mobbed-up ex-husband, her film director/sometimes lover, her lover's wife - who was also a film actress, or a dangerous gangster.

If she'd been murdered, the studio bosses didn't want to know. Many of the Americans who paid to see the movies wouldn't tolerate yet another Hollywood scandal. They might stop going to the movies, and in 1935, that would be a disaster for the studios and, in turn, for city leaders and the police, both of which had a long history of accommodating the film industry to the profit of all. There was only one big business in Los Angeles before World War II - the movies - and it wouldn't do to have the money-making machine slowed down because of a starlet's death, no matter how popular she was.

The official version of events was neat and tidy - and there's no way it could be true. If Thelma was trying to stay warm, why would she get into a convertible instead of the sedan parked next to it? The Packard was not running, and there were two gallons of gas left in the tank. How did that happen? If she was suicidal, why hadn't she used the closed-up sedan, which would have been easier and much quicker? Why had she personally wrapped 100 Christmas presents two days earlier? And why had she just started work on a new film?

And there were more holes in the coroner's theory. If she had climbed the 270 stone steps, why were her feet unmarked, and why didn't her new, delicate shoes show scuff marks or any signs of wear from the narrow stairs? If Thelma had climbed all those stairs, opened the garage door, and started the Packard at 3.30 a.m. in the morning, why didn't the bookkeeper who lived upstairs hear anything? He later testified that he was up reading until 2.30 a.m. He was sure that he would have heard something below him, but he heard nothing at all.

The coroner also had no explanation for the blood on her face, clothing, and in the car. Her clothing was in such disarray that it suggested a struggle, but the coroner took no account of this. During the autopsy, it was revealed that Thelma suffered a broken nose, several broken ribs, and had bruises on her body and inside of her throat. A veteran reporter noted the bruising inside of her throat - as well as the knocked-out tooth - could be caused by someone shoving a bottle down her throat.

And that could explain the high level of alcohol in her body. The autopsy revealed that the food in Thelma's stomach had been eaten just a few hours before at the Trocadero party. But the autopsy also revealed more alcohol in her system -- .13 percent - than would have been possible from the four drinks she had at the party, two before eating dinner and two after.

The coroner's attempt to fix the time of death at early Sunday morning was undermined by the weather that night. It had been unseasonably cold, and there had been a strong sea breeze throughout the night. This cold air might - or might not have - slowed the decomposition of Thelma's body.

That became important because the coroner insisted that Thelma's driver, Ernest Peters, had been the last person to see her alive. However, no less than four people came forward to say they'd heard or spoken to Thelma in the time between 3:30 a.m. Sunday and 10:30 a.m. on Monday.

There was Jewel Carmen, who was still married to Roland West. She knew Thelma very well and told the police she saw her on Sunday morning in her Packard convertible at the corner of Hollywood and Vine. There was a handsome, swarthy, well-dressed man in the car with her. Jewel said she'd never seen him before.

Mrs. Wallace Ford claimed she heard from Thelma at 4:00 p.m. on Sunday afternoon. Thelma called her from a payphone to tell her that she would be attending Ford's cocktail party that evening with a surprise guest. "When you see who's coming with me, you'll drop dead!" Thelma laughed. A pharmacist swore that Thelma made the call from a payphone in his drug store.

There was also a report from a man named Person, who owned a liquor store on Figueroa. He told the police that Thelma had come into his store on Sunday evening around 11.00 p.m. She was wearing the same gown she had worn to the Trocadero but without a hat or a coat. Seemingly dazed, she asked him to dial a telephone number for her on the payphone. Person didn't remember the prefix, but the last four digits had been 7771. He said she then left the shop and joined a handsome man who appeared out of the alley with her fur coat. She walked across the street with the man, and they sat down together on the front steps of a church. They talked for around a half-hour and then left.

Everything about the case seemed to be a mess, suggesting this was no accidental poisoning in a garage filled with exhaust fumes.

But if Thelma had been murdered, who had killed her?

Even today, Roland West seems the most likely suspect, and his actions on the night of December 15 are certainly mysterious. Sid Grauman called him at the roadhouse about "2.00 or 3.00 in the morning." He told West that Thelma was leaving soon and would be home in under an hour. West closed the restaurant, sent the staff home, and went upstairs to bed. And he admitted that he bolted the heavy door between the stairwell and the apartment from the inside so that Thelma could not get in, even using her key. Why would he do this? West claimed that after their fight about the café earlier on Saturday, he had warned her that if she was not home by 2.00 a.m., he would lock her out. Some have surmised that Thelma's telephone call during the party had been to West, hoping for a reprieve. When it didn't come, she asked mutual friend Sid Grauman to call for her later. But West stubbornly refused to back down. He said he likely would have let her in if he'd heard her knocking, but the sounds of the wind and surf drowned everything out.

Or so he said. Because then he told the police that a barking dog awakened him at 3.30 a.m. after he had fallen asleep. He also said he heard water running in the apartment and assumed that Thelma was home. But how could she have gotten into the house through the manually bolted door?

West said that he realized Thelma wasn't there when he got up the following day. Was he worried? Did he call the police? He said later that he assumed she had gone to her mother's house. He never checked, though, and he never became alarmed after several telephone calls for Thelma came on Sunday and none of her friends could locate her.

When questioned, neighbors said they heard West in a bitter argument with Thelma when she came home from the party. West now completely changed his story and downplayed the disagreement at the same time. Yes, she had come back, but he wouldn't let her in. Thelma then beat on the door for the next 10 minutes with her fists and screamed obscenities at him. After that, he said, he thought she had gone to her mother's house.

The police never pressed the matter with West, and there was no actual evidence to tie him to the scene of Thelma's death. But Thelma's friends recalled that West had an affinity for convoluted murder mysteries. Some of them called it "an obsessive interest in the perfect crime." Some made the wild suggestion that he had hired an actress to play the role of "Thelma Todd" in the heard-but-not-seen argument on Sunday morning. While that was happening, Thelma was already lying dead in the garage. West had killed her because he was angry that she had a new boyfriend.

But West may have had another motive - greed. After Thelma's death, he asserted that her only investment in the restaurant was her name, for which she received half the profits. None of her heirs ever contested this. The space occupied by the restaurant and the apartment above were leased from the building's owner - Jewel Carmen, West's wife.

Interestingly, it had been the sighting of Thelma by Jewel Carmen - with the swarthy man in her convertible - that the police took most seriously. If she had been lying, it's possible that Thelma was already dead.

But, of course, we'll never know for sure.

What we do know is that Thelma's death ruined West's career. He never directed another film in Hollywood. He and Jewel Carmen divorced shortly after Thelma's death, and later, he sold the café. In 1950, he suffered a debilitating stroke and endured an emotional breakdown. On his deathbed in March 1952, he confessed to Chester Morris that he had always been haunted by Thelma's death and felt that he was in some way responsible for it.

Although exactly what he meant by that is unknown.

Thelma's death barely caused a ripple in Hollywood, especially after the inquest ruled that she had died accidentally from carbon monoxide poisoning.

But Thelma's attorney, who attended the inquest, was sure that the police had been on the wrong track all along. He requested a second inquest, in which he would be able to prove his theory. He believed that he could pin her murder -- not accidental death -- on Lucky Luciano. He was sure that when Thelma had turned down the gangster's offer to take over the gambling at her café, she had unknowingly signed her own death warrant. The attorney was convinced that Luciano, or someone who worked for him, had beaten Thelma, put her in the car unconscious, and then started the engine. With the garage door closed, she had been poisoned by the fumes.

The district attorney agreed to the idea, and a second inquest was scheduled. However, when movie producer Hal Roach learned of the plans for the second inquest, he begged the D.A. to drop the matter. We'll never know why but he urged the District Attorney to reconsider. Reluctantly, he agreed, and the case was closed for good.

Thelma died leaving a will that paid $1 to her ex-husband Pat DiCicco and the rest to her mother. When Thelma's mother first learned about her daughter's death, she insisted that someone had murdered her. Soon after the will was read, she changed her story and publicly accepted the coroner's official version of Thelma's death.

And it wasn't just the coroner's version of events; it was the Hollywood version, too. Although it's a story that no movie producer would ever be allowed to put on the screen. The audience would never be able to suspend their disbelief beyond the first reel.

With the case of Thelma Todd officially wrapped up, her spotlight faded to black. No matter how many unanswered questions remained, no one wanted to try and answer them. Roland West's career was ruined by Thelma's death, and no one wanted to join him on the unemployment line.

The mystery of what really happened to Thelma has lingered for decades. Most believe this is the reason why her spirit is still so restless.

Although nearly nine decades have passed since Thelma entertained guests at the roadhouse, her ghost has been frequently reported in the building. It still stands today along the Pacific Coast Highway and has been used as offices and creative spaces for many years.

Staff members at a production company that used the space several years ago said they often saw a filmy image that resembled

Thelma. It was usually seen near the concrete steps leading to the garage and outside in a small courtyard area.

More tragic are the sightings of Thelma's ghost, as well as other strange events, at the garage on Posetano Road. For many years, people complained about the sound of an engine running when the space was empty. Others said they have smelled - and been nearly overwhelmed by - what seems to be exhaust fumes. The garage is always empty when this happens.

Or at least empty of anything they can see.

The terrible events of long ago have left an indelible impression on this place, just in the way that Thelma Todd has.

Will she ever rest in peace? It seems unlikely. Unless new evidence would miraculously come to light after all this time, her murder will always remain unsolved. And as a result, her lonely spirit will continue to linger for many more years to come.

"SHE WALKS THESE HILLS"
MAMIE THURMAN

Although Mamie Thurman died nearly 90 years ago, her spirit lives on in the mountains of West Virginia.

The legends say that when the winds wail in the dark of the night, Mamie's ghost still walks the hills of Logan County. There are stories of an apparition that has been seen, while others claim to have picked up a lonely young woman near Trace Mountain, only to find later that the seat beside them in the car is mysteriously empty.

But why does she still walk? Many say that her spirit cries out for justice. The story of her murder is one of mystery, sexual depravity, and even a missing grave. It is a story of horror and darkness that touched the lives of some of the area's most prominent citizens in 1932.

And Mamie's ghost serves as a dark reminder that her death continues to go unpunished.

On June 22, 1932, the lifeless body of a pretty, dark-eyed woman with brown hair was found dumped along a road near Trace Mountain in Logan County, West Virginia.

The gruesome discovery was made by Garland Davis, a deaf-mute who stumbled over the body while picking blackberries.

The authorities were alerted, and the dead woman was quickly identified as a local woman named Mamie Thurman. She was married to a police officer, Jack Thurman, which made the discovery even more shocking.

R. L. Harris, the undertaker from the Harris Funeral Home who acted in the position of a coroner, arrived on the scene that afternoon. He later stated that Mamie's body was found facing downhill and that she might have never been discovered if some bushes had not kept her from sliding down the mountainside.

She was found wearing a dark blue dress with white polka dots and one shoe. The other shoe was found near the body. Her handbag was found a short distance away. It contained a pack of cigarettes and about $10. She was wearing a watch, a diamond ring, and a white-gold wedding ring, which suggested that robbery was not the reason for her death.

When Harris bent down to examine the corpse, he clearly saw that her neck had been broken. She had also been shot twice in the left side of the head with what would turn out to be a .38-caliber weapon. The bullets had been fired at close range, and both passed through her brain. There were severe powder burns on her face. In addition, her throat had been cut from ear to ear.

Someone had wanted to make sure she was dead.

Harris noted that she had been dead for several hours before she was discovered. The investigation would later reveal that she had last been seen the previous night around 9.00 p.m.

Mamie's remains were moved to Harris' undertaking establishment, and he embalmed her later that afternoon. He believed that Mamie was already dead when her throat was cut and that she had not been killed at the scene. Most likely, whoever killed her had not expected her to be found for quite some time - if ever. In such a remote area, where paved roads didn't exist, animals would more likely carry away the remains than a person would stumble across them. Garland Davis had just been lucky, although it's unlikely he felt that way.

Within hours of Mamie's body being discovered, a warrant was issued by Magistrate Elba Hatfield for the arrest of local resident Harry Robertson. A separate warrant called for the capture of his African American handyman, Clarence Stephenson. Both men were soon behind bars.

Robertson was a politician and well-known in the community. He worked at the National Bank of Logan and served as treasurer for the local public library. He seemed to be liked by everyone who knew him, and he and his wife moved within Logan's highest social circles. She was the treasurer for the local Women's Club, and both were active in their church.

On the other hand, Stephenson was a native of Chattanooga who had been in Logan County for the past nine years. He had worked in several area coal mines before going to work for Robertson. Prior to being arrested for Mamie's murder, he had never been in trouble with the law. He mainly worked around the Robertson house, acting as a caretaker and doing odd jobs. His primary responsibilities were to feed and care for Robertson's hunting dogs.

What initially sent the authorities to Robertson remains unknown, but he admitted that he had been sleeping with Mamie Thurman when questioned. He often arranged to rendezvous with her with help from his handyman, Stephenson. Robertson would tell his wife that he was going hunting - he was an avid sportsman - and then Stephenson would drive him to one of the places where he had arranged to meet Mamie.

Affair or not, to those who heard about his arrest Robertson seemed like an unlikely killer. Rumors flew about Robertson and Mamie. Everyone considered her an active church worker, kind lady, a young woman of "quiet demeanor," and "a very nice lady who minded her own business."

But soon, locals would learn that this was the public version of Mamie - she had many secrets. And as those secrets began to be revealed, tongues would wag about her many affairs with married men and her sexual escapades around town. Many started to believe that the "Vixen of Stratton Street," as she became known, may have gotten exactly what she deserved.

The murder was startling news all over the region, galvanizing a community that had just begun to feel the pain of the Great Depression. At a time when many families could barely afford to put food on their tables, the strange death of Mamie Thurman would provide an unwelcome but desirable distraction.

She was born Mamie Morrison on September 12, 1900. Her father, George, was a carpenter and struggling contractor who had once lived in Logan County. By the time Mamie was born, though, he and his wife had moved to the tiny town of Bradfordsville, Kentucky, not far from Louisville.

Mamie was only three years old when her mother died. Little else is known about her childhood. It couldn't have been very stable because Mamie left home early, and her father abruptly died in 1928 following a gun battle with police officers in Ashland, Kentucky.

What is known is that Mamie married Jack Thurman around 1922. He was 16 years older than his young bride. Two years later, they had moved to Logan, West Virginia, which was located in the heart of coal country. By 1932, they had been living in Logan for eight years, renting a two-room garage apartment behind Harry Robertson's house on Stratton Street. Jack had a position on the city police force, which he'd gotten just 15 months before Mamie's death. The job came about thanks to Harry Robertson, who was the president of the city commission - and the man who would soon be charged with Mamie's murder.

As we'll soon see, the Mamie Thurman murder case would become hopelessly entangled between families, friends, and politics in a small town where everyone knew everyone else.

Mamie was often described as having a pleasant smile and a soft voice. She was likable, attractive, and kind. She wore her dark-brown hair neatly curled, and tucked under on the sides, a fashionable look of the early 1930s. She had olive skin, a pert, turned-up nose, high cheekbones, a long neck, and dark eyes. Women envied her looks and envied how men looked at her in her stylish, tight-fitting dresses. When Mamie walked down the street in Logan, it would later be said, all eyes - men and women - watched her as she went by.

Mamie had worked at several businesses around town, including the Logan National Bank and a car dealership. At the time of Mamie's death, she had been enrolled in a summer business school held in Logan and offered by the West Virginia Wesleyan College.

Mamie was well-liked, but there were rumors - rumors that claimed that the sweet, church-going woman had a secret side. Mamie liked to drink, as many people did during the fading years of Prohibition, but Mamie also liked to get a little wild - and not always with her husband.

The rumors about Mamie's double life ran amok after her murder, even intruding on her funeral, which took place on June 24.

Without a doubt, it was probably one of the most bizarre services ever held in Logan County. Strangely, the cost of the funeral was more than $7,200, a staggering amount in 1932. The services were paid for in cash by her husband, a city patrolman. Jack made a meager $175 a month, and it was never explained where the money for the funeral came from.

There were about 550 women and 30 men in attendance at the funeral. It was conducted at the Nighbert Methodist Church, the most prestigious church in town. Mamie had been a faithful member. The church's pastor, Reverend B. C. Gamble, and the Reverend Robert F. Caverlee of the First Baptist Church both officiated.

Oddly, Reverend Gamble chose not to deliver a sermon. Instead, he read a scripture from the Book of John. The verses told of a woman brought before Jesus, having been caught in the act of adultery. Her captors intended to stone her to death. Jesus replied that the one of them without sin should cast the first stone, and the once angry crowd left the woman alone. In the moments that followed, Jesus didn't condemn the woman for her actions but simply told her to go and sin no more.

"This is the text," Reverend Gamble said, and then he paused for a few moments before he added, "develop your own sermon on that basis."

His words were met with stunned silence from the congregation. Only the sound of weeping could be heard. After that shocking moment, Mamie's obituary was read aloud, and the service was concluded. What happened next, though, remains a mystery to this day.

Mamie's death certificate was filed at the courthouse, and it stated that she was buried at Logan Memorial Park in McConnell. In addition, it listed her cause of death as "unknown." According to records and a search of the cemetery, though, Mamie was never buried there. To make matters even more confusing, records at the Harris Funeral Home showed a charge of $35 for moving Mamie's body to Bradfordsville, Kentucky. However, the cemetery in Kentucky had no record of the internment of her body either.

So, where is Mamie Thurman buried?

No one knows; it's another unsolved mystery in this already perplexing case.

On the day of the funeral, West Virginia State troopers searched the home of Harry Robertson, the lead suspect in the case and one of the most prominent and influential men in town.

In 1932, Harry Robertson was 40 years old. He worked for the Logan National Bank and was the Chairman of the Board of Commissioners of Logan. He was, by all appearances, a staid and respected bookkeeper. He was a small man with close-set eyes and a receding hairline. His remaining hair was kept in place with tonic and was precisely parted on the left. He was commonly dressed in serious business suits with bow ties and wore a pair of thick-rimmed, round glasses when he worked, poring over the bank's numbers.

In other words, he certainly didn't fit the stereotype of a murder suspect.

Robertson and his wife had two children and lived in a three-story, dark brick home on Stratton Street. Behind the house were two separate buildings - a small shed and a garage with an upstairs apartment. The Robertsons also took in boarders on occasion, and there had been several of them living in the main house during the worst years of the Depression. One of them was handyman Clarence Stephenson, and another had been a fellow bank employee named Oscar Townsend.

At the bank was where Mamie first caught Harry's roaming eye. When she had started working at the bank, Harry had trained her as a teller. Their interactions eventually led to an affair, and soon, Harry became her landlord, renting out the garage apartment to Mamie and Jack. He also got Jack a job for the police department, which conveniently kept him out of the house. After Mamie quit working at the bank to become a "full-time housewife," Harry was around "to watch out for her" when Jack had to work the late shift as a patrolman.

During the search of the Robertson house, the police made several alarming discoveries. They found several bloodstained rags in the basement and several places on the floor where it looked as though someone had attempted to clean something up. That "something" was believed to be blood, a belief that was later confirmed by a Charleston chemist named T. A. Borradaile. His tests showed the blood to be human; however, none of his tests were admitted as evidence during the trial that followed.

The troopers also found a razor hidden in the basement and discovered a hole in the wall that appeared to have been made by a bullet.

The investigators also found bloodstains on the window, fender, and Robertson's Ford sedan seat. The car was mostly used to transport hunting dogs when Robertson traveled up to Trace Mountain, where he owned a hunting cabin. The vehicle's back seat had been removed, and a tarp had been placed over the back of the front seat and on the rear portion of the vehicle. This was supposed to protect the car from the dogs when they were in the back, but investigators also believed it would have made the perfect way to move Mamie's body. They didn't believe it was a coincidence that her remains had been found just over a mile from Harry's cabin.

On June 27, Harry was released from jail on a $10,000 bond guaranteed by his defense attorney, C. C. Chambers, Bruce McDonald of the McDonald Land Company, and by T. G. Moore and C. L. Estep, two other prominent men in town.

Harry's handyman, Clarence Stephenson, would not be so lucky. He had also been charged with Mamie's murder, and even though he had the same attorney as Robertson, he was not released on bail prior to the hearing. It was for a simple reason - he was, as the newspapers called him, "the Negro general handyman." It didn't pay to be poor and black in West Virginia in the 1930s.

Clarence had been born and raised in Chattanooga, Tennessee, and had little formal education. He had first come to Logan in 1923 and managed to get a job at the Draper coal mine. He had worked in several other mines in the area, and in late 1930, he began boarding with the Robertsons. Harry hired him to be a driver, an odd-jobs man, and his "go-between" - which meant picking up Mamie and dropping her off in out-of-the-way rendezvous spots around the county. Clarence never married but did have a sister, Josie, who worked as a maid at the Pioneer Hotel in Logan.

Clarence always maintained that he was treated well by the Robertsons, washing dishes, running errands, and taking care of Harry's hunting dogs. Harry usually took Clarence with him when he went hunting.

The newspapers unkindly described Clarence as "the funniest-looking man you ever seen." He was quite short, generally regarded as unattractive, and his looks were further complicated by a protruding forehead that had been caused when he was struck by the shaft of a grocery delivery wagon. The contusion had swollen and simply never went down again.

Despite all this, he was likable, friendly, and well-known to just about everyone in town. So it was hard for most to believe that he had anything to do with Mamie's murder.

On July 5, the *Logan Banner* newspaper announced that Judge James Damron of Huntington would aid in the Thurman investigation without pay. He was one of the state's most distinguished criminal lawyers and judges, and he offered to serve as a prosecutor in the case. In a letter to the county's prosecuting attorneys, L. P. Hager and Emmett F. Scaggs, he wrote, "Mamie Thurman's brutal murder was a drastic deed and the handiwork of a well-laid out conspiracy." He also said that he believed the perpetrators of such a "foul and damnable murder" should be apprehended and brought to justice. The district attorneys readily agreed to his sentiments and gave him a seat at the prosecutor's table.

In the meantime, the investigation into the murder continued, and detectives were making some rather unsavory discoveries about some of the county's most prominent citizens. The most sensational revelation confirmed the existence of a "Key Club" in Logan where married businessmen would meet with their girlfriends in secret. The men and women all had secret keys to get into the club, which was located in a building "in the heart of the city."

Both Mamie and Harry had been members of the club and frequently visited there. Clarence Stephenson later reported that Harry had paid him to watch the club and make sure that Mamie wasn't going there with anyone else.

Jack Thurman - who had never been suspected of Mamie's murder - naively stated that he was under the opinion that his wife had "always been true to him." If he was telling the truth, he stated that she always waited at home for him on nights when he was on patrol duty. In addition, he always praised her in the courtroom and during police interviews. When questioned about her affairs, he responded by saying, "She was a perfect wife to me, and I cannot imagine she would do such a thing."

This was much different from the way that Harry Robertson described Mamie. The Mamie that he knew was a "lusty, lewd, unfaithful woman, who had been sneaking around with more than a handful of secret lovers at any given time."

As the case heated up even further, it began moving toward a trial. Pressure was being felt by the men of the district attorney's office from all sides - especially from the side of the business community in Logan. Every city leader was terrified of his own name being leaked as a member of the city's sensational "Key Club."

In a press statement on July 26, though, Assistant D.A. Emmett Scaggs announced that his office had no intention of dragging the names of anyone into the case merely to satisfy the curiosity-seekers. He knew that many people were more interested in the scandal than in finding out who killed Mamie Thurman, but his office was not. In addition, he assured the public that just because some "prominent people" might be involved, his office was moving forward on the case as quickly as possible. Scaggs added, "Murder carries an extreme penalty, while adultery is only a misdemeanor." They would, he promised, get to the bottom of the case.

Scaggs followed this with another startling announcement. Believing that many honest people in the county could shed some light on the case but were afraid to get involved, he had asked the court to offer a $1,000 reward for new evidence that would lead to a conviction. This crime, Scaggs stated, was the "most brutish crime in Logan County history," and he was determined to see it solved.

Not surprisingly, several people came forward with information. One of them was Oscar Townsend, who rented a room from Harry Robertson and had worked with him at the bank. He said that there had been "ill feelings" between Mamie Thurman and Harry Robertson's wife, Louise and that the two ladies, who had once been friends, had not been "going around together" for some time. He also informed the police that he had traded a .38-caliber gun to Harry Robertson in exchange for a smaller pistol some time back.

Shortly after receiving the information, another search was carried out at the Robertson home. Police found a .38-caliber pistol under Robertson's pillow, where he kept it at night. They also found a knife and a bloodstained piece of canvas that led them back to the car. Inside the vehicle, a more thorough search revealed a blood clot underneath the rubber floor mat. It appeared an attempt had been made to wash out the car, but the blood clot was missed because it was attached to the underside of the mat.

Things looked bad for Harry Robertson, but it was not because of information given to the police by Clarence Stephenson. He refused to say anything bad about this employer. From his cell, he sent a letter to his sister, Josie. He wrote that he "would die before he would lie on" Robertson and his wife. He asked that Josie get a message to Mrs. Robertson and tell her that he had been moved to the Williamson jail to keep anyone from seeing him. He also wanted her to know he "will not do anything to hurt Mr. Harry or her." He wanted Josie to tell Louise to stand up and help him and Mr. Harry. He knew that things would go hard for himself and his employer, but he said that the police didn't know anything that would hurt them.

But Clarence Stephenson didn't know yet that he had already been chosen as a lamb to the slaughter.

On July 29, a huge crowd of people, numbering as many as 1,000 and many carrying their own chairs, began gathering in front of the Logan County courthouse. Some came as early as 6:00 a.m., all hoping to gain admittance to the hearing.

Magistrate Elba Hatfield was in charge of the proceedings. He was already in place when Jack Thurman arrived and when Harry Robertson and Clarence Stephenson were brought in under guard. Stephenson had his hands cuffed in front of him, but Robertson's hands were free. Both men sat calmly at the witness table, and while Stephenson stared straight ahead, Robertson constantly wet his lips and looked around the room.

A few minutes later, Louise Robertson was escorted into the grand jury room by Robertson's boarder and police witness, Oscar Townsend. She walked to her husband's side and kissed him lightly on the cheek. Then, she sat down next to him and placed an arm around his shoulders. Huddled close, they proceeded to whisper back and forth to one another for about 10 minutes. They were then joined by Judge Estep and C. C. Chambers, attorneys for Robertson and Stephenson. Prosecutors Hager and Scaggs sat down at the other end of the long table.

The Grand Jury panel was made up of many of the county's prominent citizens, and many were associated with Harry Robertson. Instructions were given to the jury, and it was added that the murder of Mamie Thurman was one of the most gruesome in the county's history. The Grand Jury was charged, "If there is enough evidence to indict the parties responsible, the court expects you to do so."

Testimony was then given concerning the discovery and autopsy of Mamie's body and the collection of the physical evidence in Robertson's house and car. Later, Harry himself was called to the stand. His testimony was the most shocking of the day. On the stand, Robertson recalled an almost two-year affair between himself and Mamie Thurman. He testified that he and Mamie often met at the "Key Club," which was frequented by many well-known and wealthy businessmen and their "lady friends." Both male and female members had passkeys to the place, and in these private rooms, they enjoyed parties, illicit affairs, and drunken orgies. Robertson also said that Mamie gave him a list of 16 different men with whom she had engaged in sex. She had given it to him about a year before when they had worked together at the bank. He noted, "One of the men is dead, all except three live in the city of Logan, and all are married but one."

Robertson went on to say that he continued to see Mamie, even though she refused to stop sleeping with other men. He testified that Clarence Stephenson was often the "go-between" for his trysts with Mamie. He also admitted to having "improper relations" with Mamie on many occasions, but he had last seen her at around 8.00 p.m. on the night she had been killed. He did not see her again after that, he said, and he had nothing to do with her murder. The jury seemed pleased with Robertson's testimony, but apparently, Stephenson was not as convincing.

During his testimony, the handyman also refuted the charges that he had been involved in Mamie Thurman's death. He corroborated the testimony of Harry Robertson and denied seeing Mamie on the day she was killed. He also told of being moved from the jail in Logan to Williamson. He was driven by a state trooper along an isolated road over Trace Mountain. At a bend in the road, they came upon two cars parked off to the side and surrounded by several men. Shots were fired in their direction, and one of the troopers told Stephenson that it was a mob and asked if he was afraid. They urged him to tell all that he knew, or it was likely that he would be "taken off." Stephenson replied, "If I was making a dying statement, it would be that I don't know any more than I've told."

One odd incident took place during Stephenson's testimony that has never been explained. At one point, he suddenly stopped talking and pointed out into the courtroom as though he were deathly afraid. However, he would not tell what he saw. Then, strangely, the prosecutor asked, "What do you see – Mrs. Thurman?"

But ghost or not, Clarence refused to answer.

At the end of the session, Magistrate Hatfield told the Grand Jury that all the evidence was circumstantial but claimed it was very damaging against both defendants. The jury ended their four-day inquiry, and the next day, a newspaper headline screamed: "Harry Robertson Not Indicted!" Clarence Stephenson, it was decided by the jury, would stand trial alone for the murder of Mamie Thurman.

The community was stunned and angered. Although it's doubtful that any mob violence was actually planned during the incident with Stephenson and the state troopers, there was talk of vigilante action after the hearing. There were several Ku Klux Klan members in the community who not only wanted revenge on the handyman for his alleged killing of Mamie Thurman but also because they believed that he was having sexual relations with her. This was contrary to Harry Robertson's statement, but rumors and whispers of violence continued to spread. Nothing ever came of them, however, and Stephenson remained safely locked away in jail.

Stephenson's trial began on Monday, September 10, at the Logan County courthouse. Hundreds of spectators packed into the building, the balcony, and the public gallery and even lined the hallways. Many others waited outside and hoped to get a seat inside at some point during the proceedings. A man who left his seat in the gallery found it immediately filled.

The first witnesses were R. L. Harris and a Dr. Rowan, who had examined Mamie's body. They described the location where the corpse was found and the condition of the body. They again pointed out that Mamie had been killed by two bullets to the head before her throat had been cut.

They were followed on the witness stand by Jack Thurman, who stated that he had worked his regular shift from 6.00 p.m. until 6.00 a.m. on June 21. He said he had last seen his wife at 5:30 in the evening. He testified, "I was working my beat with Hibbard Hatfield, and I telephoned my wife shortly before one in the morning. When she didn't answer, I went home and found that her bed had not been slept in." Thurman would not see his wife again until the next day when he identified her body at the Harris Funeral Home.

Thurman had to constantly be told to speak up throughout his testimony as his voice rose and fell in volume. Even when he was cross-examined by the defense, who tried to portray his relationship with his wife as rocky, Thurman remained quiet. He stated that he and Mamie did not argue on the afternoon of her death and that they were on good terms. He repeated his earlier assertions about Mamie's faithfulness, which caused a newspaper writer to later describe his statements as "pitiful."

The next witness was Fannette Jones, an African American woman who lived on High Street. According to her testimony, Robertson and Mamie often met at her house for their rendezvous. Jones testified that Mamie had come to her house about 8:00 p.m. on the evening she was killed. She stayed for only about 10 minutes and then left.

Other witnesses included Mattie Bell, a laundrywoman who worked for Mrs. Robertson. There was also Nadine Mabney, a drugstore employee who sold Mamie a pack of cigarettes at about 8:30 p.m.; Jack White, a teenager who said that he saw Mamie shortly before dark; and Clyde White, who testified to seeing Mamie enter the house of Fannette Jones and stay there "several minutes." All these witnesses were used to create the prosecution's timeline of events on the night of the murder, as was the testimony of W. L. Brand, who saw Mamie about 9:00 p.m. on the night of her death.

The following witnesses were much more damaging to Stephenson. The first was E. F. Murphy, a local businessman who lived close to the Robertsons. He testified that he saw Stephenson alone when he came home from work on the day Mamie was killed. He also stated that he saw Clarence and Mamie together around 6:00 or 7:00 that evening. Another witness, Sherman Ferguson, also claimed to have seen Mamie with Stephenson that same night. He spotted the handyman driving a Ford sedan while he was downtown that evening.

Harry Robertson provided the most stunning testimony of the entire trial. The newspapers reported that Robertson's testimony "almost brought the crowded courtroom to its feet on several occasions when he revealed the sordid details of his relationship with Mamie Thurman."

Robertson slowly began to reveal the truth behind his "hunting expeditions" with Mamie Thurman and the two-year deception he and Mamie had perpetrated on his wife and Jack Thurman. He began by testifying that he had known the Thurmans for seven or eight years and that he and Mamie began their affair while working at the bank. His relationship with Stephenson had been as a friend and an employer. The defendant maintained an apartment in the attic of the Robertson home, and they often went hunting together at the cabin on Trace Mountain. Stephenson usually accompanied him to the cabin, bringing along the dogs in the back of the sedan. Stephenson had always been welcome to use the automobile when it was not being taken to the cabin.

Robertson testified that the last time he saw Mamie was around 8:00 p.m. on the day she was killed. He left his house shortly after that to take his children to a swimming pool in Stollings. That was the last time that he saw her, he said, but added that Stephenson was in the house at that time. After returning to town, he said he dined at the Smokehouse Restaurant until 9:00 p.m. with his son, where they had listened to a prizefight on the radio. The Ford was gone when he returned home. His wife later confirmed his whereabouts on that evening.

Harry explained that he and Mamie would often meet at the mountain cabin and that sometimes she would take a taxi to meet him. Incidentally, all the taxi bills were found to be charged to Jack Thurman. So if he ever even once looked at the bills, then he was undoubtedly lying about his belief that Mamie had been faithful to him.

Mamie always returned home around 11:00 p.m. After leaving the cabin, Stephenson would meet her at 21 Holden Store and take her back to Logan. He said that Mrs. Robertson didn't know about the routine but probably "suspicioned."

He also said that he went hunting at Crooked Creek the Saturday before the murder and that Mamie was with him at the time. He said that he had no "engagement" with her at that time but later went to Fannette Jones' house and was with Mamie for about an hour. Stephenson then took her home. He testified that this was the last time he had sex with her before her death, and while he and Mamie had planned to go on another "hunting trip" the following Tuesday, he had called it off on the afternoon of her death—which was very convenient.

On October 13, Louise Robertson took the stand. The newspaper reported that the crowd anxiously awaited her testimony and that "they strained to hear every word." She stated her name and address and said that she had been married to Harry Robertson for 18 years, and they had a 14-year-old daughter and an 8-year-old son. She admitted that she knew Mamie Thurman and had been friends with her, but the relationship had cooled off. She said, "I stopped going around with Mrs. Thurman last January... I had reasons to believe that she and my husband were intimate, and I wouldn't be around with a woman that was intimate with my husband."

When questioned about where her husband was on the day Mamie was murdered, she explained that her husband had left for work that morning, returning home for lunch, and then came home in the evening at the usual time. She then added that he took the children to the swimming pool in Stollings that evening. After their return, all of them had dinner together, and then Robertson drove his Packard "around the block" because he had recently had some work done on it and wanted to test it out. After that, he and his son left to listen to a prizefight and promised to be back around 9:00 p.m. She went on to say that her husband had uncharacteristically washed the dishes after dinner. This was a job that Stephenson usually did, but her husband told her that the handyman was ill. She also noted that she saw Stephenson in the dining room after her husband left and that he "was in the kitchen a time or two." She said that she heard him leave the house later and that he returned a little while after the family went to bed. She told the prosecutor: "I heard him come upstairs and close his door. I never heard Clarence anymore that night after 11 o'clock."

The defense, still trying to throw suspicion onto Robertson, questioned Louise about the guns that her husband kept in the house. She simply answered that she didn't know anything about guns, other than that they were kept put away and out of the reach of the children. She stated, "My husband had a gun, but I don't know what kind, as I don't know anything about pistols."

Mrs. Robertson's response, when questioned about her husband's alleged affairs with Mamie, was described as "very unusual." She replied to the questioning, "I learned they were intimate with each other because I had cause to believe they were. A woman doesn't have to be told these things." She claimed that no one told her about the affair, but her "woman's intuition" caused her to become suspicious.

She was then asked if she had ever spoken to Mamie about the affair. She replied, "No, but I was talking to Mrs. Thurman once, and she told me that someone had told her that she had better watch her husband. I told her that if her husband is ever untrue to you, you won't have to be told, you'll know it. I had an enmity toward Mrs. Thurman. Of course, I cared and was hurt... but what was the use to be mad about it?"

While there was nothing very damaging in Mrs. Robertson's testimony against Clarence Stephenson, the same could not be said for the police officers that testified. Of course, these men were friends and co-workers of Jack Thurman and undoubtedly wanted to see the man they believed to be the killer properly punished. That's not to say that they lied about the investigation, but things certainly became heated during the examinations. One intense moment came when defense attorney Chambers began baiting Logan patrolman Bill Bruce about the bloody rags found in Harry Robertson's basement. He suggested that the police had planted them there, and Bruce became angry. He shouted at Chambers, "If it wasn't for paying a fine, I'd slap your face!"

Chambers snapped back, "Oh, no, you wouldn't slap my face here or any other place!"

The judge banged his gavel and shouted down to both of them, "If you men don't hush, I'll have you both sent to jail!"

In addition to Bruce's testimony, Police Chief Smeltzer testified that he saw Stephenson cleaning out the inside of Robertson's Ford Sedan at about 8:00 a.m. on Wednesday, the day that Mamie's body was discovered. Patrolman Bruce was with him when they drove by the house.

After both the defense and the prosecution rested in the trial, the judge began his final instructions to the jury.

But a rather strange event occurred in the last few minutes of the case. Several women discovered two envelopes in the gallery addressed to one of the prosecutors, John Chafin. The notes were signed by "A Voter" and "A Citizen," and each claimed that the writer had seen the murder of Mamie Thurman committed. They also went on to state that the writer believed the crime would be "whitewashed" and would go the way that other crimes had gone in Logan County. The notes added, "We believe there are people here who saw that woman get in the car and go to her death. We believe there are those who saw her get into the car and go up Trace Mountain." The prosecutors later announced that they didn't think there was anything to the letters.

Stephenson was allowed to make a statement to the court before the jury began its deliberations. He insisted, "I am not guilty. I have no knowledge of the crime that I am accused of. I tried to tell the truth... I hope the law won't stop until they find the guilty parties."

The jury was only out for 50 minutes before returning with a "guilty" verdict against Clarence Stephenson. However, they did pass on a recommendation of mercy, charging against the death penalty and opting for life in prison instead. A life sentence was handed down on October 13, and Stephenson was given 90 days to appeal to the Supreme Court.

On November 15, pleas from the Logan County Branch of the NAACP went out across the county to raise the $600 needed for

Stephenson's appeal. Many churches in Logan began accepting donations, and more than 3,000 people attended a meeting in Stephenson's support. The money was raised, but despite all the efforts on his behalf, the Supreme Court turned down his appeal in 1933.

Stephenson remained in the Logan County Jail for some time and was later transferred to the West Virginia State Penitentiary at Moundsville. The state prison was a horrible place in those years, but Stephenson strangely never served "hard time." One Logan resident, Normal Sloan, who served time with Stephenson both in the Logan County jail and at Moundsville, said that Stephenson received catered meals while incarcerated in Logan County. Sloan said, "Everything was carried to him three times a day from the New Eagle Restaurant."

After being transferred to Moundsville, Stephenson served as Warden Oral Skeens' chauffeur. Thanks to this, he was kept away from the often brutal conditions of the prison. According to Sloan, Stephenson continued to deny that he committed the murder, but he did admit that he played a hand in Mamie Thurman's demise. Sloan recalled many years later, "He told me he was hired to take the body to 22 Mountain, and that he didn't do anything to Mamie Thurman. He never did say who killed her, but he said that he didn't do it. Stephenson told me it was all politics."

On June 11, 1939, Stephenson was transferred out of Moundsville and was sent to the Huttonsville Prison Farm, where he died of stomach cancer on April 24, 1942. He never spoke to the authorities of the things he knew about Mamie's death, and he carried the secrets of the crime to his grave.

As time has passed, most have realized that Stephenson was little more than a scapegoat in the case - and that Mamie Thurman's real killer was never punished.

The story of Mamie Thurman has never really ended. There are many strange events, mysteries, and unanswered questions that have followed Mamie to the grave. Investigations into her death continued for years, and most believe that it's still officially unsolved.

There are dozens of questions that still linger about what took place in 1932. Unfortunately, most of these questions will never be answered, thanks to the fact that many of the details were so conveniently erased from history shortly after the trial occurred. Even the courtroom transcripts and 17 deposition copies have disappeared.

Many believe that Stephenson took the blame for events that were set into motion by prominent citizens of the area, working to cover up their own illicit activities. Who killed her and why so brutally? Was her death caused because of something she knew or something she had done? Was her broken neck a key to her death? Was her slashed throat, so unnecessary after two bullets to the head, intended as a warning to others about talking too much? Why was the list of 16 men that Mamie slept with suppressed at the trial? What was Harry Robertson's real role in her death? Why didn't Louise Robertson divorce her husband after learning of his affair with Mamie? Why wasn't Louise Robertson ever suspected of the murder of the woman who was sleeping with her husband?

And the list goes on and on.

Later inquiries, while not answering any of these questions, have discovered several rather unusual things that took place and were learned after the trial of Clarence Stephenson. Regrettably, many of these strange facts have triggered even more unanswered questions.

After the trial was over, Prosecutor Chafin appeared before a board of city commissioners on behalf of Jack Thurman, who had been refused bond to return to work as a police officer. After a closed-door session, Thurman was returned to duty as a Logan patrolman. However, it was reported that he died a few years later in an insane asylum in Louisville, Kentucky.

Although Mamie's funeral services were conducted at the Nighbert Memorial Church and even then described as "the most unusual funeral ever in Logan County," a check of the records at the church showed no listing of Mamie Thurman ever having been a member, having been baptized there, or married there. Defense attorney C. C. Chambers was placed in charge of these records. Shortly after the murder case, Reverend Gamble of the Methodist Church left Logan and was not heard from again. R. F. Caverlee, the pastor of the First Baptist Church, who also officiated at Mamie's funeral, transferred to a church in Fredericksburg, Virginia, soon after the trial.

On Friday, December 30, 1932, a road crew discovered several bloodstained garments and a long-bladed hunting knife near the spot where Mamie Thurman's body was discovered. The knife was covered with what was thought to be blood. Foreman Joe Buskirk said, "It is only a miracle that my men discovered the rags and knife." Whatever became of these items is unknown. Could they have cleared Clarence Stephenson? We will never know.

And things got even stranger in 1985. In that year, a man named George Morrison, who was a half-brother of Mamie's, came to Logan looking for his sister's grave. Morrison lived in New Mexico and had only just learned about his half-sister and her violent death. He wanted to erect a proper headstone on her grave, and it was at this point, it was learned that her correct burial records were missing. Some said that she was buried in the Logan Memorial Park in McConnell, and others claimed that she had been moved to Kentucky. No cemetery records existed to prove anything either way, and no marker could be located to show where she had been interred.

Morrison placed a legal advertisement in the *Logan Banner*, searching for information. He received several calls from the ad, all of them strange.

One of the callers claimed that a prominent doctor had paid him to exhume Mamie's body back in 1962. He refused to identify himself.

A woman called and said that she had once owned a cemetery map that marked the location of Mamie's grave. She no longer had it because someone had purchased it from her for $1,000. The man who bought it did not give his name.

Another man wrote in reply to the advertisement and asked Morrison to phone his home. He gave his name simply as "George." Morrison said that the man sounded elderly, and he claimed to be a retired Logan businessman. He also claimed to know everyone involved in the original case, including Mamie, the Robertsons, Stephenson, and others. "George" told Morrison that a woman had killed Mamie and that the deed had been covered up.

Morrison was skeptical about all the calls and began to realize that Mamie's death was a mystery that would probably never be solved.

What really happened to Mamie Thurman? How did she spend her last terrifying moments? We will never know for sure, and perhaps, for this reason, her ghost has long been reported to walk the hills around the town of Logan. Some believe that her ghostly appearances are caused because she cries out for justice, while others believe that she wants her final resting place to be found. Perhaps it is both - but regardless, her crying phantom has long been a part of local lore.

The ghostly tales began not long after the dark events of the murder trial started to fade from immediate memory. Hikers, motorists, and even Boy Scouts who had any reason to be near Trace Mountain began to tell of seeing a woman in white wandering in the woods near where Mamie's body had been discovered. The reports claimed that she could be heard crying and that the smell of flowers always accompanied the sightings. The strange scent would even occur in the winter when no flowers were in bloom.

A man who used to deliver supplies to a coal mine located near the murder site once had a rather startling experience in his truck. One night, as he was driving along the old road, he was suddenly overwhelmed by the smell of flowers, and an ice-cold chill swept through the cab of his vehicle. He had never heard the stories of Mamie Thurman's ghost, but when he mentioned the incident to a friend, she quickly filled him in on the story. He decided then and there that he would never travel that road again.

According to some, the old bridge near where Mamie was found is also haunted by her ghost. The road across the bridge leads back to some old coal mines, and a driver must travel down a steep incline before reaching the bridge. The stories say that if a car is parked on the bridge and shifted into neutral, the vehicle will roll backward up the hill. No one has been able to explain why this occurs, but local lore has it that the spirit of Mamie Thurman causes it.

And these are not the only stories. Perhaps the most famous and most commonly told are the accounts of the spectral woman who has been picked up along the old mine road. She is described as wearing a white dress and having dark hair that curls under her ears in the style of the 1930s. The pale woman is often given a ride back in the direction of Logan, but then she vanishes from the car long before it reaches its destination.

Could this phantom hitchhiker be Mamie Thurman?

Many believe so, and a general belief in hauntings would suggest that it might possibly be - but then again, what about the tale of Mamie Thurman is truly as it seems? That is another question about this strange case that will probably never be answered.

THE SAUSAGE MAKER'S WIFE
LOUISA LUETGERT

On May 1, 1897, Louisa Luetgert - the wife of one of Chicago's premier businessmen and sausage-makers - vanished without a trace. She was last seen in the company of her husband, Adolph. They walked across the street from the Luetgert home and into the sausage factory.

Her disappearance and probable murder caused a sensation in Chicago, especially when word leaked out about where she was last seen. It became the only crime in the city's history that affected the sales of a food item for an entire summer and even spawned a wicked little rhyme about Luetgert's missing wife.

As the years passed, a legend has grown, stating that not only does Louisa still haunt the neighborhood where she died but that she hounded her murderous husband from Joliet Penitentiary to the grave.

But the story of Louisa Luetgert cannot be told without first recounting the history of her husband, Adolph. Born in Germany on December 27, 1845, he came from a well-off family that had been selling animal hides, tallow, and wool for four generations. He came to America after the Civil War, landing in New York with just $30 in his pocket. He lived for a time with family friends in Quincy, Illinois, and then moved to Chicago.

He didn't know anyone when he arrived in the city. "I had three cents then," he later said. "A stranger handed me a quarter that morning. I bought my breakfast and then went out to hustle for jobs."

Luetgert began visiting leather shops, looking for a tannery where he could ply the trade he'd learned back home in Germany. He soon found a job with Union Hide and Leather Company, but the business closed a month later. He spent the summer looking for work. When the weather was warm, he worked as a mover. When winter arrived, he got a job in a meatpacking plant. He spent the next few years working for tanneries, saving his money, and planning for the future.

On October 8, 1871, the Great Chicago Fire leveled most of the city, destroying the downtown area. When the fire finally stopped moveing northward at Lincoln Park, several hundred people were dead. It had stopped just short of the place where Luetgert lived. When Chicago began to rebuild a few days later, Luetgert decided he was ready for a change.

Having saved $4,000 from his tannery work, he went into business for himself in 1872 and married Christine Roepke. They bought a lot on the North Side and had a cottage moved there. Luetgert began a wholesale liquor business in the basement. The couple had a son named Max, who died before he was two. Another boy, Arnold, was born, and then Caroline died from peritonitis in November 1877. Luetgert sent his son to live with Caroline's family until he could find a new wife.

His search only lasted two months. In January 1878, he married Louisa Bicknese, who had arrived from Germany just five years earlier. She was a beautiful young woman with light hair and a pale complexion and was nine years younger than her husband. She barely spoke a word of English. She worked as a household maid in the Fox River Valley and met the man who would be her husband by chance. He was immediately taken with her, entranced by her diminutive stature and tiny frame. She was only five feet tall and looked almost child-like next to her burly husband. As a wedding gift, he gave her a unique, heavy gold ring. Inside of it, he had her new initials inscribed, reading "L.L."

Little did he know at the time that this ring would prove to be his undoing.

In 1879, they sold their property for $10,000, moved to Clybourn and Webster in the Lake View neighborhood, and opened a saloon and liquor store. It would be here where Adolph Luetgert would have his first brush with the law.

On the morning of September 11, 1879, the body of a millwright named Hugh McGowan was found in a barn on Luetgert's property. His head had been cut open, and a huge plug of tobacco had been shoved down this throat.

McGowan had been missing for two days. He'd last been seen drinking in Luetgert's saloon. Around 10:00 p.m. that night, a man named Fred Butler was supposed to take the very inebriated McGowan home but left him in the barn to sober up instead. Hugh's 17-year-old son, James, went searching for this father later that night, visiting the old man's favorite places to drink, including Luetgert's place, but the bar was closed by the times James got there at 11:00 p.m.

It was Luetgert who found the body on September 11. The newspapers reported that McGowan had died from an overdose of whiskey. James McGowan admitted that his father was a "hard-drinking man," but it was unusual for him to stay out all night. In addition, he couldn't imagine how the tobacco had gotten jammed in his throat. His father never used plugged tobacco. He believed that someone had hit his father over the head and then strangled him by shoving the tobacco into this throat. McGowan's body had been found in an unusual position, too - propped up in a sitting position against a pile of boards.

According to Luetgert, Hugh had gone into the barn to sleep because he was afraid to go home in such a drunken state. But his family said they had never given him trouble about his drinking. Why would he have feared coming home? James McGowan was convinced that his father had met a violent end - and he believed Luetgert had something to do with it.

The coroner held an inquest, calling Luetgert as a witness. The jury ruled that McGowan had died "from asphyxia caused by a large quid of tobacco lodging in his throat and bronchial tubes while he was in a state of intoxication."

James disagreed with the coroner's jury. The jurors, he said, had been Luetgert's neighbors and friends. James demanded a postmortem examination. He chose a physician to represent him at the examination and go with him to the morgue. When they arrived, though, they found the postmortem had already taken place. James protested, but the coroner refused to investigate any further.

Adolph and Louisa had three children in the 1880s; Louise, who died from cholera when she was ten months old; a boy named Louis, who had a long life; and then Elsa, who died when she was 14 months old, another victim of cholera.

Luetgert's saloon remained profitable, and expenses were low since the family lived in a small apartment above the saloon, but Luetgert wanted more. He sold the business for $10,000 and bought a butcher shop and meat delivery route on North Avenue. He also sold meat out the back door to neighbors and began making sausage on the side. After a short time, the sausage sales were making more money than his regular meat business. At this point, though, he hadn't figured out how to store the sausage during the warm months. He shut that part of his business down on April 1 each year, sold what remained in stock, and started making sausage again in the fall.

He was making good money, but it was hard work and required a lot of his attention. Worse, he suffered from poor health. He had frequent indigestion and sometimes coughed up blood. His doctor blamed it on liver congestion. The only thing that seemed to help was drinking Hunyadi mineral water, which was claimed to help those with stomach and liver problems and cure constipation.

The work seemed too much for him, and he decided to quit and buy a 60-acre farm in Elgin, a town northwest of Chicago. It was a significant change from the city, and Louisa hated it. After a mental patient escaped one night from a nearby asylum - and Louisa had a close encounter with him - she put her foot down. They had to return to Chicago.

Luetgert decided to return to the meat business, or specifically to sausages, which had been his biggest money-maker. He built a packing house and factory at North and Sheffield Avenues in Chicago, which employed about 50 men. He became the first sausage-maker in the city to manufacture his product in the summer and winter. Serving as his own foreman, he was soon selling over $100,000 worth of sausage each year.

The family lived in a flat on the factory's third floor, but Louisa hated the smell, the smoke, and the constant noise, so they moved out. They lived in a few other homes over the next couple of years, and in 1892, Louisa gave birth to their last child, Elmer.

That same year, Luetgert bought a five-acre parcel of land at Hermitage and Diversey for $30,000. He then spent an additional $140,000 building a factory and a large home for the family on the land. He subdivided what was left into 18 smaller lots on which houses would eventually be built. It was here that he would achieve his greatest success - and his continued infamy.

Luetgert had a terrible reputation in the neighborhood where he established his home and family. He became the source of many rumors - some true, some not - that would eventually lead to an easy belief that he had committed murder. Neighbors considered him arrogant and boastful. He didn't associate with people in the local taverns or even with other Germans. Luetgert would later say this was because he was so busy building his business that he didn't have time for friends and acquaintances.

But he seemed to have time to carry on affairs with some of the women in the neighborhood, though. He was not a happily married man. He had a roaming eye and often bragged of his enormous sexual appetites. He was said to have been involved with a wealthy German woman named Christine Feldt and Mrs. Agatha Tosch, who owned a nearby saloon with her husband. He later became involved with Mary Simerling, a household servant and his wife's niece, and this proved to be the breaking point in his marriage.

In 1893, Chicago hosted the World's Columbian Exposition, but this was of little interest to Luetgert. He encouraged his family to go and enjoy the fair, but he claimed to be too busy to attend himself. He didn't set foot on the fairgrounds, but his sausage was on sale in a German restaurant there in the Manufacturer's Pavilion. The restaurant disguised his sausage as an import from Europe, and no one knew the difference.

When the World's Fair closed that fall, the financial problems that had been looming over the economy during the exposition caused a full-blown panic and depression. Factories shut down, stores closed, and one-fifth of Chicagoans lost their jobs. Families came close to starving. Children were sent out to steal food or to look for scraps in garbage cans. The destitute tried to earn change by sweeping sidewalks and opening doors for businessmen. At night, sleeping men occupied the corridors of City Hall.

Until the time of the Columbian Exposition, Luetgert had been making a fortune in the sausage business. But now, many of those who had ordered from him were unable to sell the product. Luetgert made deals, shaving money off outstanding bills and trying to keep the factory open. Louisa constantly harassed him about sinking all their savings into the packing plant. The Lake View laborers who had lost their jobs still imagined that Luetgert was rich but the men still working in the factory saw how Louisa worked day and night, despite having a servant. She never appeared to spend any of her husband's money.

Luetgert had taken out a $50,000 loan to pay for his building. In 1896, he still owed on the entire note and was paying 6-percent interest on it. He often found himself a few thousand dollars short of making payroll or covering supply costs, so he would go to   the bank for another loan, paying it back a week later.

He was soon in desperate straits and tried to sell the business to a friend, William Charles, for $200,000. Charles accepted the offer and even drew up the papers, but the sale was never closed. Luetgert later said the deal fell through because he could not clear the property of the $50,000 mortgage.

Just as Charles' option on the factory was about to expire in the fall of 1896, Charles introduced Luetgert to an Englishman named Robert Davey, who said he wanted to invest in the Luetgert sausage business. Davey claimed to have nearly $37 million in backing from banks and investors all over Europe. He carried letters of credit from many banking firms.

"And I, as a damned fool, took it for granted they were all right," Luetgert later said.

Davey turned out to be an experienced con artist and had even been profiled in the *Chicago Inter Ocean* in 1893. If only Luetgert hadn't been "working too hard to read the papers," he might have recognized him. Davey had been chased out of Chicago by police detectives and newspaper reporters three years earlier but had returned in 1896, much to Luetgert's bad luck.

Using information he'd gathered from other businessmen, he specifically chose Luetgert as a target. He first worked out a deal with Charles to drop his option to buy the A.L. Luetgert Sausage and Packing Company. Luetgert then met Davey at his hotel to sign papers to incorporate the company and issue $225,000 in bonds. Davey claimed that he already had buyers for the bonds in Antwerp and other distant cities. Luetgert would get $200,000 in cash and $100,000 in stock while continuing to run the business with an annual salary of $5,000.

It seemed too good to be true, but Luetgert's lawyers were the only ones who thought it was. When Davey wanted to take the bonds to New York himself, they insisted on sending the bonds through a banker, holding them in escrow until Luetgert had received money from the investors. Davey tried to convince them he was a legitimate businessman, but they weren't convinced.

Adolph Luetgert was, however. The business property that had been Luetgert's - including the "buildings, boilers, engines, all certain formulas, special mixtures, trade secrets" - now belonged to the newly incorporated A.L. Luetgert Sausage and Packing Company.

The expenses of incorporating the sausage company needed to be covered, and Davey expected Luetgert to do so. Luetgert said he gave Davey between $3,000 and $4,000. Increasingly strapped for cash, Luetgert mortgaged 18 residential lots for $3,000 on February 25, 1897, with Christine Feld as the lien holder - even though he had already sold some of the lots to other buyers. The next day, he borrowed $30,000 using the factory as collateral. The loan was due in six months. On March 5, he went to a different bank and again used the factory as collateral to get an additional $7,000.

In late February, Davey took a trip to New York - paid for by Luetgert to "meet investors." Soon afterward, Luetgert received a telegram from a Dr. John Phillips of New Haven, Connecticut, claiming Davey was sick with rheumatic fever. Luetgert went to New York to search for Davey but found that he was not at the hotel he had given as his address. Luetgert went to New Haven and discovered that Dr. Phillips was an elderly man who had not practiced medicine in more than 15 years. The doctor had never heard of Davey and had sent no telegram.

Davey was gone and with him went most of Luetgert's remaining money.

A month passed before Luetgert told Louisa what had happened. She had been very excited about the company's reorganization because the influx of cash meant that they could move away from the factory. Luetgert later said that he just couldn't break the bad news to her. When he did, Louisa was heartbroken. She was angry, hurt, and upset - and she didn't know the whole story. "I didn't tell her everything," Luetgert admitted, "because I was afraid it would make her far worse."

Luetgert closed the factory and laid off most of the workers. The butchers and salesmen who were in Luetgert's debt were unable to help him. Notes were coming due, and, without any income, it was almost inevitable that creditors would seize the factory. All of Louisa's predictions were coming true. She continued to worry and pester him for allowing their debts to overwhelm them in the way they were doing.

Luetgert later insisted that he continued to provide for his wife, even in their dire financial state. He gave her money, he said, whenever she needed it. She always had a "washerwoman and a hired girl," and during a time when the children were sick, a nurse was there to help. "Louisa never needed to do hard work," Luetgert claimed. "She had all the help she wanted."

But people in the neighborhood told stories about the arguments between the couple. Luetgert's business losses took a terrible toll on his marriage. Louisa scolded her husband for his ways with other women. He was using them as solace from his troubles. As Matthew W. Pinkerton of the famous detective agency later stated: "He was an immoral man and was visited often by women of extremely doubtful character."

Friends and neighbors frequently heard him and Louisa arguing. Their disagreements became so heated that Luetgert eventually moved his bedroom from the house to a small chamber inside the factory. He used the excuse that he had to keep an eye on the empty building or, more unlikely, that he slept there to improve his health. Mary Simerling made Luetgert's bed in the office, and Louisa suspected she did more than just tuck in his sheets. The loud argument between Adolph and Louisa that followed the voicing of her suspicions gave the neighborhood a lot to talk about.

And soon, there was even more gossip. One night, during another shouting match with Louisa, Luetgert responded to her criticisms about business by taking his wife by the throat and choking her. Before she collapsed, Luetgert calmed down after seeing alarmed neighbors looking at him from the parlor window of their home, and he released her. A few days later, Luetgert was seen chasing his wife down the street. He was shouting at her and waving around a revolver. After a couple of blocks, Luetgert broke off the chase and walked silently back to the factory.

On February 13, one of the banks from which Luetgert had borrowed money became concerned that the factory might not be worth as much as his debts and took an inventory of the property. Fred Mueller, a nephew of Louisa's, was the treasurer for the company and later stated that Luetgert approached him on the day before the inventory and told him, "I have fixed up a scheme so that the same sausage will be weighed a couple of times."

When the inspector from the bank had finished his work on the fifth floor, he asked for lights on the fourth floor, but Luetgert told him they were broken but would be fixed the next morning. When the inspector left for the day, Luetgert had his men move all the meat that had been counted on the fifth floor down to the fourth and third floors of the factory so it could be counted again.

Mueller also said Luetgert had ordered him to fill out a false set of accounting books, making it seem as though the business was profiting $30,000 and $40,000 each year when it was actually losing money. Mueller tried to tell him that the bank would not believe it, but Luetgert told him they would - he had done it before. He later got nervous, though, and burned the books, although he did continue a scheme that he had to pad the payroll by withdrawing cash for himself under various names.

Later that same month, Luetgert told Louisa's brother, Diedrich Bicknese, that Davey's swindle had left him in a bad place. He said the "damn Jews" at the bank were going to close him down, so he wanted to take some of his property to Bicknese's farm to hide them from his creditors.

Louisa overheard the conversation and pointed out that her husband's deception made him just as reprehensible as the man who had swindled him. Diedrich later remembered Luetgert's reaction: "Luetgert jumped up and looked as if he meant to strike her and then began walking up and down the room. I went out to the stable and directly Luetgert came out and said, 'I guess we'll drop that. The old woman is liable to go and report me.'"

On April 3, Luetgert told Diedrich that he had given up all hope of saving his company. He only wanted to salvage what he could from it. He said he had managed to get $8,000 out of the business and would get more if he had the time. He told Diedrich that he hoped to buy a farm and get into the chicken business.

In mid-April, Foreman Brothers bank - which held the mortgage on the factory - called Luetgert to their offices and demanded money. Luetgert protested because the loan was not due for another five months, but the bankers were adamant that at least $5,000 of the debt needed to be paid by May. Luetgert reluctantly agreed to try and come up with the money.

When he returned home, he told Louisa what had occurred at the bank. When she became upset, he assured her that everything was fine.

"Yes," she replied. "That's the same thing you told me when you came back from New York and you said everything is all right and I found out afterward everything was all wrong."

According to Luetgert, he still resisted telling her the truth, but when she pressed him for more information, he finally spilled the details of how bad things really were. He revealed how much money he lost to Davey, the amount he owed the banks, the money he owed to suppliers, and the money he owed to Swift and Company. "I was more afraid of the meatpackers than I was of the bank," he later said.

Louisa was in tears. She asked him if they were going to lose everything, and Luetgert lied once more. "No," he told her, "I don't believe the Foreman Brothers would take any act."

But Louisa didn't believe him. Her marriage had been built on lies, she now thought. Little by little, many believed, Louisa began to go mad.

A week or so after her confrontation with Luetgert, Louisa had to summon a doctor because their son Elmer was sick. When the family physician, Dr. Clarendon Rutherford, came to see the boy, he noticed that Louisa was "less tidy" than usual and appeared to be worried. She wore a vacant stare, he said, and sometimes seemed unaware of her surroundings. Rutherford surmised that she was going through "the change of life." Afraid to leave Louisa in charge of managing Elmer's medicine, he insisted that the family hire a nurse.

He soon learned this was not the first time that Louisa had behaved oddly. She had recently purchased a pair of dark red satin slippers. They were much too small for her feet, but she refused to return them. Instead, she placed them at her side and sat on the front porch, admiring the shoes.

Mary Simerling usually straightened Louisa's room each day, but in early April, Louisa began spending more time there, making it difficult for Mary to do her work. When Mary tried to clean, she usually found the door locked.

Or so she claimed.

One of Louisa's in-laws, Louis Balgamann, a farmer who lived south of Chicago, visited her the last week of April. He noticed nothing unusual about her mental condition. When Diedrich talked to his sister around this same time, he also saw nothing strange about her state of mind. He would come to believe that Luetgert convinced friends and employees to make up stories about Louisa's mental state so that he would have witnesses to her odd behavior when she suddenly disappeared.

And Diedrich was possibly correct. On April 27, Adolph Elandt, a delivery driver for the sausage company, stopped by the house and talked with Louisa. He said that she told him that "everything was gone, and she didn't think she could stand it any longer." She said that she was going to leave, and when he asked her where she planned to go, she said that she "would go out in the country and work as a hired girl, so no one would know her."

On April 28, another conveniently placed employee named Charles Bahanke claimed that he also spoke with Louisa. He was also told, he said, that she planned to run away to the country.

Frank Dettler, a friend of Luetgert's, also said he talked with Louisa that same day. He said, "She was crying and laughing, kind of shaking all over." Dettler asked her what was wrong, suggesting she seemed worried, and she replied, "Everything is gone now, everything is lost. I will not stay here anymore, I will go!" He stated that he tried to comfort her, but she seemed inconsolable.

That same week, Marcus Heineman, a former salesman for the company, came to the house looking for Luetgert. According to his statement, Louisa said that her husband was upstairs but wanted to be left alone. He was up there worrying about his business troubles. After that, she blurted out, "I am going away!"

Mary Charles, the wife of Luetgert's close friend William Charles, also spoke with Louisa during the last week of April. She testified that Louisa told her that if her husband were unable to repair his business, she would leave him.

Mary Simerling said that Louisa slept very little during the last week of April. She worried constantly. She claimed that three or four times in the night, Louisa came to Mary's bedroom and asked her to make her some whisky punch. Mary added that Louisa spent hours sitting in front of a window, looking out at the factory, or she walked from one room to another. She often muttered, "Everything is gone. I must leave."

Twice that week, Mary said she saw Louisa crying. She claimed that the other woman spoke dreamily of living in a castle on the lakeshore and wearing extravagant clothes. At other times, Louisa talked about going to the country, changing her name, and working as a servant girl.

One day, she recalled that Louisa helped her to gather up the dirty dishes after a meal. Louisa carelessly threw the dishes into the sink, breaking a cup. Mary said, "You want to be a little careful - you will break all of our new cups."

"Oh, I don't care," Louisa allegedly replied.

The last day of April was a Friday, and it was cleaning day in the Luetgert home, but Louisa told Mary not to worry about the housework - or so Mary told the police.

According to the young woman who was having an affair with Adolph Luetgert, Louisa said, "Never mind about the cleaning. I won't stay here long anymore."

Louisa's prediction turned out to be correct.

On May 1, 1897, Louisa Luetgert disappeared.

Mary Simerling - no surprise there - would later tell the police about Louisa's alleged actions on the day she vanished. She described how Louisa had buttoned her dress wrong that morning and wore it that way all day. "There was something wrong with her mind," Mary noted. Later in the day, she claimed that Louisa was constantly wringing her hands and saying that she wanted to go someplace where no one would find her.

Two more of Luetgert's employees - once again, no surprise - said they saw Louisa on May 1. William Follbach, a teamster, and Anton Schuster, a butcher, said they saw her sitting at a window knitting around 8:00 a.m. Follbach said that she seemed to be working around the house all day but offered no reason as to why he would have been watching her. In the afternoon, Schuster said that he filled some barrels with tallow and bones to be hauled away and looked across the street to see Louisa washing some windows. At least neither man claimed she was acting peculiar.

That evening, around 7:00 p.m., one of Louisa's neighbors, Amelia Kaiser, brought over a bowl of German cheese spread for the Luetgerts. She also noticed nothing out of the ordinary about Louisa's behavior.

Mary Simerling, who said she witnessed no quarrels in the Luetgert house that evening, went to bed around 8:00, while Louisa and Mrs. Kaiser were still talking. Louisa walked her neighbor home around 8:30. "She gave me four oranges and said I should take them to my children," Amelia later recalled.

Around 9:00 p.m. - which seems late for such a call - Louisa allegedly showed up at the home of Luetgert's friend, William Charles. His wife, Mary, said that Louisa wanted to know if any money had been raised from the sale of the factory. Mary said no money had been found. When Louisa left, she was said to have murmured that she couldn't stand it any longer. "I will go," she said in German.

One of the Luetgert children, Louis, had gone to the circus that evening with a friend, William Esau. Howe's London Circus had set up its tents a few blocks away at the corner of Diversey and Herndon. Louis later remembered that he got home that night around 10:00 p.m. He testified, "I went into the house by the rear door. My mother let me into the kitchen door."

Louis said that his mother was wearing a thin brown robe with red and blue figures on it and slippers on her feet. "She then went back to her chair. She sat down under the gas jet by the sink on the east side of the kitchen and started reading the newspaper again. The gas was lighted. There was no other light in the kitchen."

Louisa joked with him, asking him if the circus was worth 10-cents. Earlier in the day, he had asked his mother for the money to attend the show, and she had teasingly questioned if it was worth the expense.

Louis went on, "I went into the pantry and hung up my overcoat, and I came out and started talking about the circus. Then I saw my father come out. He carried a lantern, a thing which he always did when he intended to go to the office. He said it was getting rather late, and I should go to bed and talk about the circus in the morning. I went to my room and undressed. This took me four or five minutes. I talked with my brother Elmer when I got to bed.

"I never saw my mother after seeing her with the newspaper."

On Sunday, May 2, Mary Simerling rose at her normal time of 5:30 a.m. She ate breakfast with Luetgert while the children were still in bed. Later that morning, she realized that Louisa was not in the house.

According to Mary, Luetgert had gone to the factory earlier that morning but returned home between 10:00 and 11:00. They and the two children ate lunch together around noon. William Charles and another business associate arrived soon after that, and Luetgert left with them.

During this entire morning, Louisa had not been mentioned.

Agatha Tosch said that Luetgert came into her tavern between 2:00 and 4.00 in the afternoon. "He asked me for a glass of beer. He didn't say anything," she said. "I asked what was the matter with him, he looked so strange and excited in his face. He didn't answer me. He just told me he was going home to his house to change clothes. He looked very pale, as if he had not slept."

Mary said that Luetgert came home, changed clothes, and drank a cup of coffee before returning to the factory for the rest of the night.

On Monday morning, Luetgert went to see his lawyer, Adam Goodrich, to discuss his ongoing business problems. Goodrich called Foreman Brothers on the telephone and talked to them about the money his client owed. When Goodrich ended the call, he told Luetgert that problems were ahead.

Luetgert shook his head. "That is not the greatest trouble I have," he sighed.

"What else has happened to you? I thought this was trouble enough." Goodrich answered.

"My wife left me on Saturday night," Luetgert said.

Goodrich would later claim that Luetgert broke down in tears but added that he wasn't certain if his client was crying because his wife left him or about his business problems. He went on to say that she left him because of all his business troubles, and he didn't know where she was but might have gone to her sister's or her brother's homes.

Even to Goodrich, this seemed odd because it meant that Louisa would have abandoned her children. He asked Luetgert if perhaps he should contact the police.

"Oh no," Luetgert quickly answered. "She is with her brothers and sisters, and if it gets into the newspapers, she won't come back to me at all."

Goodrich thought about this for a moment and then said, "There is a better reason than that why you should not get it in the newspapers. If it gets in the newspapers, it will not help you in your trouble between you and your wife, and you will not be able to raise the money that you need. You had better look quietly around yourself and see where she is and try to get her to come back to you."

Before he left the office, Luetgert said that he would, but unless he planned to use a medium to contact the spirit world, he wouldn't be able to reach his wife.

On that same day, William Follbach, the teamster from the sausage factory, later told police that he stopped at the Luetgert house that morning and spoke with Mary Simerling. He asked about Louisa and was told she was "upstairs asleep."

Obviously, she wasn't.

On May 4, the Foreman Brothers bank seized control of Luetgert's factory. Frank Moan, from the Cook County Sheriff's Office, served the papers on Luetgert and began guarding the factory. He inspected the building and found it to be clean - it hadn't been producing anything for weeks - but Moan did notice at least 50 boxes of the kind of soap used for scrubbing the floors at the courthouse.

At 1:00 that afternoon, Diedrich Bicknese came to the Luetgert house looking for his sister. He spoke with Mary Simerling because Luetgert was not there. Mary told him that Louisa had been missing since Sunday morning. Diedrich asked her if Adolph and his sister had been fighting lately, and Mary said they had not quarreled for at least ten days.

At this point, Diedrich began what would become a fruitless search for his missing sister.

He went to the home of his other sister, Wilhelmina Mueller, and learned that Louisa wasn't there either. He returned to the Luetgert home around 4:00 p.m., and this time, his brother-in-law was home. Luetgert and two of his employees were putting some sort of incubation device that Luetgert had designed into the house's basement. Diedrich greeted him, watched for a few minutes, and then motioned Luetgert over to talk to him. They walked over near the gate to the yard, and Luetgert seemed anxious to tell Diedrich about the money they could make with this incubator, but Diedrich had more important things to discuss.

"Where is Louisa?" he demanded to know.

Luetgert shrugged, "Isn't she out at your place?"

"No. If she was out to my place, I wouldn't have to look for her here."

Diedrich asked where Luetgert thought she was, and he simply said he didn't know. - she might have gone away or wandered away. He didn't seem concerned at all about the fact that his wife, and the mother of his children, was missing. He didn't check to see if her clothing was still in the closets, he told Diedrich, but he knew she had a little money with her.

"When did you last see her?"

Luetgert said that she had returned from Amelia Kaiser's house at about 10:00 on Saturday night, and then he had taken his key and gone to the factory. That was the last time he had seen her. He was convinced that she had gone off with another man.

Diedrich found his story hard to believe, knowing his sister would not have run away with anyone and would not have left her children behind. "Have you done anything or tried to find out where she is?" he asked. "Are you going to do something?"

Luetgert told him that he had paid two private detectives $5 each to look for her - which was a lie - because he believed they could accomplish more than the Chicago police. He said it was no use to have anything published because Louisa would probably be coming back soon.

Diedrich was unsure what to think of Luetgert's behavior. He said to him bluntly, "Well, I think she is not alive. If she was, she wouldn't leave the children for three days. You know that."

Diedrich left Luetgert standing there in the yard. He said that he'd let Diedrich know if he found out anything in the next week or two, but Louisa's brother told him that wouldn't do. He'd be back in the morning - and every day after that until Louisa turned up.

Diedrich did return to the city on Wednesday, first going to Wilhelmina's home and then showing up on Luetgert's doorstep.

"I don't know anything new," Luetgert told him and then asked about a man who was selling a farm in Elgin. Diedrich impatiently turned the conversation back to his sister, but Luetgert left the room and lay down on the couch as if he were going to sleep.

Diedrich then questioned Mary again. He asked if any of Louisa's clothing was missing, but Mary told him that she was afraid to go into Louisa's bedroom because she was afraid Louisa would return and be angry at her for going in there. Diedrich said that he'd take the risk, and they entered the room together. All of Louisa's clothing was in its place. Only the nightdress and robe she had been wearing the previous Saturday night were gone.

Diedrich now feared the worst.

He wasn't ready to stop looking yet, though. He went to see Amelia Kaiser, visited cousins, and went to Kankakee to visit a relative with a farm in the area. He went to see Mary Simerling's parents, who lived in the same neighborhood. Louisa was nowhere to be found.

On Friday, he returned to Chicago and went to Wilhelmina's home. Together, they went to the Luetgert house around noon. Adolph was gone, so they decided to stay there and wait. One of the boys, Louis, asked his uncle, "Is mama at your house?"

Diedrich sadly told him that she was not.

"Well, I know where she is. She is at Mrs. Tew's on the West Side," Louis replied. "Mary told me so. Papa took her there in a buggy."

"How do you know that?"

"Mary told me that, too," the boy added. "Mama and Papa went downstairs together" after he had gone to bed on May 1.

Luetgert did not return home until 5:00. As he walked up the street, Diedrich got up and met him on the sidewalk. He told Luetgert that they needed to go inside because his sister wanted to talk to him. Wilhelmina confronted him in the kitchen, demanding to know where Louisa was. "If you do, say so," she snapped, "and save my brother from spending time and money."

Luetgert said they wouldn't believe him if he told them the truth.

"How can you be so still, and act like nothing happened?" Wilhelmina demanded.

Diedrich added, "Your wife is gone, and you act like nothing happened. Now, there is got to be something done. I have been all over. I can find nothing. If you don't report this matter to the police, I will. I want it cleared up."

Luetgert told them to go ahead and notify the police. He said it was no disgrace to him. Louisa's behavior would bring shame to the Bicknese family. Diedrich told him that he didn't care - he just wanted his sister to be found.

Diedrich and Wilhelmina left. After eating supper, Diedrich went to see Fred Mueller, Wilhelmina's son. At 8:00 p.m., they went to the Sheffield Avenue Police Station. They reported Louisa's disappearance to Captain Herman Schuettler, one of Chicago's rare honest police officers and an officer known for being "an honest but occasionally brutal detective."

The detective and his men began searching for Louisa the next morning. Two officers, Walter Dean and Martin Qualey were sent to the sausage factory to interview Luetgert. He wasn't there, and they spent two hours looking for him. At noon, they gave up and went back to the station.

At 5:00, Schuettler went to the Luetgert home with Inspector Michael Schaack and Lieutenant George Hutchinson. They arrived at the same time as Luetgert, and they all went into the house for some questions.

Captain Schuettler asked him about Louisa, and Luetgert blamed her disappearance on the fact that she had been "acting strange." He added, "I think she got crazy - one of her crazy spells."

He didn't report her disappearance, he claimed, because he didn't want the embarrassment when the story ended up in the newspapers. But Schuettler told him it was his responsibility to report that his wife was missing, adding that he didn't see how they would be embarrassing. If Louisa had gone insane, Luetgert had to take care of her, and the police would do whatever they could to help.

"Don't you know that we would assist in getting her?" Schuettler asked. "You've known me for a long time. We have been acquainted. Why didn't you come and tell me about it?"

Captain Schuettler was familiar with Luetgert and had dealings with him in the past. Schuettler recalled a time when the Luetgerts had lost their family dogs, an event that prompted several calls from Luetgert, but when his wife had gone missing, Luetgert had never contacted him. He later remembered, "It seemed strange to me that Luetgert, who had a short time recently insisted on a vigilant search for two great Dane dogs, should fail to report the disappearance of his wife."

After the interview with Luetgert, the search began in earnest. But the police were no longer convinced they were searching for a missing woman - they started to believe she was dead.

The police began searching alleyways and dragging the river, which was just a short distance west of the sausage factory. They also searched the clay pits, many of which were filled with water. They also looked through large piles of terra cotta at a factory down the street. The searches turned up nothing.

Men were sent to find out where Luetgert dumped the ashes from his factory. They found piles of ashes along Hermitage Avenue and sifting through them, one officer found half-burned strips of metal that looked as if they might have been part of a woman's corset. More officers with rakes came back on May 9 and found more pieces of metal. One officer also found a hairpin.

As some of the detectives were searching the neighborhood for clues, others were questioning neighbors and relatives. They soon heard all the accounts - as well as many rumors - about Louisa, Luetgert, and their noisy and violent quarrels. They also questioned many of Luetgert's employees.

While most of them backed up the accounts given by Luetgert, the teamster William Follbach - who had come back to the Luetgert house to check on Louisa but was told she was upstairs sleeping - told a story that no one else was telling - at first anyway.

According to Follbach, he had seen Louisa at the sausage factory around 10:30 on the night of May 1.

And he wasn't the only one. A neighborhood girl named Emma Schimke walked past the sausage factory with her sister that same night, and she recalled seeing Louisa and her husband walking toward the factory.

Soon, Frank Bialk, a night watchman at the factory, confirmed both of these stories. He had also seen Luetgert and Louisa at the plant that night. He only got one glimpse of Louisa but saw his employer several times. Shortly after the couple had entered the factory, Luetgert had come back outside and had given Bialk a dollar and asked him to get him a bottle of celery compound from a nearby drugstore. When the watchman returned with the medicine, he was surprised to find the door leading into the main factory was locked. Luetgert appeared and took the medication. He did not comment on the locked door and sent Bialk back to his post in the engine room.

A little while later, Luetgert again approached Bialk and sent him back to the drugstore to buy a bottle of Hunyadi water, the medicinal spring water that he used to treat his stomach ailments.

While the watchman was away running errands, Luetgert was apparently working alone in the factory basement. He had turned on the steam under the middle vat at a little before 9:00 that night, and it was still running when Bialk returned. The watchman reported that Luetgert had remained in the basement until about 2:00 a.m.

Bialk found him fully dressed in his office the next day. He asked whether the fires under the vat should be put out, but Luetgert told him to bank them at 50 pounds of steam pressure. This was an odd request because the factory had been closed for several weeks. But Bialk did as he was told and went down to the basement.

When he entered the basement, he saw a hose that was running water into the middle vat. On the floor in front of the vat was a dark-brown, sticky, glue-like substance. Bialk noticed that it seemed to contain bits of bone, but he thought nothing of it. Luetgert used all sorts of waste meats to make his sausage. He thought nothing further about it at the time.

On May 3, another employee, Frank Odorowsky, known as "Smokehouse Frank," also noticed the slimy substance on the factory floor. He feared that someone had boiled something in the factory without Luetgert's knowledge, so he went to his employer to report it. Luetgert told him not to mention the brown slime. If he kept silent, Luetgert told him, he would have a good job for the rest of his life.

Frank went to work scraping the slime off the floor and poured it into a nearby drain that led to the sewer. The larger chunks of waste were placed in a barrel, and Luetgert told him to take the barrel out to the railroad tracks and scatter it there.

Following these interviews, Schuettler made another disturbing and suspicious discovery. A short time before Louisa's disappearance -- even though the factory had been closed -- Luetgert had ordered 325 pounds of crude potash and 50 pounds of arsenic from Lor Owen & Company, a wholesale drug firm. It was delivered to the factory the next day.

Another interview with Frank Odorowsky revealed what had happened to the chemicals. On April 24, Luetgert had asked Smokehouse Frank to move the barrel of potash in the shipping room to the factory basement, where there were three huge vats were used to boil down sausage material. Luetgert warned him that the potash was extremely dangerous and that he should avoid contact with it. However, he did need it to be cut up into small pieces.

Frank, along with another employee, crushed the potash with a hatchet and a hammer. Both men were badly burned when small pieces of it came into contact with their faces and hands. The pieces were all dumped into the middle vat, and Luetgert turned on the steam beneath it, dissolving the material into liquid.

Combining this information with the eyewitness accounts from employees and Emma Schiemicke, Captain Schuettler began to believe that he knew what had happened to Louisa Luetgert. To find out if he was correct, a search would have to be made of Luetgert's factory.

It would be a search that would lead to one of the most gruesome discoveries in the records of Chicago crime.

The search of the sausage works began on May 15. The factory was actually two connected buildings, with the shorter wing hidden from Diversey Avenue behind the main structure. The south building, where most of the manufacturing took place, had an open cupola on each corner to allow in fresh air. The odor during sausage-making was often described as "overpowering." The building was filled with scraping machines, cutters that reduced meat into small pieces, steam-operated propellor cleaners, vats, boilers, engines, racks, and machines that stuffed meat into casings.

Police officers searched the building and sifted through a pile of ashes in the corner of the engine room but found no evidence of what had happened to Louisa.

The search moved on to the north wing, which mainly was used as a warehouse where sausage was stored. The front part of the first floor included Luetgert's office and a large retail salesroom where the company had sold groceries and meat. The front part of his office contained several desks. A massive fireproof safe was in the back. Behind that was a nine-foot by five-foot windowless room where Luetgert usually slept. The dark chamber was fitted with a bed, mattress, sheets, a blanket, a washstand, and a toilet. The door that led into this sad apartment had a placard on it that said "This Room for Mr. Luetgert Only" in rough, black letters.

Not far from that doorway was a staircase that led down into the basement, where Luetgert had been working alone on the night of May 1. There were six large furnaces in the basement that were used for smoking sausages on the west end. Their flues extended the entire five stories of the building, and on each floor, they opened onto chambers where the sausages could be placed for smoking. The basement also had three large wooden vats, each about 12-feet long and divided into two sections. Luetgert's employees used the vats for dipping the sausages into a salty solution that preserved them - usually.

The officers discovered that the middle vat was filled with a brownish fluid. They put some of the liquid into a bottle. They also found a false tooth, which they gave to Inspector Schaack.

With officers holding candles and a lantern, Schaack peered into the vat. He put some of the liquid in his hand and saw that it was dark brown. He asked for a stick, and one of the men handed him a scraper. Feeling around for a place to let out the water, Schaack discovered a plug. He knocked it out, and the murky water began pouring out onto the floor. He directed one of the officers to grab a gunnysack that was hanging on the next vat and hold it under the open drain to catch anything solid that came out. Several men lifted the vat about three inches on the opposite side to help it drain. Finally, they used a broom to drain it as much as they could.

One of the men, Officer Walter Dean, climbed into the vat to look around. He later testified that the substance in the vat had a "very sickening smell," as if there was "something dead around it."

Searching through the muck, Schaack found a light-colored clump of hair on the top edge of the vat. The men kept searching inside the tank, and Schaack took the gunnysack over by the window to look at what they'd caught. The window was so dirty that it barely let in sunlight, so Schaack forced it open. Examining the sack, he found several fragments of what looked like bone, including one that he thought was a piece of a skull.

As he held the bones up the light, he heard Officer Dean call out from inside the vat. "Wait! What is that?" he said loudly. He bent over, picked something up from the bottom of the vat, and handed it out to Schaack.

He'd found two gold rings. One was a small, plain wedding ring, but the larger one was much heavier, and as he peered closely, he saw that it was inscribed with two initials in German Gothic script - "L.L."

Louisa Luetgert had worn both rings.

In the days that followed, Luetgert was in a frenzy. He was asking his employees what the police had been looking for in the factory, but none of them knew - the police were keeping silent.

After hearing rumors about Louisa's disappearance, Christine Feld went to the Luetgert home and asked Mary where Louisa was.

She told Mrs. Feld that Louisa was downtown shopping. When Luetgert came by later, Christine confronted him. She asked, "Why is Mary telling lies that your wife is downtown?"

Luetgert said that he didn't want everyone to know that his wife was missing. He claimed that she had disappeared for a few days on several previous occasions and then returned.

Christine was upset. She wasn't sure that she could trust Luetgert anymore, and her suspicions would come back to haunt him at his trial.

The lies didn't help. Word rapidly spread about the missing woman, and a story appeared in the *Chicago Tribune* on page one. The article gave no indication that Luetgert was suspected in Louisa's disappearance. In fact, it incorrectly claimed that Luetgert had notified the police. Without citing any sources, the article claimed Louisa had abandoned her family.

But that all changed the next day. In a follow-up article, the *Tribune* changed its mind and first suggested that Louisa had met with foul play.

Luetgert was furious when he read the story. He rushed to the Sheffield Avenue police station with the newspaper in his hand and angrily confronted Captain Schuettler. "I can't control the newspapers," the detective waved him away. "You'll have to go talk to the editor."

Many of his friends and even some of his own employees had already turned against Luetgert, and now the public was starting to do the same thing. In the days that followed, Luetgert was told that he might be arrested anytime.

Witnesses came in and out of the police station on Chicago Avenue, refusing to answer questions from reporters. Mary Simerling was brought in for questioning and kept in a cell overnight. Louisa's niece, Frieda Mueller, left the station under police escort. She appeared to be "deeply agitated," reporters wrote. She was unable to speak, but friends said that she had broken down sobbing several times while Inspector Schaack was interviewing her.

The next morning, Luetgert stayed at home. He complained of feeling ill. Around 1.30 in the afternoon, Captain Schuettler, along with Detectives Dean and Qualey, arrived at the house and rang the bell. They had come to see Luetgert on important business. They found him in the sitting room, laying on the sofa, with Fred Mueller and a reporter from the *Chicago Journal.*

"What do you want?" Luetgert asked. "I am not feeling well today."

It was Detective Qualey that answered. "We have come to arrest you, Mr. Luetgert, on the charge of murdering your wife."

Luetgert's face turned white. "Take me if you want!" he cried as he jumped up from the sofa, "but I am innocent. God knows I am innocent!"

The arrest warrant was read aloud, and Luetgert remained silent until it was finished. He asked permission to go upstairs and get some clothing. They allowed him to do this, and he soon returned and put on his hat and a light overcoat. As he stepped out on the porch with the detectives, his little boy, Elmer, called out after him. "Goodbye, Papa!" he shouted. "Bring Mama back with you!"

Luetgert hurried to the policemen's carriage, his face ashen.

Curious neighbors stood on the sidewalk and stared at the house. Little groups gathered in front of the taverns and outside the gloomy, abandoned sausage factory. Newsboys walked around the neighborhood, selling extra afternoon editions that contained the news of Luetgert's arrest.

The papers, which quickly sold out, reported that the police were accusing Luetgert of using a solution made from crude potash to dissolve his wife's body - but rumors spread that he had ground Louisa up as sausage instead.

Sausage sales in Chicago plummeted in the summer of 1897.

Luetgert was confined at the Cook County Jail. His cellmate was an old acquaintance, a North Side butcher and saloonkeeper named Nic Marzen. He had been charged with killing a butcher and cattle buyer named Fritz Holzhueter, who had vanished on January 30, 1895. His body was found, partially cremated, a month later. Marzen was arrested, tried, convicted, and sentenced to death but was back at the county jail while his case was appealed.

He told reporters, "Luetgert is surely innocent. He will surprise them all when it comes to a trial... The woman is alive today and she will show up."

His fellow inmates may have believed Luetgert was innocent, but the grand jury didn't. He was indicted on June 5 for killing his wife and dissolving her in the sausage vat. Louisa's body had not been found, and there were no witnesses to the crime, but the police and District Attorney Charles S. Deneen believed the evidence would prove the case.

The bones that had been found in the vat were human -- a third rib; part of a humerus, or great bone in the arm; a bone from the palm of a human hand; a bone from the fourth toe of a right foot; fragments of bone from a human ear; and a larger bone from a foot. Of course, the forensic science of the time did not offer anything further, but there was no question the bones had belonged to a person.

The trial began in late August. Louisa's family, including Diedrich Bicknese, were often in the courtroom, and so were Luetgert's children. When the trial was not in session, Luetgert often picked up Elmer and kissed him.

The jury was selected by August 28 and included two clerks, a butcher, a manager, a building contractor, a salesman, a soap-maker, a railroad watchman, a collector, a sewing-machine maker, an unemployed printer, and an unemployed railroad engineer. Many of the potential jurors tried to get out of their duty with excuses about their jobs, but Judge Richard Tuthill was seldom sympathetic.

The courtroom was packed each day, mostly with women, and they fought for seats each morning when the bailiff opened the doors. Everyone wanted to be part of the trial and to get a glimpse of the man who was being called a murderer all over the city.

The prosecution brought in a long parade of witnesses, including Frank Bialk, who testified about the events of the night of May 1 and the middle vat in the factory's basement.

Police officers and detectives also took the stand, describing their searches of the factory. Captain Schuettler produced the two gold rings that were found, both of which had belonged to Louisa. They had been identified by some of Louisa's relatives and long-time friends.

During the prosecution's portion of the trial, Luetgert's mistresses turned on him. Agatha Tosch took the stand on the morning of August 31, testifying in German with a reporter from a German-speaking newspaper translating for her. She testified about conversations she had with Luetgert before and after Louisa disappeared.

She said that Luetgert had once told her that Mary Simerling was the only reason that he could stand to remain in his house. He said that he couldn't eat Louisa's cooking and had thrown meals at her feet several times. Louisa had wanted Mary to be removed from the house, but Luetgert refused. He wanted Mary to stay and told Agatha that there were many times when he wanted to take Louisa and "crush her." Another time, she heard him bitterly complain about his need to call a doctor to take care of Louisa when she was sick. "If I had waited a little longer," he told her, "the dead, rotten beast would have croaked."

She added that she had asked Luetgert where his wife had gone shortly after Louisa had disappeared. He was in her tavern, gulping down huge quantities of beer at the time. She said that he became pale and very excited and exclaimed: "I don't know! I am as innocent as the southern skies!"

She wondered if Luetgert had no idea where his wife was, why he would have a reason to proclaim being innocent of anything.

Christine Feld entered the courtroom to testify, dressed all in black. She had been the subject of many rumors that she was preparing to flee to Germany to avoid testifying. There had also been a lot of speculation about whether she would remain loyal to Luetgert.

She wasn't.

In fact, when she took the stand, Luetgert's previously bold demeanor collapsed. A *Tribune* reporter wrote that his "eyes bulged out with terror and thick drops of greasy sweat formed on his flabby cheeks and neck." When she sat down in the witness chair, "Luetgert bowed his head as though to shut out the whole horrible nightmare of the courtroom."

Luetgert had once told this woman that if she betrayed him, that he would not care to go on living. Christine apparently did not feel the same way about Luetgert. She exposed all the lurid secrets that he had been keeping from everyone.

Prosecutor Deneen asked her about conversations she'd had with Luetgert before Louisa disappeared. "He said he could not any longer live with his wife," she said. He told her that he had too much trouble in the factory, but once that was over, "I will settle with her." She also testified that Luetgert said he preferred Mary to his wife.

Moreover, he had told her that he could make his wife angry by simply mentioning Christine's name.

Deneen then showed Christine some papers and identified them as letters written to her by Luetgert. When Luetgert saw the packet of letters, he became livid for a moment, and then all the color drained from his face. He whispered to his attorney, William Vincent, who had apparently been unaware of the letters' existence until then. The state's attorney handed one of the letters, scrawled in German, to Vincent, and Luetgert grabbed it. He saw what was written on it, and he knew that his fears over the contents of the packet had been justified.

The letters were all poorly written, gushing love letters that Luetgert had sent to Christine. Some were written before his arrest, and others from the county jail. He called her "his beloved" and said that if not for her, he would have ended his life already. In other letters, he asked her for money, stating that "lawyers were bloodsuckers." That letter was followed by several that went unanswered, each time begging her for money. Luetgert blushed as the letters were read aloud in court.

During her testimony, Christine also revealed that Luetgert had given her $4,000 for "safe-keeping" shortly before Louisa's disappearance, but the most damaging evidence came with her production of a bloody knife that Luetgert had also given her. He left it with her, without explanation, on the day after his wife disappeared. The knife had been tested by the police, and while there was blood on the blade, experts were unable to determine if the blood was human or animal. Luetgert claimed the blood on the knife was fake - planted by the police.

The line of witnesses continued. The prosecution called the young girls who had seen Luetgert and his wife enter the factory on the night Louisa disappeared, as well as the workers who had also spotted them.

Mark Delafontaine, a chemistry teacher at South Division High School, was the expert who had determined that the bones found in the factory vat were human. He brought several boxes of evidence with him to the courtroom. They were opened and examined by the jury. Some of the people in the courtroom noticed an "indescribable sickening stench."

Luetgert laughed when he saw a jar that contained clumps of what Delafontaine said were lumps of putrid and disintegrating flesh. The bone fragments were also passed around. Luetgert didn't flinch when he picked one of them up. He laughed and turned to a reporter and said, "This is a bit of cow's shoulder bone."

The spectators in the courtroom pressed forward until the judge had to order them to sit back down.

The prosecution walked Delafontaine through his findings about the bones and declared, without question, that the bones were human. On cross-examination, Vincent was able to get him to admit that he was not an expert on anatomy, but that was all.

On September 9, George Vincent Bailey, an osteologist at the Field Columbian Museum of Chicago, also identified the bones as human. He was an expert on anatomy, and not only did he state that the bones belonged to a human, but he demonstrated that they were those of a woman or at least a small person.

George Dorsey, an anthropologist who was also from the Field Museum, agreed with his colleague. He was also able to state that the bones were human and added, "From its apparently small size, I should judge it to be that of a woman."

After calling the bone experts, the prosecution also put corset makers on the stand. They testified that the burnt piece of metal that the police had found in the ashes from the Luetgert factory was indeed the remnants of a woman's undergarment. There was no way to definitively link the metal to a corset that belonged to Louisa, but the damage was done.

A dentist named Carl Klein, Jr. testified that he had made a full upper aluminum denture for Louisa in July 1893. He examined one of the small pieces of matter that the police found inside the vat and identified it as a false superior lateral incisor. However, he was unable to say if the false tooth the police found had belonged to Louisa.

After nearly a month, the prosecution finally rested their case.

When William Vincent began the defense's case, he did everything he could to attack the witnesses that the defense had presented. He disputed the findings of the experts, cast doubt on the credibility of the police, and largely did all that he could to create doubt that Louisa was dead at all.

Louisa was a constant part of the defense's case.

They attempted to show that she was afflicted with a "peculiar malady" for five or six months before she vanished. One defense witness said that it was "evident that Mrs. Luetgert had an alternating melancholia of degeneracy which had very slowly developed to become accentuated at that period of female life which is so generally critical to neurotic women - the menopause."

Louisa was supposed to have had two cousins and a brother who had gone insane, which clearly meant that insanity ran in her family. The witness, J. Sanderson Christison, also claimed that the shape of her ear had been a bad sign, indicating that she was likely to commit crimes or go insane. He declared that all of Louisa's relatives had the same kind of ear.

Judge Tuthill ended up cutting his time on the stand short and didn't allow Vincent to put any other insanity "experts" on the stand. "I am not going over her whole life history and let you pick out isolated circumstances," Tuthill told the attorney. "You can show anything queer that she did, but that's all."

Several witnesses testified that Louisa said she would leave home if Luetgert's business collapsed. When Vincent tried to demonstrate Louisa's insanity with the fact that she had given Amelia Kaiser four oranges, Tuthill blew up.

On September 25, Mary Simerling took the stand. She never looked at Luetgert as she testified, but he kept his eyes on her the entire time. She described how Louisa had behaved in later April, saying over and over again that she would run away. She described how Louisa rubbed her hands together nervously and spent too much time in her room. When the defense tried to ask Mary about Louisa's behavior in the months leading up to the last week in April, the judge refused to allow it.

Mary claimed Luetgert had treated his wife well. She denied ever seeing him strike her or threaten her with violence and added that he always gave Louisa whatever money she needed. Mary also said that Louisa beat her children nearly every day during the six months prior to her disappearance. The prosecution objected to this, and the judge sustained it.

She went on to describe how terribly she had been treated by the police, claiming they kept her in a cell for 48 hours without food and only gave her a wooden plank to sleep on. A police matron had made her strip when she was brought to the station, she said, and officers watched from the door while she stood there naked.

Mary also denied the rumors of her affair with Luetgert, saying that she never went with him to the factory office at night. The only time she had been there, she lied, was when she made his bed during the daytime.

The prosecution attacked every part of her testimony, forcing her to admit that she had told the police the opposite of what she was saying in court. Even though she would not admit to having an affair with Luetgert, she did confess that she had once told friends that Luetgert was going to "make her his wife." She was also asked why she had told a judge that she had been treated well at the police station and then told a different story in court. She had no answer for that.

She also denied telling the police about the fights the Luetgerts had or how Luetgert had chased his wife down the street with a pistol. She also denied telling William Follbach on May 3 that Louisa was sleeping in the house when she had been missing for two days. She denied admitting to the police that she had told Follbach that story because she feared the disgrace that Louisa's disappearance would bring to her husband. She denied telling the police that she had noticed nothing peculiar about Louisa's behavior.

Over and over, Mary's sullen answer was "No, sir." The incessant questioning was taking its toll on her. Her face grew paler, and her voice began to falter. Literally, everything she had once said was now being denied from the witness stand. She refused to be shaken, though. It was only at the end of the day when she lost her temper.

The prosecutor asked her, "You say that she used to beat the children. With her hands or stick or club?"

"With her hands, stick - anything she could get hold of, her slipper."

"She used anything she got hold of?"

"Anything she got hold of."

"Broom?"

"Yes, sir."

"Poker?"

"Yes, sir."

"Anything - pick up a chair?"

"Anything she got hold of."

"Just as apt to use a chair as anything else?"

"Yes, sir."

"She would have hit them with a stove leg and beat them with it?"

"She would if she could have lifted the stove."

"She would have hit them with the stove if she could have lifted it?"

'Yes, sir."

"You know she would have done that?"

"Yes, sir."

"You're not a clairvoyant or a mind reader? That is not your business?"

"No, sir."

"Just a plain domestic girl?"

"Yes, sir."

Mary was asked about statements that she had made to the grand jury that contradicted the testimony that she was giving now. She didn't deny having given the earlier testimony but claimed she had lied to the grand jury because Inspector Schaack had forced her to do so.

"They made me say it," she blurted out. "Inspector Schaack told me I had to say everything. If I would not, he would punish me for it."

When Mary left the stand, she sat down near Luetgert. He looked over at her and gave her a wide smile.

As mentioned, Louisa Luetgert was a constant part of the defense's case. Not only were her alleged actions and subsequent disappearance studied, talked about, and dissected, but the defense even went so far as to claim that she was not dead.

Rumors had spread as early as May 3 that a mysterious "woman in black" had shown up in Kenosha, Wisconsin. Many people saw her in town, but she refused to talk with anyone. Then, one day, she was just gone. Two weeks later, people in town read about the disappearance of Louisa Luetgert and wondered if the strange woman might have been her. The woman was never seen again, and the Chicago police didn't take the sighting seriously - because they received hundreds of letters from people who claimed they'd seen Louisa in hundreds of different places.

Since disappearing, Louisa was said to have boarded a train in Fon du Lac, Wisconsin. She had walked into a saloon in Decatur, Illinois, with an umbrella and ordered a beer. She had asked a lawyer in Nebraska for help getting a divorce. She was working as a cook on a boat in New York. She had stayed with a family in Ashland, Wisconsin. She had stopped into an employment office in Peoria, looking for work. It seemed that "Louisa" had been in most of these places at the same time, crossing back and forth across the country.

Some of the sightings were obvious hoaxes. Bottles containing notes signed by women were found floating in Lake Michigan near Chicago, Racine, and Valparaiso, as well as in the Rock River near Rockford. One letter, signed by "Louisa," said she wanted to die because she couldn't stand to see her husband with another woman. Another said, "I have been imprisoned by some unknown persons, and in an unknown place."

A woman on the city's North Side found a ring inscribed with the name "Louisa Luetgert" and turned it over to the police. Captain Schuettler looked at it and discovered it was brass. The lettering was crude, apparently scratched onto it with a penknife.

One story claimed that Louisa was working as a servant in Summit County, Ohio, and being paid to stay out of sight by business rivals of her husband, who wanted Luetgert to go to the gallows.

Alexander Carl Grottey, a man who claimed to be an old sweetheart of Louisa's, said he had encountered her walking in Manhattan on May 7. He added to the story by saying that she had sailed for Europe. He wrote to Luetgert's lawyers and offered to testify.

Captain Schuettler went to New York to check out the story, and it quickly unraveled. The two men who were with Grottey when he supposedly saw Louisa contradicted his story. No record could be found of Louisa buying a ticket to Europe. Grottey turned out to have a history of reporting seeing people who had gone missing. He was also too young to have been Louisa's former sweetheart - he was only 15 when she and Luetgert had gotten married.

Other sightings of Louisa were cases of mistaken identity. One September 15, several farmers in a town west of Chicago saw a woman running through the woods. After they chased her, she sat down on the ground and started digging in some gravel. She was very dirty, and her hair hung in a tangled knot down her back. When she finally spoke, her words were incoherent. The farmers took her to the Melrose Park police station, where some officers thought she looked like Louisa Luetgert. However, it was soon discovered that she was Caroline Johnson, who had been admitted into an insane asylum in 1896. She had been released and had disappeared.

Local police officers also spent a few days in October trailing a mentally ill woman in ragged clothing through eastern Indiana. Descriptions of the woman vaguely matched those of Louisa, but she turned out to be Lillian English, who had been roaming the area for months.

Women identified as Louisa were seen most frequently in Wisconsin. She was usually said to be hiding out on a farm, working as a servant, or held against her will. To some, the detectives and reporters tracking her down always seemed close to finding her but always missed her.

On September 25, three boys from Oshkosh were hunting hickory nuts south of town and ran into a woman in the woods. At first, they believed she was somehow connected to a farm where they wanted to gather nuts and asked her for permission to do so. She replied that it was not her land; she was only visiting. The woman, who said she was from Chicago, told the boys her name, and they later said it was "Luetgert" or something similar. She said that her husband was a butcher and that she had fled because he had threatened to cut her up. People were looking for her, but she had friends to protect her. The sighting was reported, but no trace of the woman was found.

The day before that, September 24, a woman in a dusty dress who appeared tired from traveling stopped in at a tavern on North Street in Chicago. The saloon owner, Arthur Mundwiller, said the woman told him, "They tried to murder me by giving me poison and throwing me into a vat several times."

Only a few of the people who claimed to have seen Louisa after May 1 were called to testify by the defense. Jacob Melber, a butcher from Wheaton, west of Chicago, thought he had seen Louisa on May 6. A woman had asked him for directions to Elmhurst, and Melber thought she was Louisa Luetgert, whom he had met a couple of years earlier when he had come to the Luetgert factory looking for work. But when he was asked if he was convinced the woman was really Louisa, he didn't sound convincing. "I would not swear, but that was pretty near the same sized woman," he said. "In weight, I cannot tell you it. I cannot tell you by her figures, the color of her hair, or anything like that."

A fruit seller named Armadale Opdyke swore he had seen Louisa on June 9. He had been driving his horse and wagon toward Janesville, Wisconsin when he met two women on the road. They asked him how to get to Elgin. Opdyke camped along the road that night and said that the women slept on the ground about 150 feet from him. Shown a photograph of Louisa, he said it was one of the two women he'd seen.

Maybe.

Several other witnesses were called to testify about the mysterious woman in black who visited Kenosha. Apparently, Luetgert's defense team thought she seemed the most likely figure to shift attention toward. When each of them took the stand, though, prosecutors accused them of having already told the Chicago police that the woman did not resemble photographs of Louisa. In court, they claimed that the woman in the photographs and the woman in black were the same person.

District Attorney Deneen fired a quick series of questions at bartender Matt Scholey, and the witness badly fumbled his description of the woman he was now claiming had been Louisa. "How much did she weigh?" Deneen asked him.

"Oh, I should judge she weighed somewhere between 100 --- between 135 and 140 pounds," the bartender replied.

Deneen smiled and shook his head as a resigned look washed over the face of defense attorney Vincent. "So, 135 to 140 pounds?" Deneen clarified.

"No, I should judge she weighed about 115 to 118 pounds. I have got mixed up," Scholey blurted out.

Deneen's smile broadened and turned into a chuckle. He looked over at his co-prosecutors, and all three laughed aloud. Some of the jurors, who rarely smiled during the proceedings, joined in the laughter. One of Luetgert's defense attorneys jumped to his feet in protest, demanding that the prosecution stop making fun of the witness.

"I am not making fun," Deneen said.

Judge Tuthill, who was trying not to laugh himself, said, "Well, the witness was smiling himself."

"Anyone would laugh at that answer," Deneen said.

"I made a mistake," Scholey spoke up.

Deneen was allowed to continue his questions and soon had Scholey denying that he had ever told police officers, "If you fellows have got any money, I will tell you all about this. My evidence is worth something, and you can get it if you have got the dough. My testimony is worth $1,500, and that's what I'm going to get for it."

As for his mistake about the woman's weight, Scholey explained that he had been confused because he thought Deneen was asking him how old the woman was.

Smiling again, Deneen asked him, "You thought I was inquiring about her age when you said 135 to 140?"

Scholey shrugged.

When the defense attorneys showed a Kenosha police officer named Henry Feldshaw a photograph of Louisa, at first, he said that it didn't look much like the woman he'd seen - but then he changed his mind. Feldshaw denied telling the Chicago police that the woman he had seen in Kenosha didn't look like Louisa. However, he did admit that he'd told them she looked like "an old sport," in other words, an aging prostitute. That is not a description that ever would have fit Louisa Luetgert.

Another Kenosha policeman, William Shaw, claimed to have seen the mystery woman at the local train station. Before testifying, he told a newspaper, "The Chicago cops think they know a lot, but we will show them a few things before we get through." But Smith also ran into problems when Deneen grilled him. He also denied telling the police that the mystery woman didn't look like Louisa. He also had to deny that he had asked the detectives for $50 before he'd tell them where the woman could be found.

Frank Scheve, a farmworker who said that he had seen Louisa walking down a country road, had to admit that the defense had given him $5 for his appearance at the trial. They'd also bought him a new suit and shoes for the courtroom and paid for his train ride to Chicago. But he did deny - with a red face -- that he'd told the farmer he worked for that he was only testifying in the trial so that he could come to Chicago and have a good time.

In the end, it seemed that Louisa Luetgert was everywhere and nowhere, all at the same time. The prosecution believed that they had proven that Louisa was exactly where they believed she was - dead.

However, they had a hard time with the witnesses that followed the wild claims of Louisa sightings on the stand. The parade of witnesses that followed included seven experts who disputed the testimony of the state's bone doctors and chemists. Each of them denied that the bones found in the middle vat at the factory as human.

Mistakes were made, though. Each of the witnesses made errors when identifying boxes of bones brought into the courtroom to test their knowledge. One of them mistook the bones of a dog for bones from a human hand, and another was unable to tell the bones of a hog - which the defense claimed was really in the vat - from the thigh of a musk ox from the Field Museum.

While this was going on, Dr. Clarence Rutherford, a Luetgert family physician, told the *Tribune* that he had declined to testify for the defense as a bone expert, despite his many years of experience as an anatomy professor. He didn't testify for Luetgert because he knew he couldn't help him - he was sure that one of the bones the police had was from a human hand.

Meanwhile, Adolph Luetgert was falling apart. First, he developed a badly ulcerated tooth that caused him considerable pain. A short time later, he began using crutches when he came into the courtroom each day. It was initially reported that damp weather had brought on an attack of rheumatism or that he had sprained his leg. However, it was later learned that Luetgert had been injured in a fight with a prisoner named William Young. It had started with a few words exchanged, and then Luetgert lost his temper. He had rushed at Young in a rage, but Young dodged, caught Luetgert low around the waist, and hurled him almost 20 feet backward against a steel door. Luetgert was unable to get up and had to be assisted back to his cell.

He also continued to give interviews to reporters who came to see him in his cell. He was now pushing the theory that Louisa was pretending to be dead until he could be executed for her murder. After that, she'd return and claim his fortune. The biggest problem with this theory is that he had no fortune - not yet anyway.

He soon began to claim that he would be found innocent and make a fortune writing a book about his life. He was innocent, he swore, and would make that clear when he testified at his trial.

Vincent was against Luetgert taking the stand, knowing that the prosecution would needle him into losing his temper in front of the jury. On October 5, as the attorney was wrapping up his defense, Luetgert came into the courtroom determined to be his last witness. After some quiet whispering, Luetgert was taken into another room by his attorneys. Vincent told him that if Luetgert took the stand, Vincent would "wash my skirts of the whole matter." He would leave the case if his client didn't follow his advice.

Finally, Luetgert changed his mind. He said he guessed he had "better keep out of it." They soon returned to the courtroom and told Judge Tuthill that Luetgert had decided not to testify. The large crowd that had gathered to see Luetgert defend himself on the stand were disappointed to hear Vincent say, "The defense rests."

For the next three days, prosecutors presented a string of witnesses to undermine Luetgert's defense, casting doubt on just about everything they'd said. They produced witnesses to counter the story that the woman in black in Kenosha was Louisa and to shake the reliability of Mary Simerling's testimony. Among them were five grand jury members who testified that Mary's story to them and the story she told in court were much different.

The defense had tried to refute the testimony of Emma Schimke, who had seen Louisa go into the sausage factory with her husband on May 1, but the prosecution brought in witnesses that vouched for where she was and when she was there on that night. Emma herself was called back to the stand again to repeat her story. As she left the stand, she stuck her tongue out at the defense attorneys, which prompted laughter in the courtroom.

Finally, seven friends and relatives of Louisa testified that she had always been a kind and good mother to her children.

Closing arguments followed, lasting for the next six days. Each side went over their case again, appealing to the jurors for justice. Days of heated discussions, votes, wrangling and compromise, and accusations of bribes followed, and on October 21, the jury announced that they were unable to agree on a verdict.

The jury was sent home. The trial of Adolph Luetgert was over - for now. But the prosecution didn't rest for long. They had already started making plans for a second trial.

Luetgert was unhappy. He'd mistakenly believed that ending the trial with a "hung jury" had cleared him. He was both outraged and basking in the attention. While he was condemning the Chicago newspapers for being unfair to him, he was also boasting about the countless offers of marriage that were pouring into the jail.

Luetgert didn't need a new wife - he needed money to pay his lawyers for a second trial. William Charles began collecting donations from Luetgert supporters and shopping around for a publisher for the book that Luetgert wanted to write. He was paid a few times for articles and statements about the case.

Before the second trial could begin, a new judge had to be chosen. Luetgert was pleased when the case went to Judge Joseph E. Gary, who was best known for presiding over the 1887 trial of the anarchists involved in the Haymarket Square bombing. Although, it seems strange Luetgert would approve of this choice. Gary was known for being unusually harsh to defendants. He was clearly biased against the Haymarket anarchists - most of whom went to the gallows. Regardless, Gary was still a respected judge, and perhaps Luetgert simply believed that he was so important that the most famous judge in Chicago was put on his case.

But one person not returning to the case was his lead lawyer, William Vincent. Apparently, one time with Luetgert was enough for him. In addition, Luetgert's son, Arnold, had paid him with three forged checks, souring him on the whole family.

Luetgert's financial troubles were growing. He now owed $176,000 on various mortgages and debts. People who bought property from him learned that he had mortgaged the land to others, causing many of them to go public about the money that Luetgert owed them. Luetgert continued to ask for donations for his defense fund, which led to the hiring of his new lead attorney, Lawrence Harmon.

Harmon worked around the clock for his new client, driving himself to exhaustion. His assistants complained that he was handling everything himself. He was absolutely convinced of Luetgert's innocence and believed his client when he told him that Louisa simply disappeared. When he ran out of money to pay stenographers, he and his assistants laboriously wrote out a record of the trial. He stretched time by making numerous objections. In time, he would even spend $2,000 of his own money to fund the defense case.

Like Luetgert's earlier lawyers, he tried to show that Louisa had a family history of insanity and disappearances. Once again, the court refused to allow any evidence about that, but Harmon kept trying. He also made repeated promises to prove that Louisa was alive - much to his client's delight - but no solid evidence ever surfaced.

Harmon did anything Luetgert wanted, including posing embarrassing questions to prosecution witnesses like Agatha Tosch. He also got into a disagreement with the judge about the two rings that had been found in the sausage vat. Harmon insisted on covering them with a sheet of paper when witnesses spoke about the rings. The judge ordered them to be left on display. As the tension over the situation grew, Harmon became more and more excited. "It is my privilege to do that, and I deny the right of the court to deprive me of it," he cried out.

After Harmon finally uncovered the rings, he questioned Louisa's friend Sophia Tews about the rings, trying to insinuate that they actually belonged to Sophia's sister, Louise Law, who had died in an asylum in Kankakee, Illinois. This, he claimed, was why the "L.L." was engraved on the larger ring. Judge Gary refused to allow him to follow this line of questioning, though.

But the prosecutor spoke up. "We shall be glad to meet Mr. Harmon on the evidence of Louise Law. He knows her will never produce anything of the kind."

"No, I won't produce Louise Law's ring," Harmon shouted at him. "You produce it! There it is!" Harmon held up one of the rings the prosecution had entered into evidence. He was waving it around in front of the jury. The district attorney stood to object, but the judge sustained the objection before he could even call for it.

Judge Gary said, "Mr. Harmon, I don't know, but it may be to your advantage to not endeavor to create so much turbulence before this jury."

"I am not creating any turbulence at all," Harmon said.

The bickering continued, and Gary threatened to fine Harmon for contempt of court. Even Luetgert, who had been in favor of turning the trial into a circus, was starting to get worried about Harmon's behavior and antagonizing the judge.

And Harmon's strange behavior didn't improve. When questioning Edward Cady, an expert on corsets, Harmon brought up the fact that Cady had never worn a corset himself.

The judge threw up his hands. "We don't care if this man wears corsets, bloomers, divided skirts, or socks. Let him proceed with his testimony."

Luetgert enjoyed the way that Harmon cross-examined Christine Feld when she returned to the stand. The letters that she had received from Luetgert were again entered into evidence. He shifted in his chair as they were read aloud but watched as Harmon then asked personal questions that Luetgert had suggested.

He asked her how she referred to Luetgert, but Christine did not understand the question. So, Harmon chimed in. "Did you ever call Mr. Luetgert 'my toosey-wootsey,' 'joy of my heart,' 'deary,' 'chickie,' 'sugar plum,' or 'gallant cavalier?'"

When the judge admonished Harmon, he changed tactics and asked her personal questions about an affair with Luetgert. The judge ordered Harmon to stop insulting the witness and threatened to turn the examination over to one of Harmon's assistants. But Harmon kept up the sharp questions, prompting Christine to call both the attorney and his client liars.

Harmon was all over the place, asking bizarre questions, badgering his own witnesses, and angering the judge. When the prosecution called a new witness, Frank Hangel, who claimed that Luetgert tried to hire him for an "unspecified job," Harmon seemed more interested in the newspaper Hangel was reading than when he stated Luetgert said to him that he'd recently had troubles with his wife but would "soon get rid of them."

At one point, Judge Gary complained impatiently that Harmon was wasting time with his questions, and Harmon replied that he took exception to the "court's unfriendly criticism."

"Go on, go on," Gary yelled at him. "Every interruption only leads to a waste of time."

The scientific testimony from the first trial was repeated with one key difference - the prosecutors were now only using four small bone fragments from a woman's hand. Deneen had decided not to use the others because they were still being disputed by sparring experts. In addition, the jawbone that had been found in the vat had been lost by the chemistry teacher Delafontaine after the trial.

But the experts who did return stated in even stronger terms that the four bones found in the vat were definitely human - a statement that Harmon made a joke about.

When the prosecutor objected, the judge blew up again at Harmon. The word around the courthouse was that the jury was also growing tired of Harmon's antics.

Things became even more heated when Inspector Schaack took the stand. Right away, Harmon threw out a series of suggestions that the police had used false evidence in the case. Schaack was amused as he rejected the accusation that the police had dug up the body of a Great Dane on the factory grounds and sent the bones to Rush Medical College for examination.

He also rejected Harmon's suggestion that he had planted the false tooth in the sausage vat after procuring a real tooth from a dentist's office. Harmon then asked Schaack if he knew that reporters had placed bones in the building once owned by infamous serial killer H.H. Holmes to create a newspaper sensation. Schaack said that he didn't know anything about it, and the judge ordered the question to be stricken from the record.

After Harmon finished with his interrogation, the prosecutor mockingly told a reporter, "Schaack had an awful hard time to get bones and went about it in a very peculiar way. He needed bones to be put in the vat and came away with a few little pieces. He needed a false tooth and made the mistake of having a natural tooth drawn from a woman."

After Schaack finished testifying, he announced he was going to take a couple of days off. "I'm afraid that I will go nutty if I have to stick this out from day to day," he told a reporter. "If I feel so tough, those jurors must be in terrible condition. They ought to have a vaudeville performance at the hotel."

The courtroom got its own vaudeville show on January 21, 1898, when Adolph Luetgert took the stand in his own defense. Responding to questions from Harmon, he essentially told his life story, from his time in Germany to his rise in the Chicago sausage industry. The jury listened keenly to every word. Luetgert listened to each question carefully and then paused before answering in a grave, impressive manner. At all the proper places, he reached into his pocket for a handkerchief and dabbed at his eyes. "Take your time, Mr. Luetgert," Harmon always whispered dramatically.

When asked about the allegations from witnesses that he had been abusive to Louisa, he denied it. He also denied ever waving a gun at her, despite the dozens of people who saw it. "Never in my life have I made a threat against my wife or any soul on earth with a revolver, nobody on earth," he said.

Luetgert described how his business had declined and how a clever con artist had tricked him. He claimed that Louisa had been disturbed by his business losses and began acting strangely in the weeks leading up to her disappearance.

He explained away everything that seemed suspicious in his case. He had bought the barrels of potash to make soap, he said. He had last seen his wife in their kitchen, not in the factory. She didn't leave the house to accompany him back to the factory, he added. He had been in the basement of the factory alone that night, working on the soap. There had been no one there with him.

"The only human being there that you know of?"

"Yes, sir."

"Dead or alive?"

"Dead or alive," Luetgert replied.

He hadn't realized that his wife was missing until he went home for breakfast the next morning.

"Had you or your wife ever had cross or angry words during the two or three years or more, or for nine- or ten-years preceding May 1, 1897?" Harmon asked him.

Luetgert replied. "Once in a while we had some. Sometimes there was matters she would say that I didn't like, but we changed our minds and spoke it over and then we were through it, and then we didn't have it."

Luetgert said he ordered his employees to clean up the basement but denied that he told Smokehouse Frank to throw the slime and debris out along the railroad tracks or offered him a lifetime job if he promised not to say anything.

Harmon finally got around to asking Luetgert about the various ways he had been accused of killing his wife, but the judge interrupted him. "Don't answer that," he snapped. "I'll have no more of this nonsensical method of conducting a case. If he didn't kill her at all, that's the end of it. You may frame your question that way or not at all."

Harmon took exception to the ruling but did turn to Luetgert and asked, "I will ask you to state to the jury whether or not in any way or manner you killed your wife, Louisa Luetgert, on the first day of May or any other time."

"I did not," Luetgert said.

"I will ask you to tell this jury whether or not you ever in your life had any intention or purpose in mind to kill your wife."

"No, sir. Never."

"Will ask you to state to the jury whether or not you have ever had any intention or purpose to harm your wife in any way by any kind of physical violence."

"Never in my life."

Harmon repeated these questions in several different ways, becoming more melodramatic each time. Finally, Judge Gary cut him off. "You have been over that."

When Luetgert was on the stand on the third day, he asked the judge for permission to add to an earlier statement. He said that he now remembered a conversation that he'd had with Louisa on the evening of May 1. While they were talking, Louisa had told him that she wanted to visit her older brother, Henry, who had disappeared several years before. When Luetgert asked how she would do that because Henry was missing, she told him that she planned to try and find him.

Luetgert maintained that he still believed that Louisa was alive. "When do I expect to see my wife?" he said. "Every minute, I hope, today."

During Luetgert's testimony, the prosecution had watched silently, only rarely raising an objection. When Deneen finally left the prosecution table, Luetgert gripped the arms of the witness chair as if bracing for a shock. But Deneen eased into his questions, peppering him with queries about cleaning the factory and what was in the vat.

Luetgert continued to insist there had been no lumps or bones in the vat, only a "soapy substance." When Deneen kept asking him about the slime, Luetgert kept saying it was "soapy."

Judge Gary interrupted. "You don't understand what he's getting at," Gary said.

"Oh, yes I do," Luetgert replied. "What he's getting at, your honor, is to catch me."

The jurors exchanged curious glances at Luetgert's remark.

Deneen scoffed. "And when you can't answer, you say, 'soapy substance.'"

The questions went on for two more days. As the third day was nearing conclusion, Deneen asked, "When did you first know that you were suspected of the crime of murdering your wife?"

"It was published by a brass band and in the newspapers," Luetgert answered.

On the fourth day, Deneen questioned him about the allegation that his company had forged its books and falsified its inventory. Luetgert denied some charges and claimed he couldn't remember some of the incidents. He repeated the phrase "I don't recollect," dozens of times. He grew exasperated with the prosecutor but only got angry once. Answering one of the accusations of fraud, he turned in his chair and turned his blazing eyes on Fred Mueller, Louisa's nephew and the only clerk who could have made the allegations. Luetgert pointed a finger at Fred and cried out, "It's a lie - an absolute lie, I say - a fabrication by that man Mueller!"

Deneen then asked about his claim that he had called hospitals on May 2, looking for Louisa. "How many hospitals did you call up?"

"All I could find in the business directory and whose telephone numbers I could find in the telephone book," Luetgert told him.

"How many did you call up?"

"I don't know."

"How many as near as you can recollect?"

"I don't know."

"Can you name any of them?"

"Give me the business directory and the telephone book and I will give you the whole list of them."

Deneen then suggested several different hospitals and he asked Luetgert if he had called all of them. "I guess I did," he answered. He claimed that he gave each of them his wife's description and asked if she had been brought in.

"Did you give your name to the hospital authorities?" Deneen asked him.

"I did not."

"Did you give her name to the hospital authorities?"

"I did not."

Deneen prodded him into admitting that he hadn't used his own name and had not given them a way to reach him if a woman fitting Louisa's description was brought it.

"Did you call up any police station on the telephone?"

'No, sir," Luetgert said quietly.

"Did you call up any morgue in the city?"

"No, sir, not to my recollection."

"Did you make any search of the clay holes about your residence when the police were searching for your wife?"

"I did not."

"Did you assist in making a search of the river near your premises?"

"I did not."

Deneen sighed. "Very well, I am through with him," he said and returned to the prosecution table.

After Luetgert testified, the defense rolled out the string of witnesses who all claimed they had seen Louisa after her alleged death. They were mostly the same people, with a few additions, but their testimony remained questionable.

A bookbinder named Otto Klatt said he had passed the Luetgert house in his buggy a few minutes after 11:00 p.m. on May 12. He claimed that a woman suddenly ran out in front of him, narrowly missing being run down by his horse, and disappeared down the street. She was carrying a small bundle in her arms. He never got a good look at her but "reckoned it could have been Mrs. Luetgert."

Another witness, Theodore Arndt, said he had been on the El train on July 14 and saw Louisa there. Everyone in the courtroom was incredulous when Arndt claimed that he had never heard about the first Luetgert trial.

Judge Gary refused to let the defense bring in testimony about the supposed threats that Louisa made about running away. In addition, Harmon was reprimanded for putting on the stand three doctors who were supposed to be bone experts but turned out to be physicians who treated some of the men on the jury. The prosecution called it a "cheap trick."

After the defense rested its case, the prosecutors brought rebuttal witnesses to the stand, including Joe Detloff, who testified that he had seen Luetgert many times with Frank Hangel, who claimed that Luetgert tried to hire him to kill Louisa. During the cross-examination, Harmon seldom gave Detloff the chance to answer a question before asking him another one. Harmon laughed as the man stumbled over his answers. Luetgert enjoyed the stunt, too.

But their smiles vanished when a clear voice came from the jury box, surprising everyone in the room. "Give the witness a chance to answer before you break in on him with another question," said a juror named Charles Snow in a loud, firm voice. He was looking directly at Harmon. The defense attorney looked as though he'd been slapped across the face. He asked Detloff a question but did it while looking angrily at Snow: "What answer was it you could not finish? What was it you said that the jury could not hear?"

"That is not a proper question to ask," the judge spoke up.

Harmon sniffed. "Well, I wanted to find out what answer it was the jury could not hear."

An angry murmur was heard from the jury box. Another juror, Thomas Gardner, exclaimed, "We cannot hear anything. It's all mixed up. We cannot tell which is a question and which an answer... We can't hear any of the answers because you break in so much."

In an irritable tone, Harmon snapped at the jury. "Well, what do you want?"

"The testimony," one of the men responded.

Harmon went on with his questions, asking them angrily, but he allowed Detloff to finish his answers.

Luetgert looked shaken by the way the jurors had addressed his attorney. Making the jury angry wouldn't do anything to help his case.

As the trial drew to a close, Judge Gary finally reached his limit with Harmon's erratic behavior and his constant exceptions to Gary's rulings. He blurted out, "I don't care for you to say that what I do or say is right or wrong. I have gotten tired of your continuous sanction, at times when I do something which you think calls for your approval. I never saw a man try a case as you do. I never heard such a thing."

Harmon was astonished by the judge's words. He accused Gary of a personal attack and of conduct that was not ungentlemanly for the conduct of a trial. He called to the stenographer to take down every word.

"Certainly!" Gary said. "Get it all in. Put down all the remarks of the court."

The closing arguments began on February 1 and were not completed until Deneen gave his final argument on February 8. He was followed by the judge's instructions to the jury, explaining that prosecutors did not need to produce a corpse to prove that Louisa had been murdered. Finally, after hearing from 146 witnesses - and 866 objections from the defense - the jury retired to deliberate at just before 4:00 in the afternoon.

That same night, around 11:00 p.m., word came from the jurors that they were returning to the courtroom. A carriage was sent to the judge's house to bring him back to court. The lawyers and reporters took their places as they waited to see what happened next.

At 11:30, Judge Gary asked the jury if they had reached a verdict. They had. The foreman handed a paper to the clerk. Luetgert, who had just arrived in court under the escort of four deputy sheriffs, was at Harmon's side as the clerk read from the paper: "We, the jury, find the defendant. Adolph L. Luetgert, guilty of murder in manner and form as charged in the indictment, and we fix his punishment in the penitentiary for the term of his natural life."

Luetgert stood there, frozen, then he closed his eyes. One observer later said he believed that Luetgert laughed. Harmon looked blankly about him in bewilderment. Then, in a daze, he clutched at his client's hand for support.

Luetgert was taken from the Cook County Jail on Saturday, March 5. He hadn't expected to leave for the penitentiary this soon, so none of his friends or relatives were there to say goodbye. Guards walked him out of the building to a waiting wagon, and he was taken to Union Station. At 5:00 p.m., he boarded a Chicago and Alton Railroad train to Joliet.

Luetgert and his guards sat in the front of the smoking car. He chatted amiably with the guards and with the newspaper reporters who followed the group. As word of Luetgert's presence on the train spread during the trip, passengers came forward to see and speak with him. He joked with them about riding the train for free, with a ticket bought by the sheriff, and spoke of himself in the third person. He was going to get a new trial, he maintained, and then Chicago would hear from him again. "Luetgert goes to the penitentiary proud," he announced. "If ever an innocent man went there, it's Luetgert."

He left the train with his guards when it stopped at Joliet Penitentiary. As the heavy stone walls loomed overhead, Luetgert was led into a waiting room, where he met Warden Robert McClaughry. It was now late, and the lights in the prison had been turned out. The night keeper led the prisoner and several Cook County officials up two flights of stairs to the upper tier of a solitary area for new arrivals. The door of the last cell on the right side stood open. Luetgert turned and took one last look at the officials from the jail. "Goodbye," he said, choking a bit. The door clanged shut, and he walked into the shadows.

He spent the next day in solitary confinement. The next day, he was awakened at dawn and taken to the assistant warden's office, where he was given a prison uniform of bluish-gray coat and trousers, coarse underwear, a striped shirt, and a cap. He put on the clothing without a word, and then a trustee sewed a tag on his right shoulder with his new identity on it - number "5969."

Luetgert was then taken to the barbershop, where his hair was shorn and his mustache shaved off. He and a gang of other new prisoners were then thumb printed, photographed, and their height and weight were noted on their official charts. Luetgert weighed in at 220 pounds. He was 53 years old, making him among the oldest in the penitentiary.

He slowly settled into the monotony of life behind bars - eat, bathe, work, and sleep. He was alone in his cell. His bunk had a mattress, straw pillow, sheets, and heavy woolen blanket. There was a stool, a small mirror, a crock that held drinking water, and a wash bucket. An electric lamp burned every day from dawn until 9:00 p.m.

It was not a pleasant place. The cells were filled with the stink of men, cooked food, and sewage. Smoke, gases, and dust from a neighboring steel mill also filled the air. Around 20 prisoners died each year, about half of them from tuberculosis.

During Luetgert's first year in prison, he retained a hopeful attitude. He always insisted on his innocence and continuously claimed he was going to get a new trial. He worked in the harness shop for a time, but he was on to the chair-making shop when it closed. Later, he was - ironically - put in charge of the meats in the cold storage warehouse. He was often described as a model prisoner that first year.

By 1899, though, Luetgert began to speak less and less and often quarreled with the other convicts. His demeanor changed, and he complained about exhaustion and lack of sleep but would never explain what was causing his insomnia.

He got into a heated argument with an agent from Armour and Company about the quality of meat they were providing to the prison, and he was placed in solitary confinement for "disobedience and quarreling." He was soon sent back to his old job in the chair shop.

July 4 was the only day of the year that inmates were free to roam in the prison yard, play sports, listen to music, and dance. Luetgert avoided everyone. Many of the prisoners who had exchanged pleasantries with him in the past came to talk to him, but he answered their greetings with a scowl.

The only person he would talk with was Nic Marzen, his former cellmate from the Cook County Jail, who had been found guilty of murder again but was sentenced to prison instead of executed. The two men went off into a corner of the yard and spoke in quiet voices for nearly two hours.

It would be Marzen who would eventually reveal what was plaguing Luetgert's sleep.

Some believed that Luetgert's behavior was caused by legal proceedings underway in Chicago. Diedrich Bicknese was seeking the guardianship of Luetgert's two young children, Louis and Elmer, who were then being cared for by Luetgert's friends, William and Mary Charles. Marzen knew otherwise, however.

Every morning at 5:30, bells rang to rouse the prisoners from their beds. They got up, washed, and dressed in their uniforms. Wall guards then marched to their positions with rifles atop the prison walls.

At the same time, 50 interior guards picked up heavy clubs - the only defense weapons inside the penitentiary - and entered the cell blocks. They hurried along the galleries, unlocking cells. Then, on a signal, the prisoners stepped out and formed lines.

On July 27, 1899, as on every morning, Luetgert and the other prisoners marched in lockstep into the yard. They emptied their waste buckets into the sewer and hung the buckets on racks. Then, they marched back to the cell blocks. As they passed the ration tables, each convict was given a quart of coffee, bread, and a plate of food. On this day, the meal was Irish stew.

Luetgert took his meal and went back to his cell - it was now No. 152 on the second tier of the east wing - and sat down to eat. As guard Peter Blone passed by in the corridor, he asked Luetgert why he hadn't closed his cell door. "I didn't know it was open," Luetgert replied. "I must be a little slow this morning."

Blone fastened the door and walked on. He passed by the cell again a few minutes later and noticed that Luetgert was sitting on the edge of his bunk, bent over. Luetgert looked up and then started eating again.

At 6:45, the work bell sounded, but Luetgert was not among the men lined up in the corridor.

The stories about what happened next differ.

One newspaper claimed a convict told the guards that he heard Luetgert grunting in his cell. Another paper said guards heard groans coming from the cell. Another said that guards simply passed by the cell and knew something was wrong.

Whatever happened to send them there, Blone and another guard, George Geissler, found Luetgert stretched out on his cot, his arms and legs convulsing violently, his face turning blue, and gasping for air. Then, with help from six convicts, the guards carried Luetgert out into the corridor, hoping that some fresh air might revive him.

"What's the matter, Luetgert?" Blone asked, but Luetgert made no reply. His eyes were half-closed, and his face was twitching as if he were trying to speak. After another moment, his eyes closed the rest of the way, his muscles relaxed, and a faint gurgling sound passed between his lips.

Adolph Luetgert was dead.

It was first assumed that Luetgert died due to heart trouble, but the coroner who conducted the autopsy stated that his liver was greatly enlarged and in such a condition of degermation that "mental strain would have caused his death at any time."

Could he have been mentally strained by the court case that would give his children to Louisa's brother, or was it something else?

Nic Marzen believed he had the answer. Everyone who knew Luetgert had seen him become a shadow of his former self. His loud, blustering personality had been replaced by a worn, exhausted, angry man who fought with other inmates for no reason and seemed constantly distracted. A few times, other convicts had reported hearing him talking angrily to himself at night in his cell.

But Marzen assured those who would listen that Luetgert had not been talking to himself. Instead, he claimed that Luetgert told him that Louisa had been visiting him in his cell at night. She had returned to haunt him, intent on having her revenge.

Was the "ghost" real or the product of a deteriorating mind? Luetgert believed she was there, which would undoubtedly have caused the "mental strain" reported by the coroner that led to his death.

Strangely, Luetgert was not the only one to report seeing Louisa's ghost after the trial.

Christine Feld had reported to Captain Herman Schuettler that she had seen two ghostly apparitions as she walked home one evening. She said the first one resembled Adolph Luetgert.

"*Adolkh, bist das Du?*" she called out, asking the man she thought was Luetgert if it was him. The figure did not reply.

She shouted for it to go away - "*Geh, weh, geh weg!*" - and ran for her life. She was nearly a half-block away when the second spirit appeared in front of her. Christine screamed in terror as she recognized the face of Louisa Luetgert.

Captain Schuettler believed she had hallucinated the whole thing, but he did assign two officers to escort her home for a while. One of them stayed on call near her home during the night.

Just in case.

But did she imagine it? And did Adolph Luetgert?

If Luetgert had lived one more day, he would have received some good news. Lawrence Harmon was on his way to see him and tell him that an earlier court order giving Diedrich Bicknese guardianship over Louis and Elmer had been delayed. Some of the wording in the petition had been wrong.

In addition, thanks to a donation of $1,500, his son Arnold had finally been able to afford to pay for a transcript of the trial. Harmon had been hopeful that this meant the Supreme Court would hear his case on appeal.

"But at that very moment, when matters were shaping themselves most favorably for this last effort to secure justice for Luetgert," Harmon said, "death suddenly called him away."

But I'll ask again, was it merely death? Or was it Louisa's spirit, making sure that her murderous husband would never go free?

After Luetgert's death, Prosecutor Deneen released an affidavit that had been given by an unnamed man who had been in jail when Luetgert was first arrested. Deneen said that trial rules had prevented him from releasing it and some others that were even more damning.

Deneen knew there were those out there who still believed that Luetgert had not received a fair trial. He had a statement that proved this was not the case. The statement from the anonymous jailhouse witness said:

> He came to my cell often to talk with me and to ask questions, and one time, he said, "I make one damn mistake - them bloody rings."
> Whenever he spoke about the rings he showed by gestures and by words that he had made a mistake as to the rings and that he worried about them more than anything else.
> "I kick her in the side," he said, showing how he did it, and then he said, "I think she will come back," meaning, as I understand it, "I think she will come to."

She didn't. But maybe, just maybe, she "came back."

Adolph Luetgert and Christine Feld were not the only ones to suffer in the wake of the murder and the trial.

Diedrich Bicknese died not long after Luetgert did, in 1901. Frank Bialk found work in a brickyard, and his son, John, became a detective sergeant for the Chicago police. He was killed in the line of duty in 1916.

Judge Gary remained stubbornly proud of his record, denying he had ever shown bias. He served as a judge until the day he died, spending 43 years on the bench. He died at age 85 in 1906. His obituary was filled with praise and gave little hint of the controversies over his record. Today, he is mostly remembered as the judge who allowed the hanging and imprisonment of innocent "anarchists" at the Haymarket bombing trial.

Judge Tuthill continued his service on the bench. In August 1919, he nearly drowned while swimming in Lake Michigan. A young girl rescued him and dragged him to the beach. Her name was never learned. She disappeared right after the rescue. Tuthill underwent surgery and became ill with an infection. He never recovered and died on April 10, 1920.

Charles S. Deneen served two more terms as state's attorney and then was elected as Governor of Illinois for the next eight years. He later served one term as a U.S. Senator. Deneen was still practicing law in Chicago when he died in 1940.

Herman Schuettler remained one of Chicago's best-known police officers for two decades after the Luetgert case. When a trio of young men known as the Car Barn Bandits terrorized the city in 1903, killing eight people, Schuettler received most of the credit for apprehending them. He served as the police department's second-ranking officer from 1904 to 1917, when he was appointed as superintendent. Later that same year, he suffered what the press called a "nervous breakdown." He took time off to recover but never did. "Old Herman," as his men affectionately called him, died on August 22, 1918.

In 1908, Luetgert's brother, Arnold, went to a house in Elgin where he had once lived and told the current occupants that he wanted to see the room in which his son had been born. Later in the day, he went to Lord's Park and went out to one of the islands in the lagoon. He drew the attention of bystanders by firing a gun into the air three times - and then fired the fourth shot into his head.

Most of the Luetgerts, though, went on to live ordinary lives. There is still a plot for the Luetgert family in Waldheim Cemetery - now known as Forest Home, the English translation of its old name - that contains the bodies of Luetgert, his first wife, and the three children who died young. Only the faded headstone of his daughter Elsa is still there.

Luetgert's oldest son, Arnold, moved to Portland, Oregon. Louis and Elmer lived with William Charles for a time and then lived with other relatives in the coming years. Elmer worked as a milkman for the Borden Milk Company. He had one son, who died before he was a month old, and one adopted daughter. He later moved to Michigan and died in 1976. Louis spent most of his life working as a postal clerk, eventually becoming the postmaster of Elmhurst, a suburb west of Chicago. He had four sons.

Both boys accepted the fact that their mother was dead but never spoke much about their father's trial, which both witnessed as children. One of Louis's sons, Howard, later expressed a strong belief that his grandfather had been innocent but Louis, who died in 1960, never mentioned the case to anyone.

And then there was Lawrence Harmon.

On July 30, an undertaker had delivered Luetgert's body to the Northwest Turner Hall at the corner of Southport and Clybourn, not far from the Luetgert sausage works. Several hundred people already surrounded the hall. The police had to push the crowd back so that Luetgert's coffin could be taken inside.

The casket was black with silver handles. A plate was inscribed with Luetgert's name and the dates of his birth and death. It was placed on a draped stand in the center of the room. The only flowers were an arrangement of pink, red, and white carnations. A crimson ribbon spelled out: "Our Father's Words - I am Innocent."

The doors to the hall were opened, and for the next two hours, anyone who cared to enter could view Luetgert's body. Thousands filed past the casket, looking down at the pale face that seemed to bear a faint half-smile. Not satisfied with one glimpse of his face, some of the women in the crowd returned to the line and passed by again.

Large groups of Germans adjourned to the adjacent saloon to discuss the crime over their beer. The tavern did a thriving business that morning.

Many in the crowd whispered that Louisa was likely to appear now that punishment had finally been given to her husband. Necks craned, and heads turned whenever a light-haired woman passed through the doors.

All of Luetgert's immediate family were at the service, but none of Louisa's family attended. Although the funeral arrangements had requested that all Luetgert's attorneys serve as honorary pallbearers, the only lawyer to show up was Harmon.

During the service, Harmon asked to speak. He placed his hand on the sausage-makers coffin and began to read from a typewritten letter about which newspaper reporters noted, "the majority of those present appeared to regard the speech as an interesting incident to an entertaining function." Harmon spoke of Luetgert's genial character, and at times, he was overcome with emotion.

As he reached the end of the letter, he dramatically cried out, "I call upon Louisa Luetgert, the missing woman, for whom he suffered without ever uttering an unkind word regarding her, to come forth and remove the unmerited stain from the name of the father of her innocent children!"

Harmon paused, and the hundreds of people in the room looked around as if expecting to see Louisa appear.

She didn't.

Lawrence Harmon never stopped believing that Louisa Luetgert was alive, and eventually, his belief drove him insane. He ended his life in a mental institution.

Louisa Luetgert was never seen alive again. At one time, though, a creditor that was suing the Luetgert family demanded her presence in court. But, despite the creditor's efforts, she did not appear.

For many years, the children in Lake View sang a gruesome rhyme that included the line, "He ground her up into sau-ha-sage meat, and Luetgert was his name."

The Luetgert house became an object of fear. The yard became wild and overgrown with weeds. From time to time, a tenant rented the house, but never for long.

Louisa did not rest in peace, the neighbors said. Her ghost was often seen in the house. Many passing by after dark claimed to see a woman in a white dress leaning against the mantel in the fireplace.

The sausage factory also stood empty for years, looming over the neighborhood as a grim reminder of the horrors that had occurred there. The windows of the place became a target for rocks thrown from the nearby railroad embankment, and it often invited forays by the curious and the insane.

Only a month after Luetgert's death, a factory caretaker discovered a man in the office, searching the safe and going through the books. The caretaker approached the man -- later identified as Albert Boyer - and told him to leave the place, but Boyer produced a hatchet and chased the guard out into the street. A police officer was summoned, and he arrested Boyer, asking him to explain his bizarre behavior. "I am looking for Mrs. Luetgert," the man replied, "and I can find her if you leave me alone. She is in the building somewhere and I think she is alive."

A court found Boyer insane, and he was sent to a mental institution.

In the months that followed his death, Luetgert's business affairs were entangled in legal litigation. The courts finally sorted everything out in August 1900, and a public auction was held for the factory and its grounds. Portions of the property were divided up between several buyers but the Library Bureau Company, founded by Dewey Decimal System creator Melvil Dewey, leased the factory itself. The company used it as a workshop and storehouse for its line of library furniture and office supplies. During the renovations, they discarded the infamous vats in the basement.

On Sunday, June 26, 1904, assistant engineer Charles Westerholm was alone in the building and, after starting the building's boilers, climbed the stairs to the fourth floor. He smelled something burning and hurried downstairs to discover that the entire first floor was filled with smoke. Flames were roaring up the staircase from the basement. After trying to put out the blaze on his own, Westerholm sounded a fire alarm.

By the time the horse-drawn fire engines arrived, the flames had climbed to the first floor, spread by the coating of sausage grease that still coated some of the walls and floors. As the fire spread, neighbors panicked and began hauling their prized possessions from their homes. Firefighters manned the 14 engines that arrived on the scene, and soon, word spread throughout the North Side that the

Luetgert factory was on fire. Newspapers estimated that as many as 10,000 people rushed to the scene. The fire department blocked the railroad line next to the building for over an hour, and passengers got off the trains and joined the spectators. It was all that the police officers on the scene could do to hold back the crowd.

It took more than three hours to put out the fire. The factory was still standing, but everything inside of it had been destroyed. No one had any idea what could have caused the fires, but strangely, investigators did figure out where the blaze had begun. It was in the basement - at the exact spot where Luetgert's middle sausage vat had been located.

Fire officials were perplexed. "There were no fires, no electrical current, no gasoline or other explosive or highly inflammable matter in the building, and we are at a loss to account for it," they said in a statement. "The source of the fire is a mystery, and none has been able to offer any better explanation than the superstitious folk who have an idea that some supernatural intervention against any commercial enterprise operating at the scene of the murder has been invoked."

The most likely earthly cause was the spontaneous combustion of mill dust and wood shavings from the furniture built inside the factory. But to neighbors, it seemed that Louisa's ghost had returned again.

And who's to say that wasn't the case?

Despite the damage done to the building's interior, the Library Bureau re-opened its facilities in the former sausage factory. It would go on to change owners many times in the decades that followed.

In 1907, a contracting mason purchased the old Luetgert house and moved it from behind the factory to another lot in the neighborhood, hoping to dispel the grim memories - and the ghost -- attached to it.

The part of Hermitage Avenue that intersected with Diversey was closed. By the 1990s, the factory stood empty and crumbling, facing a collection of vacant lots that were only broken by the occasional ramshackle frame house.

In 1999, though, around the 100th anniversary of the death of Adolph Luetgert, the former sausage factory was converted into loft condominiums, and a brand-new neighborhood sprang up to replace the aging homes of the Luetgert days. Fashionable brick homes and apartments appeared around the old factory, and rundown taverns were replaced with coffee shops.

But that isn't the end of the story.

Legends on the Northwest Side of Chicago say that the spirit of Louisa Luetgert still walks. If she does, she probably no longer recognizes the neighborhood where she once lived. They say, though, that if you happened to be in the street by the old sausage factory on May 1 -- the anniversary of Louisa's death -- there is a chance that you might see her lonely specter still roaming the area where she lived and died.

If you do, speak a kind word in passing to the woman whose life was one of hardship, trauma, and abuse and who died many years before her time.

BIBLIOGRAPHY

Albee, Sarah - *Poison: Deadly Deeds, Perilous Professions, and Murderous Medicines,* New York, NY, Random House, 2017

Arthur, Stanley Clisby - *Old Families of Louisiana,* New Orleans, LA, Harmanson, 1931
--------------------------- - *Old New Orleans,* New Orleans, LA. Harmanson, 1936

Asbury, Herbert - *The French Quarter,* New York, NY, Alfred A. Knopf, 1936
--------------------- - *Gem of the Prairie,* New York, NY, Alfred A. Knopf, 1940

Barry, Michael Thomas - *California's Deadly Women,* Atglen, PA, Schiffer Publishing, 2018

Blum, Deborah - *The Poisoner's Handbook,* New York, NY, Penguin Press, 2010

Bruce, Curt - *Great Houses of New Orleans,* New York, NY, Alfred A. Knopf, 1977

Burt, Olive Woolley - *American Murder Ballads,* New York, NY, Oxford University Press, 1958

Cable, George - *The Creoles of Louisiana,* New York, NY, Scribner & Sons, 1884

Chicago Daily Sun
Chicago Daily News
Chicago Inter Ocean
Chicago Times Herald

Chicago Tribune

Cimino, Al - *Women Who Kill,* London, UK, Arcturus Publishing Limited, 2019

Cincinnati Enquirer

Cohen, Anne B. - *Poor Pearl, Poor Girl! The Murdered Girl Stereotype in Ballad,* Austin, TX, University of Texas Press, 1973

Coletta, Sue - *Pretty Evil New England,* Guilford, CT, Globe Pequot, 2020

Darkis, Fred R., Jr. - "Madame LaLaurie of New Orleans", *Louisiana History,* Fall 1982

Davis, F. Keith - *The Secret Life and Brutal Death of Mamie Thurman,* Logan, WV, *Logan Banner,* 2001

deLavigne, Jeanne - *Ghost Stories of Old New Orleans,* New York, NY, Rinehart & Company, 1946

Gregory, Ted - *Mary Jane's Ghost,* Iowa City, IA, University of Iowa Press, 2017

Gribben, Mark - "Poor Pearl" from *The Malefactor's Register*

Hofmeister, Rudolph - *Germans of Chicago,* Champaign, IL, Stripes, 1976

Hynd, Alan - *Murder, Mayhem, and Mystery,* A.S. Barnes & Co., New York, NY, 1958

Jones, James Gay - *Appalachian Ghost Stories,* Parsons, WV, McClain Publishing, 1997

Kane, Harnett - *Queen New Orleans: City by the River*, New York, NY, William H. Morrow, 1949

Kendall, John - *History of New Orleans*, New Orleans, LA, Lewis Publishing Co., 1922

Kunheim, Anthony - *The Pearl Bryan Murder Story*, Alexandria, KY, Campbell County Historical and Genealogical Society, 1996

Lhotka, Bill - *St. Louis Crime Chronicles*, St. Louis, MO, Reedy Press, 2009

Liebling, A.J. - "The Case of the Scattered Dutchman," *New Yorker*, September 16, 1955

Loerzel, Robert - *Alchemy of Bones*, Chicago, IL, University of Illinois Press, 2003

Love, Victoria Cosner and Lorelei Shannon - *Mad Madame LaLaurie*, Charleston, SC, The History Press, 2011
--- - *Missouri's Murderous Matrons*, Charleston, SC, The History Press, 2019

Lyle, Katie Letcher - *The Man Who Wanted Seven Wives*, Chapel Hill, NC, Algonquin Books, 1986

McBrayer, Mary Kay - *America's First Female Serial Killer*, Coarl Gables, FL, Mango Publishing, 2020

Miller, Donald - *City of the Century*, New York, NY, Simon and Schuster, 1996

Murphy, S. Kay - *The Tainted Legacy of Bertha Gifford*, Washington, D.C., PublishAmerica, 2008

Musick, Ruth Anne - *Coffin Hollow and Other Ghost Tales*, Lexington, KY, University of Kentucky Press, 1977

Mysterious Murder of Pearl Bryan, or The Headless Horror,
Cincinnati, OH, Barclay & Co., 1897

Nash, Jay Robert - *Look for the Woman,* New York, NY, M. Evans
and Company, Inc., 1981

Ogden, Tom - *Haunted Hollywood,* Guilford, CT, Globe Pequot, 2015

Palmer, Dr. Hollis A. - *Curse of the Veiled Murderess,* Saratoga
Springs, NY, Deep Root Publications, 2004

Parascandola, John - *King of Poisons,* Washington, D.C., Potomac
Books, 2010

Poock, L.D. - *Headless, Yet Identified: A Story of the Solution of the
Pearl Bryan or Fort Thomas Mystery Through the Shoes,* Columbus,
OH, Hann & Adair Printers, 1897

Saxon, Lyle - *Fabulous New Orleans,* New Orleans, LA, Robert L.
Crager and Co., 1928
----------------- Robert Tallant and Edward Dreyer - *Gumbo Ya-Ya,*
Boston, MA, Houghton Mifflin, 1945

Schechter, Harold - *Fatal: The Poisonous Life of a Female Serial
Killer,* New York, NY, Simon & Schuster, 2012
--------------------- - *Psycho USA: Famous American Killers You Never
Heard Of,* New York, NY, Ballantine Books, 2012

Stampp, Kenneth M. - *The Peculiar Institution: Slavery in the
Antebellum South,* New York, NY, Vintage Books, 1956

Taylor, Troy - *Haunted Chicago,* Decatur, IL, Whitechapel Press, 2003
--------------- - *Haunted New Orleans,* Charleston, SC, The History
Press, 2010
--------------- - *Over My Dead Body,* Chicago, IL, Whitechapel Press,
2013

Telfer, Tori - *Lady Killers,* New York, NY, Harper, 2017

Vronsky, Peter - *Female Serial Killers,* New York, NY, Random House, 2007

Wilson, David - *Henrietta Robinson*, New York, NY, Miller, Orton & Mulligan, 1855

Wolf, Marvin J. and Katherine Nader - *Fallen Angels*, New York, NY, Facts On File, 1986

Young, Andrew - *Unwanted: A Murder Mystery of the Gilded Age*, Yardley, PA, Westholme Publishing, 2016

Special Thanks to

April Slaughter: Cover Design and Artwork
Lois Taylor: Editing and Proofreading
Becky Ray: Editing and Proofreading
Lisa Taylor and Lux
Brianna Snow
Orrin and Rachel Taylor
Rene Kruse
Rachael Horath
Elyse and Thomas Reihner
Bethany Horath
John Winterbauer
Kaylan Schardan
Maggie and Packy Lundholm
Cody Beck
Tom and Michelle Bonadurer
Samantha Smith
Lydia Roades
Susan Kelly and Amy Bouyear
Cheryl Stamp and Sheryel Williams-Staab
And the entire crew of American Hauntings

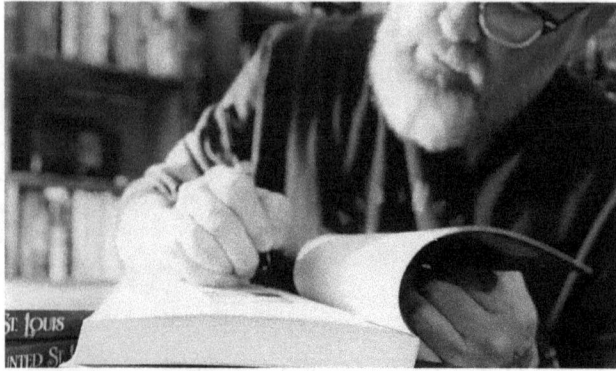

ABOUT THE AUTHOR

Troy Taylor is the author of books on ghosts, hauntings, true crime, the unexplained, and the supernatural in America. He is also the founder of American Hauntings Ink, which offers books, ghost tours, events, and weekend excursions. He was born and raised in the Midwest and currently divides his time between Illinois and the far-flung reaches of America.

www.ingramcontent.com/pod-product-compliance
Lightning Source LLC
Chambersburg PA
CBHW062044080426

42734CB00012B/2553